Jewish Migration and the Archive

Migration is, and has always been, a disruptive experience. Freedom from oppression and hope for a better life are counter-balanced by feelings of loss – loss of family members, of a home, of personal belongings. Memories of the migration process itself often fade quickly away in view of the new challenges that await immigrants in their new homelands.

This volume asks, and shows, how migration memories have been kept, stored, forgotten, and indeed retrieved in many different archives, in official institutions, and in heritage centres, as well as in personal and family collections. Based on a variety of examples and conceptual approaches – from artistic approaches to the family archive via 'smell and memory as archives', to a cultural history of the suitcase – this volume offers a new and original way to write Jewish history and the history of Jewish migration in the context of personal and public memory. The documents reflect the transitory character of the migration experience, and they tell stories of longing and belonging. This book was originally published as a special issue of *Jewish Culture and History*.

James Jordan is Karten Lecturer at the Parkes Institute for the Study of Jewish/non-Jewish Relations at the University of Southampton, UK. He is currently researching the role and representation of Jews in British television (1936–1979).

Lisa Leff is an Associate Professor at American University, Washington D.C., USA. She is the author of the book *The Archive Thief: The Man Who Salvaged French Jewish History in the Wake of the Holocaust.*

Joachim Schlör is the current director of the Parkes Institute and Professor for Modern Jewish/non-Jewish Relations at the University of Southampton, UK. His book on the Rosenthal family's emigration from Heilbronn/Germany to England was published in summer 2015.

Jewish Migration and the Archive

Edited by
James Jordan, Lisa Leff and
Joachim Schlör

LONDON AND NEW YORK

First published 2016
by Routledge
2 Park Square, Milton Park, Abingdon, Oxfordshire OX14 4RN

and by Routledge
711 Third Avenue, New York, NY 10017, USA

First issued in paperback 2017

Routledge is an imprint of the Taylor & Francis Group, an informa business

© 2016 Taylor & Francis

All rights reserved. No part of this book may be reprinted or reproduced or utilised in any form or by any electronic, mechanical, or other means, now known or hereafter invented, including photocopying and recording, or in any information storage or retrieval system, without permission in writing from the publishers.

Trademark notice: Product or corporate names may be trademarks or registered trademarks, and are used only for identification and explanation without intent to infringe.

British Library Cataloguing in Publication Data
A catalogue record for this book is available from the British Library

Typeset in Times New Roman
by RefineCatch Limited, Bungay, Suffolk

Publisher's Note
The publisher accepts responsibility for any inconsistencies that may have arisen during the conversion of this book from journal articles to book chapters, namely the possible inclusion of journal terminology.

Disclaimer
Every effort has been made to contact copyright holders for their permission to reprint material in this book. The publishers would be grateful to hear from any copyright holder who is not here acknowledged and will undertake to rectify any errors or omissions in future editions of this book.

ISBN 13: 978-1-138-09894-7 (pbk)
ISBN 13: 978-1-138-93721-5 (hbk)

Contents

Citation Information vii
Notes on Contributors ix

1. Jewish Migration and the Archive: Introduction 1
   James Jordan, Lisa Leff and Joachim Schlör

2. Reading between the lines: artistic approaches to the family archive 6
   Katy Beinart

3. 'Personal letters – to keep': managing the emotions of forced migration 27
   Esther Saraga

4. Smell and memory as Jewish archives: the case of Russian Jewish writers 43
   Henrietta Mondry

5. Heritage centres in Israel: Depositories of a lost identity? 55
   Hilda Nissimi

6. Means of transport and storage: suitcases and other containers for the memory of migration and displacement 76
   Joachim Schlör

7. Private archives and public lives: the migrations of Alexander Weissberg and the Polanyi archives 93
   Judith Szapor

8. The making of a South African Jewish activist: the Yiddish diary of Ray Alexander Simons, Latvia, 1927 110
   Veronica Belling

9. Harvard man, American dough boy, Mississippi Jew: the papers of Samuel (Sam) Leyens Switzer in Virginia 124
   Maura Hametz

Index 141

Citation Information

The chapters in this book were originally published in *Jewish Culture and History*, volume 15, issues 1–2 (April–August 2014). When citing this material, please use the original page numbering for each article, as follows:

Chapter 1
Jewish Migration and the Archive: Introduction
James Jordan, Lisa Leff and Joachim Schlör
Jewish Culture and History, volume 15, issues 1–2 (April–August 2014) pp. 1–5

Chapter 2
Reading between the lines: artistic approaches to the family archive
Katy Beinart
Jewish Culture and History, volume 15, issues 1–2 (April–August 2014) pp. 6–26

Chapter 3
'Personal letters – to keep': managing the emotions of forced migration
Esther Saraga
Jewish Culture and History, volume 15, issues 1–2 (April–August 2014) pp. 27–42

Chapter 4
Smell and memory as Jewish archives: the case of Russian Jewish writers
Henrietta Mondry
Jewish Culture and History, volume 15, issues 1–2 (April–August 2014) pp. 43–54

Chapter 5
Heritage centres in Israel: Depositories of a lost identity?
Hilda Nissimi
Jewish Culture and History, volume 15, issues 1–2 (April–August 2014) pp. 55–75

Chapter 6
Means of transport and storage: suitcases and other containers for the memory of migration and displacement
Joachim Schlör
Jewish Culture and History, volume 15, issues 1–2 (April–August 2014) pp. 76–92

CITATION INFORMATION

Chapter 7
Private archives and public lives: the migrations of Alexander Weissberg and the Polanyi archives
Judith Szapor
Jewish Culture and History, volume 15, issues 1–2 (April–August 2014) pp. 93–109

Chapter 8
The making of a South African Jewish activist: the Yiddish diary of Ray Alexander Simons, Latvia, 1927
Veronica Belling
Jewish Culture and History, volume 15, issues 1–2 (April–August 2014) pp. 110–123

Chapter 9
Harvard man, American dough boy, Mississippi Jew: the papers of Samuel (Sam) Leyens Switzer in Virginia
Maura Hametz
Jewish Culture and History, volume 15, issues 1–2 (April–August 2014) pp. 124–140

For any permission-related enquiries please visit:
http://www.tandfonline.com/page/help/permissions

Notes on Contributors

Katy Beinart is currently working on a practice-based PhD at the Bartlett School of Architecture, University College London, UK, and is a senior lecturer in Architecture at the University of Brighton, UK. She trained as an architect at the Bartlett, UCL and Oxford Brookes, Oxford, UK, going on to develop an artistic practice that includes installations, performance and projects which explores links between material culture, migration, memory and place.

Veronica Belling was the Jewish Studies librarian at the University of Cape Town Libraries, and the Isaac & Jessie Kaplan Centre for Jewish Studies & Research at the University of Cape Town, South Africa, for 31 years, from 1981 to 2012. She has a Ph.D. in Historical Studies for a thesis entitled 'Recovering the Lives of South African Jewish Women During the Migration Years, c1880 to 1939'. She is the author of *Bibliography of South African Jewry* (1997), and *Yiddish Theatre in South Africa: a History from the late Nineteenth Century to 1960* (2008).

Maura Hametz is Professor of History at Old Dominion University, Norfolk, Virginia, USA. She is the author of *Making Trieste Italian* (2005) and *In the Name of Italy* (2012), and is the co-editor of *Jewish Intellectual Women in Europe, 1860–2000*. She has explored Jews and national identity in a variety of European and American contexts.

James Jordan is Karten Lecturer at the Parkes Institute for the Study of Jewish/non-Jewish Relations at the University of Southampton, UK. He is currently researching the role and representation of Jews in British television (1936–1979).

Lisa Leff is an Associate Professor at American University, Washington D.C., USA. She is the author of the forthcoming book *The Archive Thief: The Man Who Salvaged French Jewish History in the Wake of the Holocaust*.

Henrietta Mondry is Professor in Russian and European Studies at the University of Canterbury, New Zealand. She has published widely on the reception of the Jews in Russian literature, and authored *Exemplary Bodies: Constructing the Jew in Russian Culture since the 1880s* (2009).

Hilda Nissimi is senior lecturer in the General History department at Bar-Ilan University, Tel Aviv, Israel, and has published on identity formation in the Mashhadi community and crypto-faith communities. Her new topic of research is the role of museums and heritage centres in identity formation.

Esther Saraga has a background of teaching and researching in the social sciences, in areas ranging from critiques of biological determinist explanations of sex differences to

NOTES ON CONTRIBUTORS

feminist analyses of child sexual abuse. She is now applying her critical social science approach to the analysis of her collection of family papers. She retired from the Open University, UK, in September 2009 to concentrate on this project.

Joachim Schlör is the current director of the Parkes Institute and Professor for Modern Jewish/non-Jewish Relations at the University of Southampton, UK. His book on the Rosenthal family's emigration from Heilbronn/Germany to England will be published in summer 2015.

Judith Szapor is an Assistant Professor of European History in the Department of History and Classical Studies at McGill University in Montreal, Canada. She received a doctorate in Modern Hungarian History from ELTE Budapest, Hungary, and a Ph.D. in Modern European History from York University, Toronto, Canada.

Jewish Migration and the Archive: Introduction

James Jordan[a], Lisa Leff[b] and Joachim Schlör[a]

[a]Parkes Institute for the Study of Jewish/non-Jewish Relations, University of Southampton, UK;
[b]Department of History, American University, Washington, DC, USA

In July 1999, Potsdam University hosted an international conference, supported by the European Council of Jewish Communities, the Jewish Partnership for Europe, the European Commission (Direction Générale X), the Alliance Israélite Universelle, and the Moses Mendelssohn Centre. 'Preserving Jewish Archives as part of the European Cultural Heritage' was not just a conference title, but the starting point of an ambitious programme: to identify Jewish archives (within Jewish communities and related organizations) as well as public archives (state, regional, municipal) containing material relating to Jewish history and culture; to encourage and support exchange and cooperation between those archives; 'to present the state of the art in the field of Jewish archives in Europe, to set the foundations for a future directory of Jewish archives, and to create a debate between the main actors of the field, including our American and Israeli colleagues'.[1]

In his opening lecture Feliks Tych, then Director of the Zydowski Instytut Hystoryczny (ZIH) in Warsaw, argued that the course of events since 1933 – the destruction of Jewish communities and related organizations all over Europe, the confiscation of archives and libraries by the Nazi government in Germany and its institutions all over occupied Europe, the deportations of Jewish people to the concentration and extermination camps, the damage caused by warfare and military action, as well the post-war emigration of many of the Jews who survived the Holocaust – have turned historians into archaeologists who try to decipher tombstones, search through the ruins of destroyed synagogue buildings and, literally, dig out lost or hidden materials in cities or forests.[2] Documents which may have been kept in secure places, in well-organized archives, in *genizot*, or even in private property, for hundreds of years, have been destroyed or, in many cases and in many different ways, displaced: from Berlin to Moscow, from Vilna (Vilnius) to New York, from Odessa to Jerusalem.

Most archivists agree today that these displacements have to be accepted as a matter of fact, and that instead of trying to 'return' documents to their places of origin, efforts should be made to 'reconstruct' archival collections only in a virtual way, through cataloguing, digitization, publication, and other forms of collaboration between archives all over the world. Already in 1999 those present at Potsdam, after having heard reports from Kiev, Prague, Sofia, Berlin, Milan, Girona, and so many other places, had the impression that there was another dimension, another meaning maybe, to be realized and understood. Historians must begin to integrate their knowledge of this history of displacement and dispersion into our work with greater awareness. It appears first as a practical issue affecting our research itinerary. It has become nearly impossible to write the history, be it in terms of culture, or politics, or economy, of any Jewish community or institution by simply 'going there' there and working one's way through the archive. But also the very fact that such displacements occurred will have to be an underlying motive for all such studies: Writing the history of Jewish families in a Berlin district, or even a single street, will force the researcher to travel – if only virtually – to London, to New York, to Buenos Aires and Cape Town, to Shanghai and Melbourne, and to take into account the transnational dimension brought about by the historical events.

International cooperation and mutual information are therefore crucial. Institutions such as the Leo Baeck Institutes in New York, Jerusalem and London, the YIVO Institute in New York, the Central Archives for the History of the Jewish People in Jerusalem, the Alliance Israélite Universelle in Paris, or the United States Holocaust Memorial Museum, to name but a few, have contributed strongly to new forms of exchange between archives and libraries, in their own interest but also for the benefit of research. Just one example to illustrate this: held on 5 February 2009, a workshop under the title 'Towards a European Holocaust Research Infrastructure? Workshop for Holocaust Archives' in London brought together senior representatives of the national archives on the Holocaust and European Commission staff to discuss the current state of cooperation between Holocaust archives (e.g. mutual access, joint research projects, exchanges of staff) and to explore ways to enhance this cooperation. All these developments form one important context for this special issue of our journal *Jewish Culture and History* on 'Jewish Migration and the Archive'.

But, obviously, there is a more general dimension to consider. Jewish history has for centuries, often by force, been a history of migrations and displacements. Jews, both individually and as a group, have moved, from rural areas to towns and cities, from inner city districts to the suburbs, from one country to another, and mobility – in the broadest sense – has been a continuously present element of Jewish life and of Jewish/non-Jewish relations. All too often this historical experience has even been treated with a kind of 'essentialism', as the key for our understanding of Jewish culture and history. It is exactly when we want to escape from such essentialist notions – and images of 'the wandering Jew' – that we need to explore and document (with the help of archives) the very concrete circumstances of Jewish migrations.

In this context, Jewish Studies can and should profit and learn from developments in related fields. In recent years, the interrelation of 'Migration and Memory' has been established as an important area of study. When people migrate, what happens to their documents (their letters and diaries, their photographs, their books or other material objects)? While the fate of community archives might be well documented, at least in more peaceful times, what happens to private collections? How can we, in our research, integrate personal memorial strategies into the general narratives of migration and transmigration? How do archives and museums today represent such narratives and such documents? How can the fragmentary character of such collections be made visible?

There is a clear – but not yet defined – relationship between the study of (Jewish) history and the preservation of, or often lack of, documentary evidence. We need more information on collections and projects related to the collection, storage and accessibility of archival material relating to the experiences of migration in the nineteenth and twentieth centuries (and even of earlier periods, but the papers in this collection refer to the modern era). And this more technical aspect, important as it is, has to be balanced by a study of the idea of the archive, of the role and meaning of archives in (the construction of) Jewish history and culture, and also on the history of archives. This entails a study of the events themselves, but also of the forms of their transmission – in stories, descriptions or documentary accounts; and in symbolic forms such as poetry, novels and songs. Archives can be seen as one way of ensuring the continuity of historical narratives during times of insecurity. In this sense, the archive functions as a method of survival.

Historical research on Jewish history cannot be seen, or done, independently from the limitations and challenges produced by the events of history and their consequences for archives. The two belong together. Why do we need to go to Cape Town if we want to study German-Jewish history? Or to YIVO in New York for Eastern European Jewish history? In general terms, this is an effect of migration. How does migration affect the meaning of the archive? What is brought (or remembered) from one place to another, and what is left behind? How is the archive preserved (or forgotten)? What role do archives play in transmitting memory from place to place and from generation to generation? How and why were established archives moved, and how has their meaning changed through migration? And how has migration enabled the creation and construction of new archives which reflect departure, destination and the journey?

These questions were put forward in a Call for Papers that invited researchers to participate in a conference on 'The Archive and Jewish Migration' in Cape Town in 2011. This conference, perhaps fittingly, brought together scholars based in Argentina, Australia, Austria, Canada, Germany, Israel, New Zealand, South Africa, the UK and the United States. Following a series of conferences dedicated to 'Port Jews', 'Jewish Journeys' and 'Jewish Families', and jointly organized by the Parkes Institute for the Study of Jewish/non-Jewish Relations at the University of Southampton and the Kaplan Centre for Jewish Studies at the University of Cape Town, our meeting has been concerned with different types of (Jewish) migrations and the question of how they relate to – or even produce – archives. In a way, the papers presented at Cape Town made us aware of the fact that we need to break out of traditional conceptions of the archive and to realize, conceptually, that the multifold events of migration created new forms of storage, transmission and representation of documentary evidence. Some of the papers we present here went beyond traditional approaches bounded by disciplinary conventions. All of them, we feel, enrich and broaden our understanding of the interrelationship between archives and migration, and inspired us as editors to think very differently about migration, about Jewish identity, and especially about the nature of the archive.

The first five essays in this special issue of *Jewish Culture and History* bring fresh eyes to the very definition of the archive. Moving beyond the image of a monumental building containing dusty documents sent there by state agencies, these essays considerably broaden what we mean when we talk about archives. Such work is essential if we are to consider the experience of migratory groups or individuals. The papers or objects that make possible the transmission of their memories across time and place are not confined to state archives. On the contrary, if we are to tell their stories, we need new ways of thinking about the archive itself.

The first two pieces in this collection draw our eyes to the problem of what constitutes an archive of Jewish migration, and present us with startlingly creative ways of thinking about how to find, build and use it. Katy Beinart's contribution is an artistic work rather than a work of scholarship traditionally conceived. The form allows the artist to bring to light the problem of memory transmission across generations and transmigrations, and, at the same time, provides the opportunity for inventing ways to recreate it. In reconstructing old voyages based on a personal archive of family photos, the artist and her sister connect to their family past without losing sight of what knowledge has been lost.

Esther Saraga's essay is also deeply personal and based on a family archive, in this case letters her parents exchanged in the late 1930s as they were in the process of migrating from Germany to England. The article brings to light the emotions involved in the process of relocation. In addition, through the author's exploration of her own emotional relationship to this history, it forces us to consider emotions themselves as another kind of archive within which lies buried evidence of the meaning of this migration.

At the start of her article, Katy Beinart writes of the 'strange dark chest' which was to be found in her family home when she was a child. She remembers how, '[o]n occasion, my father would open it, a strong smell of camphor would emanate, and he would bring out treasures which seemed to come from a distant place and time – silverware, porcelain, linen, prayer shawls and even a battered fox fur'. That connection between smell, memory and imagination is central to Henrietta Mondry's thought-provoking contribution to this volume. In this essay Mondry pushes the boundaries of traditional conceptions of the archive to include a more personal type of repository than a public collection of documents. She explores how certain Russian writers have worked with the idea that smell constitutes a sort of archive, and asks us to consider both the limits and the possibilities of such a theory for transmitting Jewish memory and identity across time and place.

Two of our essays use museums as a jumping off point from which to further broaden, and even to challenge, our definition of the archive. Hilda Nissimi examines heritage centres in Israel. These museums commemorate the communities from which different Israeli ethnic groups originated. As such, they can be considered archives of the Diaspora and the many different experiences of migration to Israel. Her essay shows the multifaceted relationship these museums have to the Zionist ethos of national integration.

Working from another disciplinary perspective, Joachim Schlör's article examines what has become the archetypical symbol of migration itself in museum exhibitions around the world: the suitcase. As an ethnographer, Schlör is interested in what these memory containers mean. Occupying something of a semiotic 'thirdspace', the suitcase stands poised between one place and another, and is linked to that movement and transformation itself. An ethnography of the suitcase provides another window into the lived experience of migration.

In the second half of our collection, we have brought together more traditional works of historical scholarship that deal creatively with the problems migration poses for the reconstruction of the past, and demonstrate how enriching an exploration of the history of the archive across time and space can be for historical research. Judith Szapor's study of the Polanyi archives uses a previously untapped set of family papers to fill in our knowledge about the family's complicated path of migration. Her essay not only sheds new light on the history of this important family as its members fled persecution in Hungary, Germany and Soviet Ukraine, it also explores with sensitivity how differently the same experience of migration is documented in its 'public' collection (held in a state archive) and in its 'private' papers.

Veronica Belling does a similar type of work with a document that could itself be considered an archive: the Yiddish diary of Ray Alexander Simons, now held in an archive far from its place of origin because of the migration of its owner. As an adult, Simons would become well known as a Communist activist in South Africa; this study focuses on the diary she kept as a small child in Latvia. Belling finds that the personal source sometimes contradicts what its author wrote of her youth in an autobiography she published, leading to interesting possibilities for thinking about the meaning of the Eastern European Jewish past in the context of apartheid South Africa.

Finally, Maura Hametz's essay on the papers of Sam Switzer uses a particular archival collection, housed in a university library in Virginia, to reconstruct the history of elite Jewish life in the American South in the first part of the twentieth century. Consciously interrogating why certain items were archived, and why the entire collection has wound up in its current location, leads Hametz to additional insights about Jewish migration patterns as well as the critical issue, addressed in so many of our essays, of how to discern and think about what is left out of these collections and why.

Archivists today understand that the meaning of records can be deconstructed and reconstructed, then used by scholars, who add other layers of meaning. The archive can be reconsidered and re-evaluated as a site for the production of knowledge according to its location, context and purpose. Studying archives in the context of migration history contributes an additional layer of sophistication by making us aware of the fact that these repositories on which we rely for our research do not provide us with 'complete' narratives. On the contrary, they tell stories about absence, fragmentation and loss, challenging researchers from all fields to develop new and creative ways to write history.

Notes

1. Jean-Claude Kuperminc and Rafaele Arditi, eds., *Preserving Jewish Archives as Part of the European Cultural Heritage. Proceedings of the Conference on Judaica Archives in Europe, for Archivists and Librarians, Potsdam, July 11–13, 1999* (Paris: Les Editions du Nadir de l'Alliance Israélite Universelle, 2001), 11.
2. Feliks Tych, "Juden betreffende Quellen und die Rekonstruktion der jüdischen Sozial- und Kulturgeschichte", in ibid., 16.

Reading between the lines: artistic approaches to the family archive

Katy Beinart

The Bartlett School of Architecture, University College London, London, UK

This paper explores artistic approaches to memorialisation and the archive in reinterpreting personal narratives of Jewish migration, through recent collaborative artworks by the author and her sister, made during a journey to and residency in South Africa in 2009–2010. Drawing on a private family archive of correspondence including over 200 postcards sent mainly between Hull, England and South Africa during the Edwardian period, it touches on migration, genealogical research and changing networks of communication and affection. With the loss of understanding of writing as a scribal (drawn) practice, this paper explores attempts to use embodied artistic actions to 'read between the lines' of archival material, creating forms of translation which remap familiar territories and tropes, shedding new light on these journeys into diasporic memory. The paper is structured like a series of 'postcards': fragmentary sections that reflect the nature of memory and archival material, in combinations of image and text that each contain a short extract of a longer dialogue, place and a relationship.

Introduction

As children, my sister and I were always entranced by the strange, dark chest that stood in our living room. On occasion, my father would open it, a strong smell of camphor would emanate, and he would bring out treasures which seemed to come from a distant place and time – silverware, porcelain, linen, prayer shawls and even a battered fox fur (Figure 1).

When I asked why some of these objects were broken and tarnished, he explained it was because they had been on several long voyages by sea made by his grandmother Edith, firstly with her mother Ann and later with her children (Figure 2).

As we grew older, he also showed us Edith's collection of postcards (Figure 3); hundreds of fading, delicately coloured images, of places, people and objects that seemed unfamiliar or even incomprehensible to my born-and-raised in the 1980s-England self.

As a practising artist, I often used archival material in my work, relating it to specific sites. My art practice evolved from a background in architecture, and I became fascinated by the way that place forms identity. How as we migrate, we write ourselves into places; we form narratives based on the places we come from and have left behind, and the new ones we encounter. Cairns describes the experience of the migrant in the city as 'rewriting the script of the city'.[1] Carter proposes that migrant

---

All images and artworks are courtesy and copyright of Katy and Rebecca Beinart.

Figure 1. Family silver.

Figure 2. Edith and Ann.

Figure 3. Kilfauns castle postcard.

place-making incorporates movement, preserving the experience of arrival, the place of potential approaches, thereby creating a layering of memory which opens up an alternative reading of public and private space.[2] The postcards seemed to describe this palimpsest of memory moving through and over places, although the locations and addressees were often unknown to us.

I became fascinated by this archive of material that obliquely described the process of our ancestors' movement through time and space, and which might provide clues to the Jewish identity and culture of my ancestors, which I knew so little about. I wanted to understand how the metaphorical 'writing' into and of place were embodied in the actual written and collected artefacts. *Origination*, the project I and my sister – artist Rebecca Beinart – developed from this archive, set out to trace our family history, and to memorialise these migrant histories, through artistic methodologies of re-enactment and re-embodiment.[3] By remaking their actions in places our ancestors travelled through, we wanted to both acknowledge our heritage, and understand how the archival narratives of the past had come to shape our own present identities. The expression 'reading between the lines' evolved from a form of cryptography, in which a hidden meaning was conveyed by secreting it between lines of text. Given the fragmentary nature of memory, and the archive, we wanted to use art practice as a means to create material that might fill the gaps or spaces in the narrative.

Figure 4. Edith Pearlman as a child.

The artworks I will describe in this paper relate to the stories of two people; my great-grandmother Edith Pearlman (Figure 4) and my great-grandfather Woolf Beinart (Figure 5).

Edith's parents Leopold Pearlman and Ann Filaratoff both came from Russia and were among the million Jewish migrants who arrived in Hull, England between 1880 and 1914.[4] They married around 1890, Edith was born in 1891 and the family emigrated to South Africa in the early 1900s.

Woolf was born in 1874 in Rokiskis, Lithuania and emigrated to South Africa around 1905, where he settled in Malmesbury, a small town in the Western Cape. His wife Gittel joined him there and they set up a general store and had seven sons.

Strategies for understanding and transmitting family history differ. A historian's approach may be to delve deeper for additional facts, or search the comparative literature to fill in context. But as artists, once the basic framework is in place, we interpret and work with this material differently. The restrictions of the discipline of history mean that whilst imagination is essential, it has to be rooted in a source. Art is not tethered: for the artist, source material can be a starting point for reading between the lines, offering different possibilities for reflection and interpretation. Like novelists, but unlike historians, we are fictionalising personal history, but unlike novelists, we are doing this

Figure 5. Image of Woolf Beinart (centre left) and family, Malmesbury.

through a visual medium. Our artwork does not faithfully recreate the experiences of our migrant ancestors. It is a personal exploration of identity, and a universal exploration of what memory means within a family.

Migration

In December 2009, we travelled to Cape Town by the container ship 'Green Cape', retracing the route of our ancestors from Eastern Europe to South Africa (Figure 6).

Figure 6. Container ship approaching Cape Town.

We then spent three months in Cape Town undertaking a residency which gave us the opportunity to do more detailed research in the sites where our family had lived and worked, and to generate artworks from these clues. Subsequently, we returned to the UK and made further work in Hull, the first point of arrival on their journey to South Africa for our family and many others.

We set off on our journey with books and texts, assorted costumes, a bread-making kit carried in a suitcase that had made the journey by ship with our father and grandparents, and a selection of our family archive (Figure 7), unsure as to how these would coincide on our journey to unravel the myth of our own identity. In W.G. Sebald's *Austerlitz*, a search for lost identity, the main character explores narratives of place to re-find memories of self:

> And might it not be, continued Austerlitz, that we also have appointments to keep in the past, in what has gone before and is for the most part extinguished, and must go there in search of places and people who have some connection with us on the far side of time, so to speak?[5]

Being on this journey, we hoped to somehow keep these appointments, to touch moments our ancestors had experienced in their migrations (Figure 8). But we became aware that our identities were performed, constructing an idea of a fictitious past based on our own (recent) histories. We have often attempted to re-inhabit certain moments through artworks – attempting to embody the past – to enter into memory in a way that

Figure 7. Setting off with suitcases.

Figure 8. The 'Green Cape'.

does not rely only upon words. In this sense, our work could be seen as a form of translation.

Translation, which derives from the Latin *Transferre*, meaning 'to bring across', can be seen as a metaphor for migration.[6] An object transferred takes on a new set of significances – or may be evoked using new objects which 'stand for' the original. Similarly, in the carrying over of language, words take on new significances; Benjamin's question of how translation can 'constitute the continued life of the original'[7] mirrors the question of how the migrant can continue the life of their 'home' in a new context. The difference between translation (word-for-word rendering) and

Figure 9. Ben and Gladys.

Figure 10. Picture of Ben and Gladys – reconstruction.

transduction (sense for sense), and therefore of en-textualisation: (extracting discourse from its original context and re-inserting it into a new context) exposes how translations and migrations can transform, as well as cross boundaries (footnote 6).

On the journey, we reconstructed family photographs taken onboard ship, and dressed in the original garments belonging to grandparents and great-grandparents (Figure 10). This re-enactment was a deliberate hotchpotch of time and place; the ship constructed in the 1980s, the clothing dating from the 1930s and 1950s. But perhaps this is a more honest attempt to explain our confused identities than a deliberate attempt to accurately reconstruct the past (Figure 9).

After all, surely our family, by leaving behind their home and community, were trying to create new identities. The idea of the diaspora can suggest either a clinging to memories or liberation from the past; a feeling of homelessness vs. an unreal sense of rootedness in a fictional homeland. Garfield writes: 'Jonathan Boyarin suggests that nostalgia is a denial of the state of sustained rediasporisation, which is the nature of Jewish history'.[8] Why, then, reconstruct a past which Jewish families have for one reason or another been forced to leave behind?

'Diasporic subjectivity offers the contemporary world a way of understanding community without statehood or attachment to territory ... the emphasis is not on where you are from, but where you are going'.[9] This makes sense in the context of our journey – we are not seeking a complete identity, and a return to the past, but rather, like our ancestors perhaps, more of a disentanglement from narratives of orthodoxy; acknowledging the complexities of heritage with Jewishness as a part of our identity, but not all.

Assimilation

Our great-grandfather Woolf Beinart emigrated from Lithuania to South Africa in the early twentieth century and settled in the Western Cape. Through our research at the

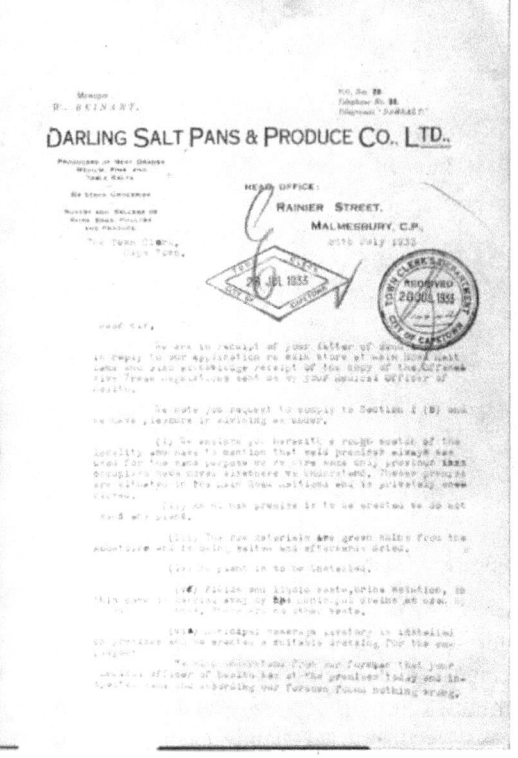

Figure 11. Darling salt pans.

Cape Town archives, we found records of the company he set up, the Darling Salt Pans and Produce Company. Plans and blueprints showed the area where he had harvested salt, between Darling and Malmesbury, two small towns in the Western Cape (Figure 11).

Through further research, looking at aerial photographs at the Department of Land Affairs, we found the exact location of Burgerspan, a naturally occurring salt pan in the Darling area, one of several from which Woolf would have harvested salt in the early 1900s. We drove down miles of bumpy tracks before we found the salt pan, and met the farmer on whose land it now stood (Figure 12).

Figure 12. Burgerspan.

Figure 13. Old photo albums.

When we told the farmer what we were looking for, and why, he said he had discovered old photograph albums in the attic which dated from the period Woolf would have been there. The albums contained faded sepia photographs of men standing proudly in front of piles of salt, men who we imagined could have been our long-distant relatives (Figure 13).

From this research, we created a series of artworks which were shown in an exhibition at the University of Stellenbosch gallery in Stellenbosch.[10] *Don't Look Back* (Figure 14) was an installation which invited the viewer to enter a recreated salt pan. The title refers to the migrant's dilemma, and particularly that of the Jewish diaspora's – whether to attempt to preserve the customs and traditions of the old home, or to leave them behind and start anew, adapting to the new environments they find themselves in. The title also refers to the story of Lot's wife, who is punished for looking back at Sodom by being turned into a pillar of salt; the work also raised a question about the very nature of genealogical research; is it wise to try and uncover one's origins? Our identities are formed so much from handed-down truths that to dig deeper can raise difficult dilemmas around identity and choices. Hilary Mantel writes: 'for some years I lived in Botswana and people there used to say that to see ghosts, you need to look out of the corners of your eyes'[11]; this artwork echoes the idea of how we try to access the past; memory is elusive and the archive is often fragmented in nature, so perhaps it is more effective to look indirectly, sideways, through a translated version of history.

Offere is a short film made on the salt pan (Figure 15). The title *Offere* means to bring across, in the sense of an offering or gift. In this case, the bringing across is an attempt to communicate with ancestors, in a place they worked. In many cultures, ancestor rituals consist of an offering, often food and wine. For example, in the Suku of south-western Congo, appeals are made to ancestors at times of crisis. The elder men go to sit on the graves at night, or at crossroads.

Figure 14. Don't look back.

Figure 15. Offere.

> The old men 'feed' the dead certain foods considered to be their favourite: particular kinds of forest mushroom and wild roots, palm wine and sometimes even manioc, the Suku staple. A small hole is dug in the ground and the food is put into it.[12]

We used porcelain belonging to Edith, as well as her dresses and table linen, and served our imaginary dinner guests with Borscht and black bread, Jewish Eastern European dishes brought to an African salt pan. The film transposes objects, rituals and cultural references to recreate an impossible scenario, an invented idea of history which combines fact and fantasy.

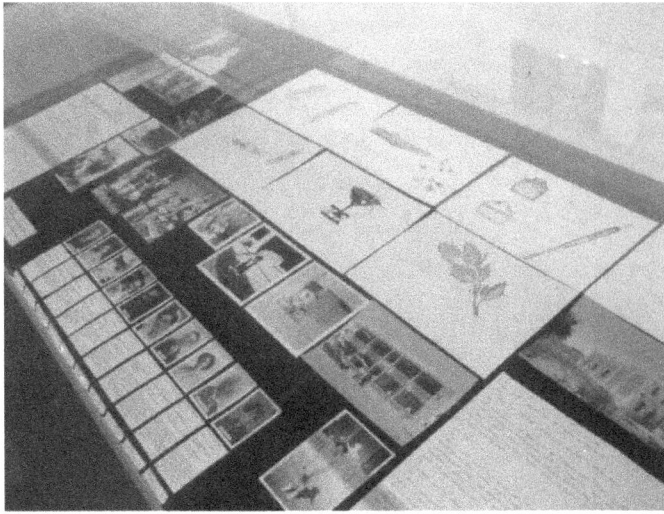

Figure 16. Transferre.

Re-presenting archival material creates questions of intention and framing. As we collected fragments of memory of place, we also created reconstructed artefacts or recordings of possible sites of significance. For *Transferre*, a collection of material presented as an archive (Figure 16), I made a series of drawings of objects found in the graveyard where Woolf was buried, a dusty and semi-abandoned cemetery in Malmesbury. The drawings also recorded fragments of objects belonging to Edith, so they became in themselves a method of processing. I also made a series of cigarette cards, referencing great-grandmother Anne's now-vanished collection; each had an image of a family member and key facts about their life. These objects were placed alongside actual letters, postcards and photographs so that the 'real' and 'invented' became indistinguishable, questioning our ready acceptance of 'authentic' archival material and the legitimacy of the reproduction. Susan Pearce writes that

> heirloom material ... is a kind of ancestor worship, where part of the point is to participate in the power which can flow from the mighty dead of one's own kin and partly, in a more limited sense, to enjoy the prestige which accrues from having ancestors at all.[13]

So, in questioning the very material of heritage, or reinventing it, do we subvert this automatic acceptance of the power of the past, and instead bring into question the relationship we have with our ancestors?

Communication

On our return to England, we took our journey to Hull, the point of arrival for Edith's parents before their subsequent migration to South Africa. Edith's postcard collection, one of the few major pieces of archival evidence to have survived our family's journeying, was used as part of an exhibition in Hull (Figure 17).[14]

Edith's father Leopold had a tailor's shop in Prospect street, central Hull, and was naturalised as a British citizen in the early 1900s. They were part of Hull's

Figure 17. Postcard of Hull synagogue.

Figure 18. Postcard from Pretoria.

2,000-strong Jewish community. Nevertheless, he left in 1902 to start a tailoring business in Pretoria, where the Boer War had led to an increase in demand (Figure 18).

Edith had trained as a pianist in Hull and was playing regularly in concerts, but from what we can deduce she left in 1910 to join the family in South Africa, although leaving behind her best friend Dollie whose closeness is evidenced through the postcard collection. We found a programme titled 'Farewell Concert', with a list of

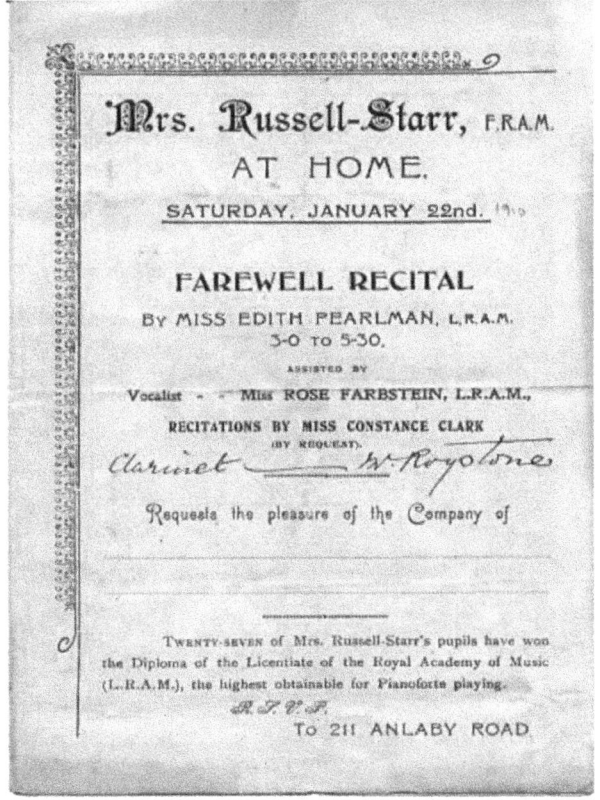

Figure 19. Farewell concert brochure.

the pieces she played in what was the final concert she gave before leaving England, at the home of her tutor, Mrs Russell-Starr (Figure 19).

For the installation *Farewell Concert* (Figure 20), we took a 78 rpm gramophone record and made a wax pressing of it, which replaces the record on the gramophone, while a recording of the music Edith played at her farewell concert is played through speakers. The wax press is another ghostly relic, of technology now defunct, and of music which marked a departure. It is not an actual artefact from our past, but instead a stand-in, a marker of absence. As part of the process of making this work, I tried to learn the pieces she played, re-inhabiting the sense of the skill that she carried in her hands. Whilst my fingers struggled to shape the notes, I could more easily work with the wax to cast the grooves of the record. This brought into sharp focus the change in identities and skills through generations – the acceptable creative choice of an assimilated young lady in 1900s Hull was classical music, but today my sister and I could pursue a career in the visual arts.

Alongside the exhibition, we made a walking tour of Hull entitled *Though I have missed you so very much*. Based on Edith's postcards, and the sites of family homes and workplaces, the walking tour was an imaginative, experiential and multi-sensory way into this material, weaving together history and myth, in an invitation for others to contribute to a narrative (Figure 21).

Figure 20. Farewell concert.

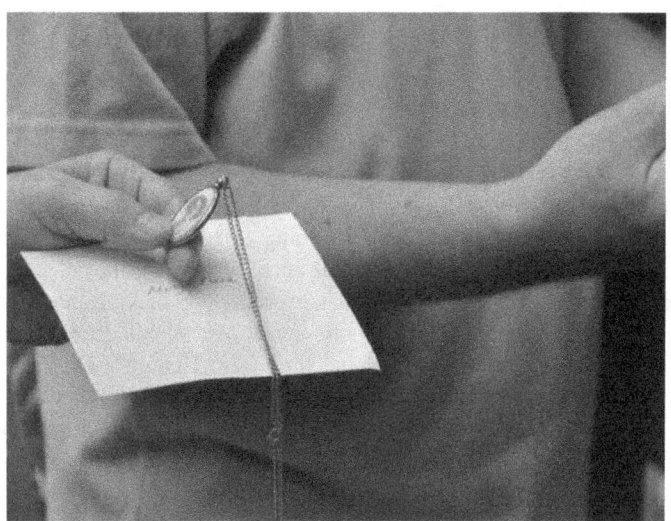

Figure 21. Walking tour – envelope.

Figure 22. Walking tour.

Figure 23. Israel's grave.

We asked participants to carry an envelope, addressed to a particular location. At these locations, they opened the envelopes and discovered one of Edith's postcards, a photograph or artefact relating to that site (Figure 22).

Figure 24.   Vodka at the docks.

As the walk meandered through the city centre and down to the docks, we became increasingly involved in the tales of the lives of Edith and her best friend Dollie, and the separation that came through migration. We encountered ships, waiting rooms, concert halls, a music box, a lost locket, lost gardens, a drowned synagogue and a forgotten brother (Figure 23).

There is added poignancy in our discovery of a truly lost family member – Edith's younger brother Israel. We came across his grave in the neglected Jewish cemetery, and looked for him in the census of 1901 where he was labelled as 'feeble minded'. He was in fact put in an institution in London during this migrant phase of family history and died there as a young man.

There is a profound sadness that emerges from tracing these now-vanished lives in a contemporary landscape. But there is also humour as secrets are revealed and

Figure 25.   Postcard of docks.

Figure 26. Ghostwriting.

interpretations of the missing facts are offered. We ended the tour at the docks (Figure 24), poured everyone a shot of vodka, raised our glasses to 'all those who have passed' and read a quote from Sebald:

> Memory, he added in a postscript, often strikes me as a kind of dumbness. It makes one's head heavy and a giddy, as if one were not looking back down the receding perspectives of time but rather down on the earth from a great height, from one of those towers whose tops are lost to view in the clouds.[15]

Postcards could be containers of condensed emotion, then vehicles for memory (Figure 25). In reading between the lines of our family archive, we may find out something about the lives of those who sent and received them, and kept them for a lifetime. For the exhibition in Hull, we produced a piece called *Ghostwriting*, for which we traced the words from a postcard onto a waxed sheet of paper (Figure 26). The faintly visible words are traces of the shapes of the letters written over 100 years ago, and through tracing the words we could imagine the motion of the writer's hand, try to deduce the sensations they felt, and try to get under their skin. Making it, I adopted a posture, noted the details of each curve and movement of the line as it formed letters. The act of tracing became an evocation of the action, a re-living of gesture and an embodiment of the intention of the writer.

Conclusion

We keep objects for certain reasons. They remind us of moments in time; they are mnemonics, or memory aids, often taking us to moments of extreme emotion or importance in our life. As we consciously or subconsciously collect this archive, we are constructing a narrative of our lives, selecting what is kept in and what is left out. The selected objects are mirrored by the places or sites they represent; these *lieux de memoire* or places of memory then take on significance for us, as symbolic of personal or

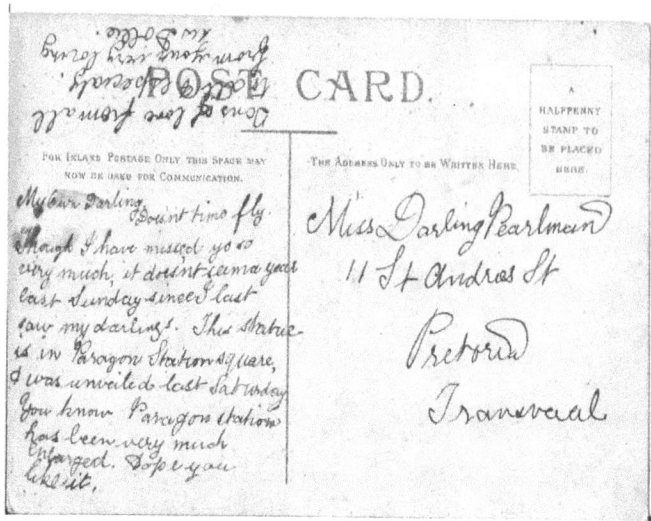

Figure 27.   Postcard from Dollie – 'Though I have missed you'.

communal heritage.[16] For diasporic Jewish families, a process of rediscovering these sites of memory has been popularised in recent times through books and films like Jonathan Safran Foer's *Everything is Illuminated*, in which a young American man 'returns' to find his family's shtetl in the Ukraine, unwittingly getting involved with the current politics of the country. Often, artefacts such as postcards are the only available guide or clue for these searches for personal identity and narrative, but according to one's discipline one can read the same object in a different way; an archivist, an historian, a curator or an artist would each produce a different reading, but perhaps could also learn from each others' approach.

We don't know why Edith kept her collection of postcards until the end of her life. Ostensibly she collected the postcards for the images on the front of them, as part of a current fashion or craze. Perhaps it was also the passion, close relationships, sadness

Figure 28.   Ghostwriting – detail.

and longing in the brief messages on the back of the cards (Figure 27). The limited messages suggest that the act of sending a postcard was in itself almost the most important element in communication. These links constituted an empire of affection – such personal ties were a result rather than cause of expanding empires, but played some role in holding it together in popular consciousness.

Ingold writes of the loss of understanding of writing as a scribal practice and how we 'fail to recognize the extent to which the very art of writing, at least until it was ousted by typography, lay in the drawing of lines ...'[17] I wonder if it is the action of writing by hand that carries an intent, a strength of conviction which invests the words with meaning (Figure 28). Could this be why our ancestors collected postcards, letters and written ephemera so preciously, not just for the words but for the action contained within the words, the physical gesture of scripting?

Perhaps it is through art practices that we can translate the postcards and other archival material to reveal 'things not said'. Gibbons describes artists working with memory in ways which 'involve the viewers affectively, positioning them at a sensory or intuitive level ... and laying the ground for more distanced critical reflection.'[18] The role of art in this case can be to give an intuitive approach to history, to remap familiar territories and tropes in such a way that new light can be shed on these shadowy journeys into diasporic memory.

Family history both reflects general trends and reveals how private experiences and entanglements inevitably corrugate broader concepts of identity. And it is this plurality and liminality which crosses between the territories of memory and history, and art and history.

Acknowledgement

The author wishes to thank Rebecca Beinart and William Beinart for their input.

Notes

1. Stephen Cairns, ed., *Drifting: Architecture and Migrancy* (London: Routledge, 2003).
2. Paul Carter, "Mythforms: Techniques of Migrant Place-making," in *Drifting* (London: Routledge, 2003), ed. Cairns, 82–98.
3. See *Origination*, Project Blog at AN Artists Talking, http://www.a-n.co.uk/artists_talking/projects/single/520058 (accessed September 29, 2013).
4. See *Moving Here: Migration Histories*. Directed by Nicholas J. Evans, http://www.movinghere.org.uk/galleries/histories/jewish/journeys/journeys.htm (accessed September 29, 2013).
5. W.G. Sebald, *Austerlitz* (New York: Random House, 2001), 359.
6. Paul Basu and Simon Coleman, "Migrant Worlds, Material Cultures," *Mobilities* 3, no. 3 (2008): 313–30.

7. Paula Rubel and Abraham Rosman, eds., *Translating Cultures: Perspectives on Translation and Anthropology* (Oxford: Berg, 2003), 7; referring to Walter Benjamin, "The Task of the Translator," in *Illuminations* (London: Fontana/Collins, 1973).
8. Rachel Garfield, "Towards a Re-articulation of Cultural Identity; Problematizing the Jewish Subject in Art," *Third Text 78* 20, no. 1 (2006): 99–108.
9. Jonathan and Daniel Boyarin, *Powers of Diaspora, Two Essays on the Relevance of Jewish Culture* (Minneapolis: University of Minnesota Press, 2002), 5. Ibid., 101.
10. Katy and Rebecca Beinart, *Origination* (Stellenbosch: University of Stellenbosch Gallery), (Exhibition March 11–27, 2010).
11. Hilary Mantel, "Ghost Writing," *The Guardian*, July 28, 2007.
12. 'Communication with the dead takes the form of a conversational monologue, patterned but not stereotyped, and devoid of repetitive formulae. One speaks the way one speaks to living people: "You, [such and such], your junior is ill. We do not know why, we do not know who is responsible. If it is you, if you are angry, we ask for forgiveness. If we have done wrong, pardon us. Do not let him die. Other lineages are prospering and our people are dying. Why are you doing this? Why do you not look after us properly?" The words typically combine complaints, scolding, sometimes even anger, and at the same time appeals for forgiveness'. Igor Kopytoff, "Ancestors as Elders in Africa," *Africa* 41, no. 02 (1971): 129–42.
13. Susan Pearce, *On Collecting* (London: Routledge, 1995).
14. Katy and Rebecca Beinart, *Origination* (Hull: Artlink Gallery, 2010) 19 June–15 July.
15. W.G. Sebald, *The Emigrants* (London: Harvill, 1996).
16. 'A *lieu de mémoire* is any significant entity, whether material or non-material in nature, which by dint of human will or the work of time has become a symbolic element of the memorial heritage of any community (in this case, the French community)' (Nora 1996: XVII) In other words, sites of memory are 'where [cultural] memory crystallizes and secretes itself' (Nora 1989: 7). These include: places such as archives, museums, cathedrals, palaces, cemeteries and memorials; concepts and practices such as commemorations, generations, mottos and all rituals; objects such as inherited property, commemorative monuments, manuals, emblems, basic texts and symbols. Pierre Nora, *Les Lieux de mémoire* (Paris: Gallimard, 1984–1992), abridged translation, *Realms of Memory* (New York: Columbia University Press, 1996–1998).
17. Tim Ingold, *Lines* (London: Routledge, 2007), 128.
18. Joan Gibbons, *Contemporary Art & Memory* (London: I B Tauris, 2008), 60.

'Personal letters – to keep': managing the emotions of forced migration

Esther Saraga

Independent researcher

This article, part of a larger project, explores ways in which a private collection of personal papers, official letters and documents can be used to construct the lived experience of the author's parents, Lotte and Wolja, two German Jewish refugees. Making use of letters written between May and September 1938, when Wolja was on a temporary visa in London and Lotte still in Berlin, the article focuses on how it felt in 1938 to be forced to leave Germany, the gendered strategies they used to manage their feelings and the importance of their letters for keeping them going through the fear and uncertainty.

I grew up in a very untidy family. My mother often apologised for the mess she would be leaving after her death, so my brother Peter and I knew there would be a lot to clear up. But we had no idea we would find so many boxes and envelopes full of papers and photographs. They were in sideboards and cupboards, in the loft and in the garage. Some were simply stuffed at the back of drawers. There were personal and official letters, unfinished drafts and carbon copies, legal documents, bills, receipts, and my father's childhood poems. They span more than 80 years from my grandmother Ester's student records in the early 1900s to post-war restitution claims, which continue until 1982. These papers constitute the 'personal archive' at the centre of my research and of this article.

Both my parents were born in Berlin. They came to the UK as Jewish refugees – my father, Wolja, in May 1938 and my mother, Lotte, four months later at the end of August. He was 29; she was 24. When Lotte died in December 1984, nearly five years after Wolja, she had lived in the same house – our childhood home – for almost 40 years. Whenever they went away, Lotte left an envelope on the sideboard marked 'to be opened in the event of our deaths'. It told us where to find their wills and was full of apologies about the mess.

We had no idea that our parents had kept these papers, or why we were not told of their existence, but it was clear from the labels on some of the envelopes that Lotte had started to sort them. Sometimes this was by topic, as with the restitution claims, but often her label would describe the nature of the correspondence: 'Private letters' or 'Personal letters', including the one that has given me my title – 'Personal Letters Lotte to keep'.

Discovering these papers raised many questions for us. Did she want us to read them? These labels, and the names written on the back of a few photographs, suggest that she did think about a time when we would find them. I remember her as someone who avoided or denied emotional difficulties; was she unable to dispose of them because it meant throwing away her past? Or was it a refusal to say 'it's over', even though the way they brought us up suggested that they tried to live in the present? Was she relying on us to finish the process for her? Was her distinction between 'personal' and 'private' a message to us; should we be throwing away the latter?

Finding the papers was emotionally overwhelming; we kept coming across them in different places during the process of clearing the house for sale. As we dipped into them, Peter said it made him feel guilty, because he hadn't known what they had been through. I responded very fiercely: 'they would not have wanted us to feel guilty; we are not responsible for their experiences; would you want your children to feel like that about your life?' But now I know that the strength of my response was a defence against exactly those same feelings in me – a sense that somehow we should have known.

Finding the papers also meant keeping them, or more specifically not throwing them away – to do so would have felt like an act of denial or betrayal, even of violence. In line with the role I had played as a child, as mediator in an emotionally volatile family, there was a tacit understanding that they were my responsibility, although I had no idea what to do with them. They were boxed up and travelled with me for the next 18 years through three house moves – 18 years of avoidance and ambivalence.

In 1994, 10 years after our mother's death, I tried unsuccessfully to read them, rationalising my failure in terms of lack of time and insufficient fluency in German. But in fact I could not manage the painful feelings, especially as I had just broken up from a long-term relationship. The letters are suffused with anxiety about loss and separation, and this triggered my own feelings of loss about my parents and about their stories, which we had only ever known in fragments.

Eight years later, in 2002, the suggestion that I could legitimately make it an academic project enabled me to distance myself a little; German courses started at the Open University where I worked; and I was now in a stable relationship. Years of psychoanalysis had helped me both to reflect on my feelings and to develop strategies for dealing with them.

As a way to start I was advised to 'immerse myself' in the papers.[1] I kept a notebook by me to record memories, thoughts and feelings triggered by the material. I also started to read about the historical context. Sometimes this was obvious – life in Nazi Germany in 1938, or the internment of Jewish refugees by the British in 1940. But sometimes it came from my responses to the letters. For example, the arrival of my new e-passport in 2010, when I was reflecting on the impact of my father's statelessness, led me to read about the history of the passport and ideas on nationality, citizenship and belonging, and to explore Wolja's negotiations of identity and the significance of identity papers.

The papers in this archive helped me to elaborate the story with which I grew up, although it was painful to recognise the losses and separations they had experienced. After 18 months, in which I had only scratched the surface of sorting and categorising the papers, I empathised with Grossmann,[2] who wonders why anyone should want to read yet another story of German Jews. However, the process of working on the papers had become as important to me as their content, and I knew I wanted to go beyond simply 'telling the story'.[3] By allowing the papers to lead me, I had developed a particular method of working: reading the letters triggers memories of family stories which then inform my interpretations, which are in turn influenced by what I can learn from historical research and archives as well as by links to wider social and political issues. My personal memories and reflections often lead me to change my original interpretation or to find a whole new layer of meaning that I had not seen before.

I decided to work with the papers in two ways: to explore what can be learned from such a personal archive, in particular about how it felt to live through particular historical events; and to reflect on the process of doing this work while negotiating the different identities of daughter, researcher and academic.[4]

The 1938 letters

In this article I am illustrating my approach to these personal papers through a focus on one set of correspondence – letters between my parents in 1938. The original letters are all in German and the translations are mine.[5]

Between 7 May and 31 August 1938, while Lotte is still in Berlin, living with her widowed mother, Wolja is in London on a one-month temporary visa with Home Office permission to look for scientific work. They write to each other very frequently, sometimes twice in one day, and sometimes with gaps of several days. Ninety letters and postcards and one telegram have survived, most of which were written by Lotte. For the first three months (May, June and July) I only have her letters; from 1 August I have Wolja's letters as well.

At this distance four months seems like a short time, but reading the letters gives me a sense of Lotte and Wolja's experience in 'real time' – it is as if I can live their story day to day as it happened. In August 2004, I wrote in my notebook:

> it is very strange and upsetting to be reading and recording these last letters, at the same time of year that it was happening ... I feel so involved and anxious about whether she will actually get out – even though I know the end of the story – indeed I am one of the ends of the story!

This reflection alerted me to the implications of reading with hindsight, knowing some of what did happen. A common feature of histories of the Holocaust is what Bernstein calls 'backshadowing', that is the use of knowledge of later events 'to impose the terms within which earlier events are analysed'.[6] In relation to the Holocaust he suggests this results in a tendency to attribute a 'gift of historical prophecy', which is then followed by judgements of people's actions at the time, in particular 'Why didn't they leave?' When I first read these 1938 letters, I experienced this myself, often feeling frustrated by what seemed to be a lack of urgency to get Lotte out. I wrote in my notebook: 'clearly war and genocide were not in their minds'. Later, when a friend described my parents as 'fleeing genocide', I recognised how this misrepresents their experience. Reading their letters more than 70 years after they were written, I have to try to understand how Lotte and Wolja themselves experienced their lives, not impose my understanding on them.

Reading with hindsight means that I also know what did *not* happen – they did get out in time – but it is easy for my interpretations to be affected by my fears about what could have happened. Within much of the 'Holocaust survivor' literature there is a strong idea of who is a legitimate person to write about, with crucial differences being made between survivors (those who suffered in camps) and refugees (those who got away). Vansant describes the way refugees may have to 'gain a sense that their stories are worth telling', since 'nothing *exceptional* has happened to them in comparison to the pain and suffering of those in concentration camps'.[7]

I find myself affected by these issues. Falling into what I think of as the 'victim trap',[8] I have found myself seeking justifications for the work I am doing by looking for examples of suffering. This can influence the choices I make – which letters to select and from these letters whether to extract passages which emphasise the suffering or those that seem to represent resistance and survival. Am I making the right choices? My mother experienced the 'guilt of the survivor', always saying 'we didn't really suffer'. Can I avoid victimhood without underplaying the discrimination, loss and pain that it is clear from these papers they did experience?

The 1938 letters tell several stories: there is a personal story of forced migration that despite its successful ending is not smooth, and which 'goes wrong' several times. Lotte's only way out of Germany is through a domestic permit and it takes Wolja three attempts to find a position for her. In mid-June Erna (Lotte's mother) is knocked over by a cyclist and badly hurt. This not only adds greatly to Lotte's distress, but delays her departure for at least a month. On 16 August her mother leaves for Palestine – to join Lotte's older sister; on 19 August Lotte finally gets her permit to come to England; on 23 August she sends Wolja a telegram: 'HURRAH VISUM KUSS = TEDDY'; and on 31 August she arrives at Liverpool Street Station in London.

We can also construct a more general story about the circumstances for Jewish refugees from information about Wolja's uncertain position in the UK, the permits and documentation that Lotte needs both to leave Germany and to enter the UK, and the rules and regulations governing export of their possessions.

Lotte and Wolja's relationship is relatively new; they are clearly lovers, but not yet married. The letters tell the story of a personal relationship conducted, for these four months, only through this correspondence. They have to fulfil multiple purposes – to convey information, negotiate decisions, and express conscious and unconscious feelings. They are also a physical manifestation of contact between people who are separated.

The 1938 letters do not 'speak for themselves'; I am choosing which story to tell, and on which of the multiple purposes to focus on. The biggest challenge was to capture the tension between the personal and the social/political in a way that recognises their mutual constitution. The strongest impact of the letters is the complexity of the emotions that Lotte expresses, so I am using this as the analytical lens through which to read them in order to explore how it felt at the time to live through these events and to identify the strategies they used to cope with and manage their feelings.

Optimism and reassurance

In the early letters Lotte is very optimistic. She constantly reassures Wolja of her love and tries to ease his anxiety, offering him both emotional and practical support. Her first letter, written on 7 May, starts: 'Isn't it strange, the first day alone in such a young marriage.'[9] She imagines Wolja having arrived in England and tells him how 'beautifully distinguished' he looked when he left. She reports conversations with her aunt and cousin, who both described him as someone who will succeed. She speaks to Wolja's parents every day, sees them regularly, and tries to protect them from worrying about Wolja.

> If you write something that your parents shouldn't know, then write on 2 separate pieces of paper, one private and one for general reading. And you know that I still see myself as your secretary and can type things for you that you don't need in a hurry.

Indeed, the following day (8 May) she is visiting a family who have a typewriter she can use to type some affidavits for Wolja:

> I miss you everywhere. On every street corner we once stood, here we had a row, there we drank Ahorn.[10] But I am so pleased that you have gone, that something new is beginning, that we live in the future, and I feel terribly optimistic about it.

She reports a conversation with the daughter of the house:

> Dita says she wouldn't let herself be exploited in this way; in the twentieth century a woman doesn't have to work so hard for her husband. When I said that I also want you to be successful there, then she nodded her head very seriously. I think, that if one spoke to her seriously more often she would be less arrogant. But this topic is unimportant.

So why did she tell him what Dita had said? Did her comment touch a nerve for Lotte? Did she feel ambivalent about how much she was doing for Wolja?

As the months pass she becomes more and more anxious, and she develops stomach problems. From Lotte's letters we surmise that Wolja is very anxious and lonely, despite having some refugee friends already in London. This is confirmed by his letters in August. He longs for Lotte to join him; indeed he does not seem to understand why she is taking so long to come. Alongside her own fears Lotte continues to reassure Wolja, whilst denying her own needs; she coaxes and pleads with him, addresses him in affectionate diminutives ('little monkey', 'little one') and uses their private names for each other 'Peter' and 'Teddy'.[11] She often tells him that she can cope with anything so long as he is ok.

Frustration, longing, anxiety and reproaches

Lotte's most powerful emotions are her frustration, exacerbated by her mother's accident, about how long it is taking to get her mother and herself out of Germany, and her longing for it all to be resolved. Variations of the phrase *Es muss klappen* (It must work out) are a constant refrain throughout the correspondence. On 3 June, she writes: '*Ach, wenn es klappen wollte!!!!!!!!!!!!!!*' (Oh, if only it would work out) and on 24 July: '*Aber es wird, u. es muss u. es soll klappen!!!*' (But it will and it must and it should work out). She makes comments of this kind so often that I wonder whether she is trying to defend herself against the fear of it not doing so. These examples also show how she uses exclamation marks to express her feelings.

On 8 July she writes two letters. In the first, she is very worried that she has not heard from Wolja for several days:

> If only something would work out for you, and you can remain strong, everything else is bearable. If only the business with Mutti's arm had not got in the way ... Darling, darling Peter, I made myself so anxious. I hear your voice in the letters – whether you're loving, whether you're worked up, whether you're angry. But I can understand that you couldn't write – you are so alone.

Here the power of the letter as a material object is also apparent. For Lotte it embodies Wolja's voice and I too can hear their voices when I read their letters – especially in their use of language and their style of writing, which I recognise from my experiences as their child. This raises questions about whether I can capture the language and style in my translations, as well as reminding me that the translations are also part of my interpretations.

My identification with Lotte's anxiety is accompanied by increasing anger with Wolja, who seems to be very critical. Lotte often refers to Wolja's *Vorwürfe*. I discovered that I had translated this at first as 'accusations'; but later, when I had read Wolja's letters too and felt more sympathetic towards him, I had used the milder (and correct) term 'reproach' instead.[12]

Conveying style through translation is never easy and in these letters Lotte uses a range of styles, including slang, idiom, humour and irony, to express her feelings. On 14 June, in response to further reproaches, she tells him he has *geschimpft wie zwei Rohrspatzen*, an idiom that I translated as 'fussed like a mother hen', only recognising later that Lotte has amended the usual version; I should have written *two* mother hens. Defending herself against his reproaches, she continues in this ironic vein: 'I really am not responsible for world history, or for the plans of the holy authorities.'

In her second letter of 8 July, written after a letter from Wolja has arrived, Lotte is more assertive:

> In relation to what you write about in principle, I say to you that you apparently don't yet know me very well if you think I am not taking your suggestions seriously. Up to now I have thought about all your suggestions very carefully, but given that this is our joint life that we are planning, you have to allow me sometimes to criticise as well.[13]

She believes it is very important that they try to discuss everything in their letters and she is explicit about the value of irony:

> I can't say anything about your tone. I think one can sometimes deal with certain questions more easily through irony than to construct them as problems. Sadly everything is bloody serious and therefore not a joke.

She is exhausted, there is tropical heat at work, and she has a bad stomach. She pleads with him not to tell her off in letters: 'I find that terribly sad'. She writes a final bit the following day, acknowledging she doesn't like the tone of her own letter, but asking him to read 'the facts'. She ends:

> With a (no many) warm kisses, and don't be such a nervous Wolja anymore. I have such anxiety that one day you'll fall apart. PS this time I have numbered the sides in your way?? (If I can't be cheeky, then I might as well hang myself.)

This use of irony is something I associate with my mother and something I loved about her. At my father's secular funeral, as we walked into the crematorium, she said to me 'I'm glad they've put the hymn books out; that will be so useful'.

Although her situation in Germany is very precarious and the future as uncertain for her as for Wolja, Lotte is often apologetic about expressing her own needs. On 28 July she writes:

> Darling Frog, I long for news from you. This whole emigration grind, which has become 100% more complicated since you left, is more than two poor women like us can cope

with. We're done in! I can't wait for the moment when I am sitting in the train. But how much has to be done before then!!!! No, but it isn't any easier for you, I am bad that I complain so much.

By mid-July the uncertainty, disappointments and fear cause them to row. In his letter of 1 August (the first of his letters that I have) Wolja tries to explain how this has happened: 'Dear little Lotte, you have written me incredibly loving letters. Why didn't they arrive sooner, then I wouldn't have written you an "angry" letter yesterday.' He has been so nervous about the domestic positions for Lotte falling through, that he was unable to work or sleep. 'And when your first letter came without a single loving word, completely cold I had to be "angry" again. Lotte, you good, dear, darling, beloved Lotte. I was so happy to get your loving letter.' I was relieved to see that across the top of this letter, he has written: 'First the most important thing – we have a position for you.'

On 3 August Lotte responds to Wolja's explanation for their rows: 'Thank goodness this period is over.' But disappointingly, the rows continue. On 18 August Lotte tries again to end them:

> It is hopefully not long until I come, and then face to face we can communicate much better. Of course at times I am imprecise. I don't have your masculine logic. But do you really believe that it is always so easy to write clearly?

Gendered communication

Extracts from Wolja's letter of 9 August show that he is able to express his feelings directly:

> I am so terribly alone despite all the people I know. I mean this superficially. Of course I know enough people to be able to invite myself to someone so long as I plan it days in advance ... I am beginning to get sick and tired of the asking and applying for jobs ... I can hardly believe that you will be here soon. And I am already angry that you sometimes won't have much time.

Wolja's style of writing, in this and other letters, is very different from Lotte's. He tends to write mainly from his point of view, usually without the subsequent apology, denial or concern about the impact of his letters that is characteristic of Lotte.

The importance of receiving letters is made apparent for both of them: for Lotte through her fantasies of disaster when she has not heard from Wolja for a few days; for Wolja through his complaints that she does not write often enough. They are responding to the fear in very different ways. Lotte becomes very sensitive and Wolja reacts with anger, usually at Lotte, which of course makes her feel even worse.

Their styles of communication seem implicitly gendered, with significant differences in the kind of 'emotional work'[14] each of them is doing. Lotte is the emotional carer who polices her own emotions in order not to stress or distress Wolja.[15] But I am also aware that this kind of interpretation is very much influenced by my own experience of Lotte and Wolja. I recognise Wolja's tendency to criticise and Lotte's need to defend herself, and because I am very like Lotte, it makes me respond angrily to Wolja's letters; how can he behave like this when she is the one still in danger in Nazi Germany?

We have also seen explicitly gendered aspects of their communication, when Lotte refers to Wolja's 'masculine logic' or to herself and her mother as 'two poor women like us'. I do not know whether such phrases are ironic or an indication of how she constructs herself in relation to him. Lotte herself has referred to her use of irony as a way of deflecting difficulties, so this may be a safe way of challenging his assumption that he knows best, even though he has been away for a long time.

Looking again across the whole correspondence I found further examples of gendered language. The most striking of these is the way in which they both describe Lotte as 'silly'. In early June, responding to his complaint that she did not understand about his work, she writes: 'Isn't it lovely to have such a silly wife?'[16] On 16 August she tells Wolja that her mother has gone to the Dolomites to recuperate; she has had a dreadful day, made worse by the fact that she hasn't heard from him and believes he simply hasn't written. She concludes: 'Peterchen, it's now 11.30pm. I want to lie next to you, and tell you so much, and just be a totally silly woman. It must be soon.' I presume that 'going to the Dolomites' is code for Erna's emigration. Lotte once told me the story of putting her mother on the train. I do not know who else was with her, but her mother asked to speak to her alone. She told her she must not cry, but go home immediately and pack everything and get to England to join Wolja as quickly as possible. Instead Lotte spent the day with a friend getting drunk. She must have felt so alone, exacerbated by not hearing from Wolja. Although Lotte sometimes also refers to Wolja as 'silly',[17] it is rarely used in an explicitly gendered context. Is her description of herself as a silly woman a way of saying that she does not want to take any more responsibility, even though in her letter of 8 July she is also exasperated by his 'knowing best' and reminds him that they are a planning a joint life together?

On 18 August Wolja responds to Lotte's desire to lie next to him and be a 'totally silly woman':

> Do you really want to lie next to me in bed? Lotteli, today for the first time I wanted to say sweet Lotte, to you. May I? ... Lotteli, if we had more money I would send you a present every day, and flowers. I think you had better bring some armour with you, so that I don't crush you with joy.

I wonder whether his cleverness and her silliness are also part of their sexual relationship.

In many of his letters, as on 1 August, Wolja addresses Lotte as '*Du Dummes Ding*' (you silly thing); and he starts his final letter of 25 August:

> You rascal, you silly thing, you, little you, you, you, you, it is so wonderful to scold you, my darling little wife. Outside in the street, I say to myself all the time 'you silly thing, you' only out of love.

This use of the word 'silly' reminds me of ways in which my parents related to one another when I was a child. My brother, my father and I were constructed as the 'clever' ones in the family, interested in science and mathematics. My father would say 'do you think Mummy would understand?' Years later, with shame, I recognised my collusion in this myth, and the way that I had enjoyed being categorised as 'clever' with my father and big brother, and I feel that shame now. Although Wolja uses 'silly' in an affectionate way, it is hard not to experience it as having derogatory undertones, and operating as a way of keeping Lotte in her place.

Possessions as the focus of emotions

A central concern of their correspondence has been the discussion, sometimes in great detail, of what Lotte should bring with her, what should be shipped, and what has to be left behind or sold. Clearly these are important practical decisions made much harder by the ever-changing regulations. My reading of their letters suggests that their discussion of possessions is about much more than this; it is also a place in which their desires, fear and uncertainty are played out.

In an early letter on 30 May Lotte describes an imaginary conversation she had with Wolja while she was eating her lunch:

> And then I wondered whether we would have enough money to furnish 2 rooms and how we would do it. And then I said I'd like a beautiful sofa, but with drawers for linen, and you were so silly and didn't understand why that's important. Ach, Wolluk, something must be resolved soon! I don't mean the sofa and the drawers, but for us two.

And real sofas also appear in a postscript to Lotte's first letter of 8 July:

> Do you still remember Mutti's sofa in her room in Franzensbader? Where your Miaou stood, in front of the radio. Shall I bring that one and my small one, or that one and your old one, or my small one and your old one? (My small one is the one from my alcove.)

At the end of his letter on 1 August, Wolja writes:

> don't forget the dictionary, the big English one, please in the transport. I need it very quickly for the article and publications that I should write. It is already a problem not having them. I am sad about the fiction, but if it is doesn't work, it doesn't.

And on 24 August, in response to her letter in which she says she has been asked by someone to bring a present for her daughter: 'I think it's preposterous to bring a bulky vase, when you aren't bringing my fiction books, because you haven't got enough money.' The next day he explains in English that if she is bringing his large Cathode Ray Tube with her, it is 'for indicating and measuring electric currents. It is a single model for a special scientific experiment, of no commercial value'. He continues in German: 'I could make good use of my two old pairs of black shoes.' Two days later, on 26 August, Lotte writes: 'I am bringing some of the novels. Your father will sell the rest, mainly several classics. They will hopefully bring in a bit of money.'

It is clear from the letters that Lotte is organising the transport of Wolja's possessions as well as her own. I presume that he took very little with him when he left Germany, not knowing whether he would be allowed to stay in the UK. He has left his home, his parents, everything that is familiar to him and he is separated from Lotte, not knowing when she can join him. It is probably very important for him in this lonely, uncertain position to imagine being reunited with his own possessions, especially those connected to his work. At the same time he does not seem to be aware that he is adding to Lotte's stress by the demands that he is making.

We have already seen that by mid-July the uncertainty and disappointments, with their accompanying fear, have helped to construct a very quarrelsome style of communication. This discussion of possessions becomes one of their main areas of conflict. Their quarrels focus on one item, not necessary for Wolja's work, the *Staubsauger* (vacuum cleaner). On 28 June, describing the furniture she is planning to bring, Lotte explains:

> The vacuum cleaner is a problem. Apart from anything else, Wolluk, we don't have any carpets; there won't be that much to vacuum for us. ... I have real romantic desires for you. Every beautiful evening, every couple I see make me burst with anger.

Wolja must have queried her decision, as on 3 July she writes: 'for your latest suggestions thank you ... by the way in relation to the vacuum cleaner you are being illogical. If you live in a furnished flat, you are responsible for cleaning the carpets'.[18] But in his letter of 1 August Wolja continues to insist that it is vital to bring a vacuum cleaner: 'The dust is here is unbelievable and it is pointless to beat the carpets.'

The vacuum cleaner even becomes an issue for Lotte's mother when, at the end of July, she writes to Wolja to ask him to stop upsetting Lotte. In response Wolja also discusses the vacuum cleaner:

> You have used the issue of the vacuum cleaner as a particular example. So, I will do this too, just as an example. And I have to say to you that all your experience as a housewife has nothing to do with it. There are housewives here too who one can ask. The bottom line is that both the way of living together in a flat or house, as well as the amount of dust here, is so different from that in Germany, that the experience from Germany is worthless.

The dust refers I believe to coal fires. In a letter to his father on 5 August 1946, advising him what to bring with him when he comes from Romania, Wolja is scathing about English heating systems: 'the houses are very badly built, only suitable for the summer, there is in our house of course no central heating and the open coal fires are a study in uselessness and inefficiency'. Wolja's pedantic style is also one that is familiar to me.

On 11 August, Lotte expresses her frustration through humour:

> You describe to me all the 'multicoloured' advantages of vacuum cleaners. I have no aversion to vacuum cleaners. I have already written to you several times that any new purchases made after 1933 carry a 100% surcharge on export from Germany.

The Nazi context

Apart from such evidence of the ever-increasing difficulties created for emigrating Jews, I was at first amazed at the normality of life. Lotte meets friends, goes to the cinema and is employed throughout, voluntarily leaving her employment at the Italian Bank a month before she emigrates. The Nazi context is of course apparent in Lotte's letters through phrases such as 'since 1933', and in her accounts of the changing regulations. Later I realised that Lotte describes the emotional atmosphere through small phrases. On 3 June: 'This sitting and waiting and trembling makes one sensitive.' On 4 July: 'It's not just me. Everyone is complaining now. It's probably in the air.' And on 8 July: 'Everything is sadly bloody serious and therefore not a joke.' Is Lotte consciously understating or avoiding what is happening around her or does she not say very much because they have become so used to it? Both interpretations are possible. In her memoir, Lily Pincus writes about how careful people had to be, and the fact that there were 'spies' everywhere.[19] On the other hand, in his diary entry of 29 June 1938, Victor Klemperer writes: 'We are so accustomed to living without rights and to waiting apathetically for further disgraceful acts, that it hardly upsets us anymore.'[20]

Lotte's phrases triggered my imagination, wondering how it did feel to be living in Berlin at this time. As I re-read the letters, looking specifically for evidence of Nazism, I realised that I had missed or avoided many examples – sometimes because the

German was difficult for me, but perhaps too because I did not want to have to think about the content. Lotte's letter of 31 May provides a good example.

> Dearest boy
>
> It is again two days without news of you. Hopefully there is nothing wrong. Here there is nothing new …
>
> I spent yesterday with Heinz. He sat here and waited for a telegram, that would tell him that the embarkation deposit had been paid, for which he has no money here. If it hasn't been done by today, which is very likely, then he must wait again until the end of August for a ship. He is very depressed, because he feels so useless without anything to do and apart from that he has no money. Two weeks ago, he told his father that he was going to Africa. Since then they haven't spoken at all. A nice state of affairs! He probably won't come to London, because of lack of money. We then went to the cinema for a bit of mutual cheering up, 'Night Club Scandal'.

She then writes about the film, and continues:

> Today my boss took a photograph of me. I was terrified, but nothing happened. He had to try out a camera, and therefore took various photos in different light. That is after all so important!! In lightning speed I had to sit at a desk, couldn't even comb my hair, had to look at him, and then it was done. If there's anything worth seeing I'll definitely send you a copy (he didn't say that, but I am saying it).

Towards the end she writes: 'There's nothing new, sadly always nearly – things', and she ends playfully with a very long signature to tease him about his complaint that she did not sign one of her letters.

This description of her boss taking the photograph gave me one of my most chilling moments. In this short paragraph we see how the social atmosphere can be conveyed so powerfully within tiny fragments of communication about simple, everyday events, as well as through phrases like 'always nearly – things'.

I tried to imagine the circumstances of the photograph; I have no idea whether Lotte's fear was a specific or a general one. It makes great sense that a Jew would be terrified of being photographed in 1938. As part of the investigation of racial characteristics many children were photographed by so-called 'race-hygienists'.[21] Referring in her memoir to an event that occurred in June 1938, Inge Deutschkron, describes this in more detail:

> A seemingly meaningless experience disturbed me much more. I sat at the photographer's. Like every 16 year old I was vain. When the photographer told me to push my hair behind my left ear, I was completely distraught and close to tears. He had spoken neutrally, without any scorn, a business-like instruction, nothing more. Nevertheless, I experienced the humiliation like the lash of a whip. But I had learned self-control. This photo must not give away what was going on in me … Racial origin could be identified from the shape of the left ear. National Socialist race scientists had discovered this. The left ear of a Jew betrayed Semitic origins, and therefore Jews' passport photos had to be taken with the left ear clearly visible.[22]

What could I learn from the history books about daily life for Jews at this time? Mid-1938 is not a period written about specifically. It is after the early waves of emigration by German Jews which took place in 1933 when Hitler came to power, and in 1935 after the Nuremberg laws were passed. But it is just before the state-organised pogroms and destruction of synagogues, shops and houses on 'Kristallnacht' (9 to 10 November 1938) which led to the arrest and imprisonment of thousands of Jews and a rapid increase in the numbers trying to get out. Yet there were many significant events in 1938: Austria was annexed in March and there were preparations throughout the year for war against Czechoslovakia; laws requiring Jews to carry identity cards and to add Israel or Sara to their names were passed in July and August respectively, both to come into effect on 1 January 1939.[23] And three days before the photograph incident with Lotte's boss, all Russian Jews were arrested and sent to concentration camps, including women, children and old men. Their property was confiscated and they were only to be released on condition that they emigrated. It is not surprising that Lotte's initial response was to be terrified.

On 10 August 1938, Victor Klemperer recorded in his diary that it was a period during which there was 'intensified Jew-baiting again and drastic new measures all the time'.[24] On 11 August, in her letter to Wolja, Lotte also refers to how much things have changed and how much harder everything has become since Wolja left. She is frustrated that like other people who have left, he doesn't understand this.

> Peterlein, you must believe me, when I write that all the regulations have changed enormously since you left, and when you don't understand something, receive it patiently and trust me, and rely on us. Please please.

Lotte's experiences are consistent with Benz's description[25] of the contradictions in Nazi policies to Jews at this time. They wanted to be rid of them – it was a policy of forced emigration, not yet genocide – but they put every possible obstacle in their way. Benz argues that even in the early years of the Nazi regime, when people apparently left of their own free will, the emigration of Jews from Germany should be seen as 'both flight from persecution and also expulsion'.[26] I wondered whether it would be possible to discover from their letters how Lotte and Wolja themselves saw their situation. Was it for them a flight or an emigration? I remember Lotte always using the expression 'thrown out'. In her letter of 28 July she refers to *Auswanderung* (emigration). They seem to believe they have no future in Germany, and they fear for themselves and their parents. On the other hand they think they have time to plan and prepare Lotte's departure. In their discussions towards the end of this correspondence, they decide that Wolja's parents, who have Romanian nationality and therefore do not qualify as refugees, should go to Romania while Lotte and Wolja get themselves settled in England, before they try to get his parents to join them. Their detailed discussions about what to bring, including presents for friends and Lotte's concern to have the right clothes which appears in many of her letters, make it feel like an emigration – albeit a forced one – rather than a flight. In his letter of 1 August, Wolja appears to believe that the situation in Germany will not last for ever. 'What are you doing with your books and silver? Also sell them? Or in the meantime leave my and your fiction with Lil until better times come?'

A return to gender

When focusing on Lotte and Wolja's personal relationship, I explored the gendered nature of the 'emotional work' in which they are each engaged. Reading the letters again through a social lens made me acutely aware of gendered aspects of other kinds of 'work' too. Wolja is actively trying to secure his residency in the UK or to obtain a visa for the USA, to find a domestic situation for Lotte and to look for scientific/research work. In contrast with the predominant picture given in the history books, Lotte was employed almost continuously after being thrown out of university, including one year in Milan. At the time of these letters, she has been working for two years as a secretary and translator for the Italian National Institute for the Exchange of Foreign Currency; she describes it as a bank. She is earning money to support both of them, caring for her own mother, seeing Wolja's parents regularly and helping them with their plans to emigrate, as well as organising her own and her mother's emigration, including the transport of their possessions. She is networking widely on Wolja's behalf, taking advice and getting hold of a *Gutachten* (an expert opinion) about his sight, which will confirm that it is not going to deteriorate further. She also drafts letters in English for him for another visa application for the USA.

Despite the amount of work that Lotte is doing, the responsibility she is taking on, and the fact that she is currently the only earner, in her letter of 11 June she is clear that Wolja is in charge and will eventually be the breadwinner. 'Look, if you suddenly get a swanky job, so that we can get married, I won't have any more problems.'

In 1932 Lotte had started to study medicine. After two semesters, she was thrown out for being friendly with communists, a few months earlier than she would have been expelled as a Jew.[27] She immediately learned shorthand and typing. In 1934 she worked in Milan as a 'governess' but she had to return to Berlin on the death of her father in 1935. She then worked in a range of clerical and secretarial jobs, and she was preparing to take on domestic work. It seems both that a range of employment possibilities were always available to women, irrespective of class, and also that she was more prepared than Wolja to take on such work.

The most explicit operation of gender and also of class can be seen in relation to the structures of emigration to UK. Wolja was allowed to enter the UK temporarily to seek work, but only because he was professionally qualified. Lotte was persecuted in Germany as a 'Jew', not as a woman; but as a woman, a 'domestic permit' offered her the only way out of Nazi Germany. Kushner shows the way in which the concept of 'domestic service' itself is constructed through both class and gender.[28]

In many letters Lotte expresses her feelings about housework. On 10 June, she writes: 'In practice I understand nothing about housework, whereas I am good at languages and also have experience with children.' With this letter she encloses her boss's photo: 'I think it's quite cute. Perhaps you can show it to families with lots of children, in case they might need me. You can tell them that I would comb my hair if I was living with them.' Four days later (14 June) she complains that he hasn't mentioned the photograph. Another week later on 21 June: 'My heroic attempts to learn to sew have failed ... On the 1st July I am taking a few cookery lessons, so that the housewives don't shake their heads at me too much'; and on 26 August (her penultimate letter): 'In relation to me, don't worry that I can do some cooking and sewing. I cannot do either.'[29]

In November 2005 I found the photograph taken by her boss in May 1938. Lotte is sitting at a desk, and although it is cut off half-way up, it is clearly Mussolini behind her. I must have seen this photograph before, but without the letter I had not realised its significance. How much it represents: a moment of fear; both flirtation and disappointment in her relationship with Wolja; her status as a professional woman; and also an advertisement of suitability for domestic work.

Excited about finding it, I carried it around with me, frightened of losing it! When I looked again at the letter of 10 June, in which Lotte sent it to Wolja, I discovered I had missed out a sentence: 'I and my photo kiss you many many times.' So it was also important for her as a physical object to connect them and convey her love.[30]

The original photo is very small. When enlarged I could see that Lotte is wearing a bracelet that she later gave to me. I still had it, thus connecting me in turn to her and to her experiences at that time. In October 2009, my brother's first grandchild was born – a girl they decided to call Lotti. So, I gave the bracelet to Lotti.

Personal letters – to keep

When I started this project I thought of the 'love relationship' aspect of the correspondence as something for me, my brother and his children to keep, or something we might eventually throw away. I had a sense of intrusion upon my parents' most personal and private feelings when I read the more intimate parts of the letters between them in 1938. I wondered whether I have the right to use their letters in this way. But I have not even thrown away the papers in envelopes marked 'private', although I know I would not feel able to use them. As I worked on the papers it became clear that Lotte had been the collector and keeper.[31] And I returned again to the question of why she had labelled them rather than throw them away herself.

Analysis of these letters in 1938 made me aware of the inseparability of the personal and the social. For both Lotte and Wolja it is their personal relationship, conducted through the letters, that keeps them going through the fear and uncertainty of their separations and helps them to survive emotionally, at the same time as their relationship is itself constrained and shaped by their circumstances. For Lotte, being with Wolja is her goal, once she and their parents are safely out of Germany. If she has professional goals, they are not consciously expressed. Wolja does have professional goals, and without his professional qualifications he would not have been granted even the one-month visa. Regular communication and reassurances of each other's love are crucial for them both. Their failure at times to meet each other's needs contributes to their rows and misunderstandings. Gender is significant not only for structuring their routes into the UK, their employment expectations, and caring responsibilities for parents, but also for the ways in which they communicate and manage their emotions.

But I still have to make decisions about what I am prepared to tell, what feels truly private, an intrusion, or even a betrayal. I am conscious of both my power and my responsibility in relation to the public images of Lotte and Wolja that I construct, though I cannot control how others will interpret the extracts that I select. I wonder whether being Lotte and Wolja's daughter gives me sufficient right to use their personal letters in this way. Should I understand their failure to throw them away as permission? Am I right to include extracts about their intimate relationship? When I decide to leave out some passages, am I protecting my parents or myself?[32]

My work on these papers has alerted me to the multiple readings of the letters and the need for reflexivity, in particular to acknowledge my emotional responses, to make connections to wider historical and current events, to use my own memories and experiences to make sense of things and to recognise what I had always taken for granted. As their daughter I am able to explore the impact of their experiences and to recognise continuities in their later lives, such as my mother's dislike of housework! In addition, I am suggesting that my personal responses as daughter offer a further resource for analysis and interpretation as the researcher and academic.

Finally, to consider the meaning of such an archive, I return to my feelings of ambivalence. Is it a gift, a wonderful legacy? I am often told how lucky I am to have it, allowing me not only to learn about my parents' experiences, but to get to know them as people in their own right, with access to their personal feelings. They also ease my own sense of loss. In the last few years of my mother's life she was very anxious and depressed; her letters put me in touch with a woman who in 1938 was strong and feisty.

Or, is it a burden? Does it mean that they could not let go or 'master the past'[33] and hoped we would do it for them? Does it force me to live in the past, in their lives, rather than in the present in my own?

The ambivalence will surely continue, as will my feelings of responsibility to care for the papers – materially as precious objects, for the lives they contain, for the memories they evoke and for the richness of what we can learn them from them.

Notes

1. My thanks here to Janet Fink – the start of her invaluable help and support to me.
2. Atina Grossmann, "Versions of Home: German-Jewish Refugee Papers out of the Closet and Into the Archives," *New German Critique* 90 (2003): 103.
3. Jeremy D. Popkin, "Holocaust Memories, Historians' Memoirs. First-Person Narrative and the Memory of the Holocaust," *History & Memory* 15, no. 1 (2003): 49–84. Popkin makes an interesting distinction between the vast majority of survivors' memoirs and first-person narratives written by professional historians who are also survivors, for whom telling the story is less important than raising the kinds of questions that I am posing in relation to my parents' papers.
4. My approach to this personal archive material is that of a feminist critical social scientist with an interest in problematising concepts, the construction of meaning, attention to gender and everyday life, and reflexivity. I find myself in sympathy with, and have made most use of, historiographical approaches which offer counter-narratives to the dominant stories of German Jewish refugees. Examples are: Marion A. Kaplan, *Between Dignity and Despair. Jewish Life in Nazi Germany* (Oxford: Oxford University Press, 1998); Louise London, *Whitehall and the Jews 1933–1948. British Immigration Policy, Jewish Refugees and the Holocaust* (Cambridge: Cambridge University Press, 2000); Wolfgang Benz, *Flucht aus Deutschland .Zum Exil im 20. Jahrhundert* (München: Deutscher Taschenbuch Verlag, 2001); Donald Bloxham and Tony Kushner, *The Holocaust. Critical Historical Approaches* (Manchester: Manchester University Press, 2005); Tony Kushner, *Remembering Refugees. Then and Now* (Manchester: Manchester University Press, 2006).
5. All extracts from letters used in this article come from the 1938 correspondence between Lotte and Wolja in our personal archive. They are referenced in the text by the date in 1938 on which they were written.
6. Michael Andre Bernstein, *Foregone Conclusions. Against Apocalyptic History* (London: University of California Press, 1994), 26.
7. Jacqueline Vansant, *Reclaiming Heimat. Trauma and Mourning in Memoirs by Jewish Austrian Reémigrés* (Detroit: Wayne State University Press, 2001), 31. Emphasis original.
8. My therapist once said to me quite sharply, 'the Jews are not the only people who have suffered'. I guessed from her name that she had Armenian origins, but only discovered many years later, from her obituary, the extent of her own parents' suffering as a result of the Armenian genocide.

9. I do not know when my parents first met; two letters in the collection from June 1937 suggest that at that time their relationship is quite new.
10. 'Ahorn' is German for 'maple', but I have been unable to find out, even from people who lived in Berlin at that time, what kind of drink it was.
11. Lotte had told us that my brother Peter was named after her favourite Teddy.
12. Although some dictionaries offer 'accusation' as a translation of '*Vorwurf*', I learned from German speakers that *Vorwurf* is only used as accusation in a legal context.
13. Underlining in the original.
14. See for example Jean Duncombe and Dennis Marsden, "Love and Intimacy: The Division of Emotion and 'Emotion Work'," *Sociology* 27, no. 2 (1993): 221–41, for a discussion of the sociological concept of 'emotional work' or 'emotional labour'.
15. Stevi Jackson and Sue Scott, "Gut Reactions to Matters of the Heart: Reflections on Rationality, Irrationality and Sexuality," *The Sociological Review* 45, no. 4 (1997): 567. The kind of emotional work Lotte is doing in this correspondence is described well by Jackson and Scott who, writing over 60 years later about public discourses of sexuality, suggest: 'women and girls are positioned as sexual carers who do the emotional work and police their own emotions to ensure that they do not place excessive demands on men'.
16. An undated letter, but its content places it in early June.
17. As in her letter of May 28, where she calls him a 'silly sheep' and on May 30, in a letter to be cited later.
18. Underlining in the original.
19. Lily Pincus, *Verloren-gewonnen: mein Weg von Berlin nach London* (Stuttgart: Deutsche Verlags-Anstalt, 1980), 73.
20. Victor Klemperer, *I Shall Bear Witness: The Diaries of Victor Klemperer 1933–41* (London: Weidenfeld & Nicolson, 1998), 1: 249.
21. Gunther B. Ginzel, *Judischer Alltag in Deutschland, 1933–1945* (Dusseldorf: Droste, 1984), 108.
22. Inge Deutschkron, *Ich trug den gelben Stern* (München: Deutscher Taschenbuch Verlag, 1983), 28. My translation.
23. Saul Friedländer, *Nazi Germany and the Jews. The Years of Persecution 1933–39* (London: Weidenfeld & Nicolson, 1997); Ginzel, *Judischer Alltag*.
24. Klemperer, *I Shall Bear Witness*, 253.
25. Wolfgang Benz, ed., *Das Exil der kleinen Leute. Alltagserfahrung deutscher Juden in der Emigration* (München: C.H. Beck, 1991).
26. Ibid., 62, my translation.
27. This is how Lotte told the story; she was always quite proud of it.
28. Tony Kushner, "An Alien Occupation – Jewish Refugees and Domestic Service in Britain 1933–1948," in *Second Chance. Two Centuries of German-Speaking Jews in the United Kingdom*, ed. Werner E. Mosse (Tübingen: J.C.B. Mohr, 1991).
29. Underlining in the original.
30. The photograph must have become significant for Wolja. Two years later, when he is interned on the Isle of Man, he writes to Lotte: 'Why don't you send me photo of you, the one you sent two years ago' (August 2, 1940).
31. This might not seem to fit with the fact that Wolja's letters to Lotte for the first three months of their separation in 1938 are missing. It is possible that she threw them away because of their rows, but perhaps more likely that she packed them with their household goods, which were never delivered. In 1961 they learned that their goods had been sold at a rock bottom price during the war.
32. What I select also depends upon my audience; people have expressed amazement at my capacity to read out some of the painful or personal material, but I found myself leaving out the more intimate passages when preparing a talk for students on my research.
33. See Bernhard Schlink, *Guilt about the Past* (London: Beautiful Books, 2010), for a discussion of the idea of 'mastering the past'.

Smell and memory as Jewish archives: the case of Russian Jewish writers

Henrietta Mondry

Russian and European Studies, University of Canterbury, New Zealand

The paper analyses the complex dynamics of the rejection of 'Jewish smells' as markers of Jewish corporeality in the context of stereotypes constructed by Russian culture. It addresses the conflicting desire to cherish and yet reject the smells of childhood as an important repository of memory in autobiographical prose by Russian Jewish writers. It theorizes the notion of smell as a Jewish archive in the context of inter-generational knowledge, displacement, space and time. How can the most ethereal of all sensations serve as an archive? How do we pass on this type of knowledge-inducing mechanism to future generations? And how do writers negotiate their national/ethnic identities on the basis of this form of remembering?

When nothing else subsists from the past, after the people are dead, after the things are broken and scattered· the smell and taste of things remain poised a long time, like souls· bearing resiliently, on tiny and almost impalpable drops of their essence, the immense edifice of memory.

Marcel Proust, *The Remembrance of Things Past*[1]

Introduction

Can smell as memory serve as an archive of Jewish knowledge and experience? Scholars note that the notion of 'Proustian memory' has become a category in a number of disciplines within humanities and the sciences, including biology and cognitive psychology.[2] Scientific experiments show that it is possible to improve autobiographical memory by being exposed to various smells of the past. Smells from childhood can serve as cues to recollections/revelations of otherwise forgotten events and spaces. This olfaction-induced memory serves as a powerful prompt in Jewish experience. Smells become depositories of knowledge and in this way are quasi-archives. The olfactory sphere in Jewish experiences is culture-specific – for centuries Jews in Europe were perceived as embodiments of unpleasant odours. In Proustian mode, odours are 'drops of essence', constructs of the Jewish body. Proust's own anxiety around his partly Jewish origins has been identified as a factor in his interest in smell-memory.[3] Moreover, Max Horkheimer and Theodor Adorno developed their hermeneutic of anti-Semitism on this notion of smell, olfaction and the construct of Jewishness in modernity by

Gentile and Jewish intellectuals.[4] The latter included such seminal figures as Sigmund Freud and Walter Benjamin.[5]

In this paper I will analyse the complex dynamics of the rejection of 'Jewish smells' as markers of Jewish essentiality and the desire to cherish the smells of childhood as an important repository of memory in autobiographical prose by Russian Jewish writers. I will theorize the notion of smell as a Jewish archive in the context of inter-generational knowledge, displacement, space and time. How can the most ethereal of all sensations serve as an archive? How do we pass on this type of knowledge-inducing mechanism to later generations? And how do writers negotiate their national/ethnic identities on the basis of this form of remembering?

The ability to perceive and emit smells is a physiological function of the human organism. The capacity to recollect events and to experience emotions via the exposure to long-forgotten smells is an empirically proven phenomenon. The olfactory bulb, the part of the brain responsible for the function of recognizing smell, sends signals to the amygdala, the 'smell brain'.[6] In a scientific experiment run in the Jorvik Viking Centre in York in 1999 groups of participants were exposed to various sensory cues which were supposed to recreate the atmosphere of a tenth-century Viking city. In addition to providing sights and sounds, the museum also provided a number of evocative smells to aid the completeness of the Viking 'experience'. This was achieved by piping a combination of seven different, highly distinctive smells into the museum. The groups had been exposed to the same set of smells six years before and in the second trial were able to recollect information on the basis of the recognition of these smells. The experiment proved that 'odours have the ability to serve as state-dependent cues for real-world memories'.[7] The notion defined by scientists as 'real-world memories' is of particular significance in application to the subject of Jewish memories. In the case of Jewish subjects, smells are often perceived not only as 'real-world memories' but also as recollections of the supra-real. Among the seven types of smells in the Jorvik Viking museum one odour – 'rubbish acrid' – recreated the smell of a Viking toilet, while all the others were either neutral or pleasant smells ('burnt wood', 'tar', 'apples').[8] All the participants experienced spontaneous disgust at the 'rubbish acrid' smell which pervaded the Viking toilet area.

This deployment of an olfactory 'experience' in a museum was recently echoed by the newly refurbished Jewish Museum in Camden, London. Among its exhibits the museum has a typical Jewish immigrant kitchen from which 'the smell of chicken soup wafts across the museum'.[9] (The museum was opened in March 2010 by the celebrity food writer Nigella Lawson.) Visitors who are blind or partially sighted are offered a 'touch tour' which also includes the experience of smelling various spices. Unlike the Viking Centre, there are no repulsive smells 'available' to visitors and the intimate area, which in the Viking museum is represented by a toilet, in the Jewish museum is represented by the *mikveh*, the ritual bath. This place of body-cleansing stands in stark contrast to the smelly Viking toilet and symbolically creates a distinction between the barbaric Europeans and the civilized Jews in early Europe insofar as the museum traces the history of Jews in Britain from the Norman invasion, approximately coinciding with the tenth-century Viking city. The *mikveh* was excavated from a site in Milk Street in London and reassembled in the Jewish museum. The new installation has mirrors and spotlights, which can be viewed as an attempt not only to glamorize but also to sterilize the territory of bathing by exhibiting its high standards of cleanliness. It is implied that no bad smells can be imagined in an intimate space inhabited by Jews. In this way the Jewish body emerges as privileged and civilized; it is a clean body accustomed to inhaling exotic sweet-smelling spices and/or such neutral smells as that of chicken soup. In the new Jewish museum, given designated status by the British Museums, Libraries and Archives Council, the cultural experience of smells and olfaction does not include exposure to unpleasant smells. The museum's identity is based on Jewish emigration to the United Kingdom. Its holdings and exhibits cover diverse Jewish émigré communities, from Europe and Russia to India and Morocco. The museum's position on archiving smells is relevant to this article with its focus on smell-memory in Russian cultural discourse in the context of migration and the Diaspora.

The concept of the body is central to the experience of smell-induced memory. The experience of recollection via the sense of olfaction creates an archive within the human body. This relationship between materiality and ethereality becomes paradoxically subverted in the experience of smell-induced memory experience. The material body as a (potential) archive is activated by an ethereal substance such as odour. Non-tactile in its physical properties, smell in this dynamic becomes paradoxically the material substance which activates the non-material mechanisms of remembering, in which case both the odour and the body can be viewed as holders of memory. In addition, in the case of Jewish exilic or Diasporic subjects, the body which the smell activates is more than the body of one individual. The historical reality of Jewish experience renders the individual body inseparable from the collective body of the Jewish people. This is both the result of the construct of the Jewish body by non-Jews and by the self-conscious Jewish subject. Consequentially, the Jewish body as an archive of cultural knowledge is always perceived as an historical body, the archive of more than 4000 years of scattered experience. This fantasy of the Jewish body leads to a non-scientific question: do Jews have memories of times immemorial? If yes, can smells trigger memories of supra-real experience, experience not of one individual life? This certainly is the case in application to the perception of the Russian Jewish body as a physical and metaphysical archive. In the following analysis I will demonstrate textual examples of the constructs of the two kinds of odour-induced memories, the real world and the supra-real, in a set of samples representing European and Russian cultural discourses of modernity and postmodernism.

Defining Jewish olfaction: from European stereotypes to the blood-libel (Heine and Rozanov)

The German poet Heinrich Heine provides an important example of Proustian memory in European Jewish discourse, in part because of the influential role which Heine played in the formation of the idea of Jewish smells, and in part because of the need to re-interpret the view that Heine treated Jewish smells derogatively. Heine also deals with the issue of smell-memory as both a Jewish individual and a collective experience.

Heine is often cited as an example of the Jewish authorial self who internalized the stereotype of the evil-smelling Jew.[10] It has also been noted that Heine projected this stereotype onto the Ostjude, the East European Jewish Other. But there remains unnoticed an important nuance: in his story *The Rabbi from Bacharach* (1840) Heine expresses a Proustian view of smell and olfaction in application to Jewish cultural knowledge. The story negotiates this knowledge in the context of the Jewish Diaspora and displacement. When a Sephardic Marano Jew arrives at a Jewish ghetto in a German town he rediscovers his Jewish identity through the smell of Jewish cooking. Significantly, the Marano Jew frames his experience in the context of Jewish history, comparing his attitude to the smells of food to that of Jews in Egyptian captivity. The logic of the narrative thus conceptualizes the Jew's body as an archive of knowledge which is ready to be activated by the sense of olfaction. The individual archive is in turn linked to the historical archive of the collective Jewish body:

> Do not look at me with disgust – said the Spaniard to the rabbi. My nose has not become a convert. When by accident I once came into the Jewish quarters and a familiar smell of the Jewish food touched my nostrils then I experienced the same longing as our forefathers in Egypt when they thought about pots with meat; tasty memories of my youth arose in me; in my thoughts I again saw carps cooked in brown sauce made of raisins which my aunt cooked for the Friday night meals; I again visualized the lamb stew with garlic and horseradish which can raise even the dead ... And my soul melted like the song of a nightingale and since then I eat in the tavern of Donna Elsa Shnapper.[11]

Despite the irony of this scene, it contains a serious subtext: Heine not only conveys a superior and derogative attitude towards the strong smells of garlic but also speculates about the decisive role that smells play in the retrieving of past memory, both individual and collective. Smells retrieve not only 'real-world memories' but also supra-real ones. If the Viking museum simulates the 'experience' of the tenth century AD, then the Bacharach experience evokes the cultural memories of ancient Israelites in Egyptian captivity.

The Russian *fin de siècle* gave birth to the idea that Jews react to certain smells in a collective way, and that the aromatics of herbs and spices of the Orient induce in Jews a certain type of behaviour. Not only have Jews preserved the cultural practice of inhaling smells of fragrant spices such as cloves and cinnamon, but the aromas of these spices also activate their collective behaviour. The 1903 tract *Judaism*, by influential Russian writer and body theorist Vasily Rozanov (1856–1919), links the inhaling of these sweet smells to the eroticism of the Jewish Sabbath. Significantly, Rozanov's fantasy of the Jewish Sabbath consists of visions of the unified behaviour of all the Jewish inhabitants of the Pale of Settlement. In his erotic descriptions the Sabbath night is an evening of simultaneous coituses of all the generations of the shtetl-Jews of the Pale, effectively presenting the Jewish collective body as an archive of sexual knowledge which can be triggered by the inhaling of traditional smells. Moreover, the smell of the Jewish ritual bath, the *mikveh*, which Jews take before the Sabbath, also receives treatment in this tract. Rozanov bases his description on two sources: the ethnographic stories of the little-known Jewish writer Savelii Litvin, *Sredi evreev* (Among Jews), and the hand-written manuscript of a Jewish convert to Christianity in the 1840s *Avtobiografiia pravoslavnogo evreia* (An Autobiography of a Christian Orthodox Jew) by Semen Tsenkhenshtein.[12] Litvin describes the repulsion experienced by his heroine, Rebecca, when her newly born daughter is put into the ritual bath, while Tsenkhenshtein claims that the water in the *mikveh* is disgustingly dirty and has a revolting smell, saturated as it is with the stench of human sweat. The author notes that although by law the water in the *mikveh* has to be flowing, the reality is that it is overused and always dirty. The convert Tsenkhenshtein was encouraged to write his autobiography by his two spiritual fathers, Russian Orthodox priests, and the notion of the foul-smelling water in the *mikveh* can be a case of stereotyping Jewish smells as foul. Certainly it is plausible to presume that both nineteenth-century Russian Jewish authors chose the notion of smell and olfaction as grounds for acculturation propaganda. Converts to Christianity, they wrote works that expressed Jewish self-hatred.[13] If these texts are part of Jewish archives on the theme of smells, should contemporary experiences of Jewish smells include these particular odours? Should we re-create them by composing odours based on collective baths with stale water? If we do, how should the bathers be chosen: from what ethnic community and background should the physical bodies be chosen? Will there be groups of participants who will recognize these smells as real-life memories, and what kind of memories will these odours induce? Should we treat these questions as fanciful?

In 'Judaism' Rozanov expresses the need to theorize the phenomena of smell and olfaction:

> This inhaling of the cloves smell is striking. What is olfaction? What is fragrance? Here is a category which has become neither the subject of philosophy, nor of art; it does not have an academic theory ... We inhale the object because of the special situation of the olfactory organ and the olfactory nerves which are linked to the brain. By inhaling we supply the brain with the particles of the chosen and loved object and by this process we come into close contact with its composition.[14]

It was clearly Jewish autobiographical accounts of cultural smells that prompted Rozanov to theorize anthropologically the notions of olfaction and smell in this essay. Ten years after the publication of this work, during the Beilis blood libel affair in 1913, Rozanov gives a race-specific theorizing of smell and olfaction. He then creates the text which became a canon of Russian anti-Semitism: *The Olfactory and Tactile Attitude of Jews to Blood* (1914). In this work Rozanov argues that it is plausible to suggest that the Jew Beilis killed the Christian boy because of the unconscious drive for the smell of human blood which Jews latently possess. In *Judaism* he classifies the impact of smell as an irrational phenomenon. This concept allows him to claim that Beilis's acts were the result of the subconscious drive of atavistic brain cells that had survived for over 4000 years. Rozanov makes this argument in the book with the fitting title *The Olfactory and Tactile Attitude of Jews to Blood*. When one Jew is accused of having a pathological drive towards the smell and the feel of human blood, the whole of the collective body of the Jewish nation is presented as an archive of this latent knowledge, knowledge which Jews are thought to pass on genetically to descending generations. The sense of smell and the smells of objects themselves become items of the Jewish biological archive. This text made an indelible impact on the interpretation of Jewish smell and olfaction as culture-specific knowledge, and Russian Jewish intellectuals responded to it as to a metatext.

From self-hatred to self-celebration: Babel, Mandelshtam and Goldshtein

In this section I will concentrate on three textual examples: two from the era of modernism and one from post-Soviet postmodernism. The first authors are the celebrated twentieth-century Russian writers Isaak Babel (1894–1940) and Osip Mandelshtam (1891–1937); the third is the award-winning contemporary writer Aleksandr Goldshtein (1957–2006). Babel, born in Odessa, fought in the Red Army during the Civil War and perished during Stalin's purges. He described in his stories scenes of devastation following pogroms in the Pale of Settlement during the Revolution and the Civil War. Mandelshtam perished in Stalin's Gulag having lived in Russia during the Beilis Affair and the two Russian revolutions. Goldshtein immigrated to Israel in 1990, the year of the collapse of the Soviet Union. He escaped from Baku, fleeing in fear of anti-Jewish pogroms which were anticipated as an aftermath to the Azeri–Armenian bloodshed in a year when the two former Soviet Republics became independent states. From Babel and Mandelshtam to Goldshtein the discursive formation of Jewish smell-memory completes a full circle. From ambivalence and self-hatred it becomes a celebration of Ashkenazi Jewish smell and odour-induced memory.

Isaak Babel was the first Jew to enter Russian literature as a Russian prose writer. Notably, his texts provide examples of the representations of Jewish self-awareness and self-hatred[15] by the trope of bodily smells. When this writer gave an autobiographical account of his childhood, his reminiscences contained a comment about the stench of the Jewish streets of his native Odessa:[16]

> Mr Zagursky ran a factory of infant prodigies, a factory of Jewish dwarfs in lace collars and patent leather pumps. He hunted them out in the slums of Moldavanka, in the evil-smelling courtyards of the Old Market ... My father decided that I should emulate them ... One day I left home laden like a beast of burden with violin case, violin music, and twelve rubles in cash – payment for a month's tuition. I was going along Nezhin Street; to get to Zagursky I should have turned into Dvorushnaya but instead of that I found myself at the harbor ... So began my liberation.[17]

Notably, the fresh smell of the sea became the metaphor for liberation and emancipation from the life of the Jewish ghetto. The fresh smell of freedom became synonymous with acculturation and assimilation to Russianness in contrasting symmetry to the evil smell of the Jewish streets – a potent trope for Jewishness in the Russian Empire. When Babel described his experience as a Red Army soldier in the post-revolutionary Civil War in his celebrated stories in *Red Cavalry* (1926), he again resorted to the trope of smell. The Russian Commander of the Division becomes for Babel the epitome of the kind of Russian masculinity that he wants to emulate. This Commander fittingly carries a pleasant smell – kind of a smell that Babel wants to appropriate as his own:

> Savitsky, Commander of the VI Division, rose when he saw me, and I admired the beauty of his giant body. He rose, the purple of his riding breeches and the crimson of his little tilted cap and the decorations stuck on his chest cleaving the hut as a standard cleaves the sky. A smell of perfume [*dukhi*] and of sweetish freshness [*pritornaia prokhlada*] of soap emanated from him. His long legs were like girls sheathed to the neck in shining riding boots.[18]

Babel's autobiographical hero expresses mimetic desire directed at the handsome Russian man's body. The fact that this giant body smells of sweet fragrance can be viewed as a way to feminize his body. What is the purpose of this feminization? Paradoxically, by feminizing the giant Russian male Babel makes him more akin to the Jew, and by proxy more akin to his own body. Babel's autobiographical narrator is small. Albeit ironically, Babel uses the stereotype of a small Jewish male body.[19] In spite of Babel's hidden desire to erase the line of difference between his own Jewish body and that of the Russian man's body through the ironic feminization of the latter, the notion of the fresh-smelling body is associated with a Russian man, not a Jew. On the intertextual level, this image of the Russian man's body as clean and fresh-smelling creates a contrast with the evil-smelling places of the Jews. Moreover, in the context of the descriptions of Jewish villages after the pogroms, this image of a clean Russian body becomes a metaphor for the difference between the Jewish and the Russian body. Decomposing corpses of violated Jewish men and women in Babel's *Red Cavalry* stories are disturbing metaphors of the fate of the Russian and Polish Jewry. The evocation of olfactory association of the dead bodies with the stench further valorizes the imagery. Babel's desire to break away from the Jewish places of the former Pale of Settlement is expressed through the complex dynamic of olfactory experiences that inform his cultural memory and identity.

Babel's contemporary, Osip Mandelshtam, also linked the recollections of childhood with smell. Importantly for the focus of this paper, he described smell as a form of the Jewish archive as he encountered it in his grandparents' home in Riga when he was an established figure of Russian modernism and a Moscow poet in the 1920s. This recollection is part of the book titled *The Noise of Time*, a title which programmatically emphasizes the sensory aspects of memory. In his essay in this book Mandelshtam singles out a bookshelf in his grandparents' apartment which consisted of old books in leather jackets, many of them written in German. The collection of books is highly representative of the German Jewish identity of his father's side of the family, with titles including those by the leading figures of Jewish enlightenment such as Moses Mendelssohn and Heinrich Heine. Both of these authors considered acculturation as a way forward for European Jewry. In addition to these authors, the Old Testament and the Talmud complete this home archive – a typical fragment of European modernity with the centrality of printed matter as an agency for the transmission of knowledge. But Mandelshtam introduces a new approach to the archive – its multi-sensory aspect. The leather jackets of books emanate a sensory form of knowledge: tactile and olfactory. The old and cracked leather has a distinct feel to the touch, and the smells of aged organic material – leather and paper – add an olfactory aspect to the sensory experience of acquiring knowledge from generations past.

The combination of the tactile and the olfactory is a strong referent to Russian modernity's perception of the Jews – a construct which finds its most powerful formulation in Rozanov's *Olfactory and Tactile Attitude of Jews to Blood*.[20] It has been noted that this is certainly the case in application to Mandelshtam's perception of his own Jewishness. Most commentators maintain that his attitude to Judaism and his Jewishness was typical for a turn-of-the-century Russian intellectual who wanted to break away from his Jewish roots but who continued to think of Judaism and Jewish identity until the end of his life.[21] Even his conversion to Christianity has elements of distrust towards Russian culture: he converted to German Protestantism and not to Eastern Orthodoxy. This move suggests that he constructed his identity as a multiple one and took into account the history of his father's family who had migrated from Germany to Warsaw and later to Riga. In his essay in *The Noise of Time* Mandelshtam negotiates Judaism and Ashkenazi Jewishness in an unmistakably Proustian and Rozanovian mode. As in Proustian memory, the inhaled aromas bring back the past but, in addition, the past is also framed as a collective supra-real experience of the Jewish nation. Like Proust's 'drops of essences' Mandelshtam writes about the 'droplets of musk' (*kroshka muskusa*) of Judaism, thus valorizing the sensory perceptions of memories: 'As a droplet of musk permeates the whole house, a tiny influence of Judaism overflows the whole life. O, what a strong smell it is!'[22] But does this passage reinforce the racial concept of the Jewish body? Indeed, if there is such a phenomenon as the 'strong smell of Judaism', how different is it from the notion of 'Jewish smell'? In the context of this article Mandelshtam's example illustrates a set of issues: he theorizes smell-memory as cultural knowledge; and he views such memory as a culture-specific Jewish phenomenon. I concur with Leonid Katsis's view that he contextualizes his own personal sensory memory experience in a dialogical relationship with the main meta-text of his time, *The Olfactory and Tactile Attitude of Jews to Blood*,[23] as the main anti-Semitic formation of Russian modernism (see footnote 22). It is important to remember, however, that Mandelshtam admits the strength of the smell of Judaism, not of

Jewishness. This choice can be read as an indication that Mandelshtam was in a dialogical relationship with Rozanov's early work 'Judaism', and not the infamous *Olfactory and Tactile Attitude of Jews to Blood*. In 'Judaism' Rozanov theorizes the sensory aspects of the perception of historical knowledge. I prefer to interpret Mandelshtam's trope of 'droplets of musk' and the 'strong smell of Judaism' as an affirmation of the multi-sensory aspect of Jewish memories, spaces and private archives. The enclosed space of his grandparents' apartment can be interpreted as a museum space. With its windows closed, its interior filled with old objects and pieces of ritual clothing, including his grandfather's prayer shawl or *tallith*, this space would have a specific odour. Anthropologists studying museum spaces have noted that contemporary museums, as air-conditioned spaces, not only remove the smells of exhibits but also eliminate the bodily odours of visitors. Did Mandelshtam think about the musk of his own body when enclosed in the apartment filled with Jewish paraphernalia belonging to his wandering family? His tragic end in a Stalin prison camp allows me to speculate about his olfactory perceptions of the public spaces of the prison and the chamber in which he and many others before him were subjected to torture. With his acute sense of historical knowledge he must have thought about the (im)possibility of archiving the sensory aspects of such spaces. Did he think about the specificity of human odours in relation to race and ethnicity in these de-humanizing spaces? Would he want those smells to be passed down to future generations as part of historical knowledge? While we do not know the answers to these questions, we know from autobiographical literature by both Jewish and non-Jewish survivals of the Gulags that they all wanted to destroy and forget bodily smells: their own and that of these others. The same applies to the experiences conveyed by survivors of the Holocaust. There is indeed a need to problematize sensory experiences in Jewish museums, archives and other spaces which purport to preserve and pass on historical knowledge and experiences in a new time and space situation.

Following the cognitive science approaches to the body, the postmodern approach to the body imbues it with all the explanatory possibilities of the mind. It rethinks the relationship between body and mind and subverts the hierarchies which stigmatize the senses of olfaction and tactility. Although Aristotle and Darwin categorized these senses as primitive,[24] cognitive scientists and linguists have now proven that sensations are part of human cognition. To use Rozanov's term, this set of sensations has been 'theorized'. With such cognition came the rehabilitation of Rozanov's views on Jewish olfaction through the work of contemporary Russian Jewish writer Aleksandr Goldshtein. Significantly, this rehabilitation became possible as a result of this writer's immigrant experience in Israel. Goldshtein's postmodern essays are informed by contemporary theorizings of the body as a site of cultural knowledge. He defines his own Jewish Ashkenazi self in Israel against what he terms 'Maghribic' Jewish culture. He maintains that Israel has destroyed all the achievements of European Jewish culture, choosing alternative odours and olfaction to represent this new Israeli culture and identity. The erasure of the Ashkenazi culinary tradition, as seen in the replacement of gefilte fish with rough falafel, is a symbol of this disappearance of cultural knowledge:

> The Jewish essence here is cheaply given away, it lowers itself for the sake of things which should be treated as a bogey but which here have become an ideal. Sweet and sour meat stews, gefilte fish, chopped herring with boiled egg and onions, honey biscuits, the conciliators (the majority of the Israeli-born Ashkenazim) gave preference to the Maghrib pita dough which bloats stomachs with its rough filling made of chickpeas.[25]

His choice of the word 'essence' to describe Jewish cultural practices is a calculated strategy. He views the aromas and smells of Ashkenazi food as a core ingredient of this culture. Goldshtein does not view North African Jewish cooking as Jewish. He hints that Israeli Jews abandoned their Diasporic European roots via the rejection of their corporeal 'essence'. This image implies that Jews in Israel, through their reactive behaviour towards anti-Jewish stereotypes, erased all those aspects of European Jewish culture which fall into the category of the senses. The internalization of the stereotypes of Jewish smells and olfaction is one key component of this cultural knowledge:

> Arabs proudly smell of themselves, Jews already have lost their smell in contrast to their olive-skinned neighbours. They are ashamed of their formerly strong sweat glands and hope to become similar to other nations sunk in sterility. Only [religious] Jews of Mea Shearim suburb still have strong smells.[26]

'Formerly strong sweat glands' is a powerful referent to the construct of the Jewish body. I have demonstrated elsewhere the intertextual polemics with Rozanov in Goldshtein's essays.[27] Here the focus is on the body as archive, a depository of cultural knowledge with its ability to activate memories through its own multi-sensory abilities. And, indeed, the image of the religious Jews from Mea Shearim suggests that the body is a depository of knowledge. As such it is not a passive archive: in order to activate this archive the body has to perform the culture by living it. This reasoning re-thinks the concept of the Jewish body as a racial body through a process of de-essentializing. As a well-read intellectual, Goldshtein is clearly familiar with the new theorizings of the body which take into account multi-sensory experience. With the erasure of elements of knowledge traditionally conveyed through practice and performance, as has occurred in Israel, the whole body of knowledge will disappear. The body is an archive of knowledge in its own right, a form of knowledge which needs to be passed onto future generations. Once smells disappear, the Proustian memory can no longer function. It is not in vain that an immigrant experience taught Goldshtein to turn to the notion of smell-memory. With no material possessions to bring over to the new land, he resorts to the sense-induced memory of smell and is incapable of identifying familiar smells in these new surroundings. The body of the Jewish immigrant from Russia is the only archive, even in the land of Israel. It remains non-perceptive to new smells as these do not activate cherished real-life knowledge.

Conclusion

Should we argue that, in the same way in which documents containing tragic events are a part of Jewish archives, unpleasant even disgusting odours also have to be catalogued? In the same way that the reading of documents constructs individual and collective memories, memories of smells can evoke a diverse range of Jewish history. Proustian memory is based not only on the smell-induced recollection of things sweet; it also covers the whole range of human emotions. Psychologists chose to conduct their experiment in the Viking museum because it provided them with the ideal technological environment: odours in the form of commercially manufactured gases were piped into theme-based areas. The ethical and political aspects of this experiment did not include matters of ethnic sensitivity. Indeed, there is no 'real-life' Viking community living in Britain to be offended by the implications that their toilet areas were not hygienic and that they carried unpleasant smells. To introduce foul smells into the Jewish museum would mean to promulgate the construct of the malodorous Jew. Racial stereotypes have essentialized both Jewish smells and olfaction. Moreover, the concept of piping gas into a Jewish museum is a controversial endeavour in post-Holocaust reality. And how many types of smells would we choose in order to reproduce the Jewish experience? The future of Jewish archives is linked to matters of intergenerational responsibility. The Viking museum experiment reveals that all the participants found the pungent 'rubbish acrid' smell repulsive. While the collectivity of this reaction to a foul smell implies its universality, the reaction to smells is a cultural construct. Freud famously argued that all barriers of disgust are the product of civilizing upbringing.[28]

As the above museums demonstrate, public spaces such as museums and archives have come to negotiate private archives as multi-sensory experiments. Sets of cultural knowledge, including memories, are stored in public and private collections as archives, and museums increasingly appeal to the public to share their 'stories' of past generations. These stories inevitably incorporate Proustian smell-memories. Oral and printed sources reflecting such multi-sensory experiences are in a complex relationship with one another, echoing as they do the complex relationships between private and public spaces containing 'memorabilia'.

We cannot control the actual composition of 'real-life' smells which we pass onto future generations via archives. Even if we pass on the documented components and ingredients of food and bathing water, the actual ingredients will change in the future: genetically modified organic matter will mutate to create a different type of smell. Moreover, we do not know in what way 'post-human' bodies of future generations will perceive smells. But we can pass on the knowledge of reactions to certain smells at various times in history. Paradoxically, our archives can influence the way in which smells will be perceived and interpreted by future generations because, fortunately, smell-induced sensations are as much cultural constructs as is the interpretation of any archival data.

I can visualize the consequences of the current advent of olfactory art for Jewish museums. The New York Museum of Arts and Design opened a new Center of Olfactory Art in 2011. The Center has a special atomizing machine whose buttons release 'the work of art'.[29] I can imagine that such machines will have a future in museums if the trend of interactivity continues to influence (decisions about) museums' viability. I would like to see an atomizing machine which allows an individual to create and compose a smell which in his or her perception best represents the smell of a chosen epoch in time and space. Can we control or predict whether the machine activators will interpret, recall or fantasize some smells as 'Jewish'? If we want future generations to react with understanding to the diversity of Jewish history and experience, we must not limit our archives to the descriptions of smells of chicken soup, cinnamon and almonds.

Notes

1. Marcel Proust, *Remembrance of Things Past*, trans. Terence Kilmartin (New York: Vintage, 1981), 1: 24.
2. M.A. Conway et al., "A Cross-cultural Investigation of Autobiographical Memory," *Journal of Cross-Cultural Psychology* 36 (2005): 739–49; A.E. Bernstein, "The Contributions of Marcel Proust to Psychoanalysis," *Journal of the American Academy of Psychoanalysis and Dynamic Psychiatry* 33, no. 1 (2005): 137–48.
3. See Julia Kristeva, "Proust: In Search of Identity," in *The Jew in the Text: Modernity and the Construction of Identity*, ed. Linda Nochlin and Tamar Garb (London: Thames and Hudson, 1995), 140–55.
4. Max Horkheimer and Theodor W. Adorno, *Dialektik der Aufklarung* (Frankfurt: Fisher, 1969).
5. See Jay Geller, "The Aromatics of Jewish Difference; or Benjamin's Allegory of Aura," in *Jews and Other Differences*, ed. Jonathan and Daniel Boyarin (Minneapolis: Minnesota University Press, 1997), 203–56.
6. John P. Aggleton and Louise Waskett, "The Ability of Odours to Serve as State-dependent Cues for Real-World Memories: Can Viking Smells Aid the Recall of Viking Experiences?," *British Journal of Psychology* 90 (1999): 1.
7. Ibid., 3.
8. Ibid., 3.
9. See http://www.thejewishmuseumorg/touch/verbal (accessed January 2, 2011).
10. See Sander L. Gilman, *Creating Beauty to Cure the Soul* (Durham, NC: Duke University Press, 1998).
11. H. Heine [G. Geine], "Bakherakhskii ravvin. Fragment," *Sobranie sochinenii* (Moscow: Akademiia Nauk, 1958), 7: 121–132, 124. My translation.
12. Semen Tsenkhenshtein, "Avtobiografiia pravoslavnogo evreia. S prilozheniem," in V.V. Rozanov, "Iudaizm," in *Taina Izrailia*, ed. F.V. Boikova (St Petersburg: Sofiia, 1993), 105–228.
13. On anti-Semitism and Jewish identity in Russia see Eugene M. Avrutin, *Jews and the Imperial State: Identification Politics in Tsarist Russia* (Ithaca, NY: Cornell University Press, 2010).
14. Rozanov, "Iudaizm," 163.
15. On Babel's Jewish identity see Efraim Sicher, *Jews in Russian Literature after the October Revolution* (Cambridge: Cambridge University Press, 1995); Alice Nakhnimovsky, *Russian Jewish Literature and Identity: Jabotinsky, Babel, Grossman, Galich, Raziner, Markish* (Baltimore, MD: The Johns Hopkins University Press, 1992).
16. On the mythology around the Odessa Jewish identity see Jarrod Tanny, *City of Rouges and Schnorrers: Russia's Jews and the Myth of old Odessa* (Bloomington, IN: Indiana University Press, 2011).
17. Isaak Babel, "Awakening," trans. Anthony Wixley, *International Literature* 3 (1935): 40.
18. Isaak Babel, "My First Goose," trans. R. MacAndrew, in *A Modern Russian Reader*, ed. R. Hingley (London: Allen & Unwin, 1959), 246.
19. On the stereotype of the small male Jew's body see Daniel Boyarin, *Unheroic Conduct: The Rise of Heterosexuality and the Invention of the Jewish Man* (Berkeley: University of California Press, 1997).
20. Before his death Rozanov asked for this book to be destroyed. He notably asked the Jews for forgiveness. Sadly, the book is used by the Black Hundreds in post-Soviet Russia for anti-Semitic propaganda. See Henrietta Mondry, *Vasily Rozanov and the Body of Russian Literature* (Bloomington, IN: Slavica, 2010).
21. See a discussion in Leonid Katsis, *Osip Mandel'shtam: muskus iudeistva* (Moscow: Mosty kul'tury, 2002).
22. Osip Mandel'shtam, *Shum vremeni* (Moscow: Prosveshchenie, 1990), 37.
23. V.V. Rozanov, "Oboniatel'noe i osiazatel'noe otnoshenie evreev k krovi," in *Sakharna* (Moscow: Respublika, 1998), 276–414.
24. For a discussion of smell in the hierarchy of senses in European philosophy in application to Jews see Kalman P. Bland, *The Artless Jew: Medieval and Modern Affirmation and Denials of the Visual* (Princeton, NJ: Princeton University Press, 2000).

25. Aleksandr Gol'dshtein, *Aspekty dukhovnogo braka* (Moscow: Novoe literaturnoe obozrenie, 2001), 25.
26. Ibid., 9.
27. Henrietta Mondry, *Exemplary Bodies: Constructing the Jew in Russian Culture* (Boston: Academic Studies Press, 2009).
28. See Sigmund Freud, "The Archaic Features and Infantilism of Dreams," in *Introductory Lectures on Psychoanalysis*, The Penguin Freud Library (London: Penguin Books, 1976), 235–50.
29. http:/www.artinfo/com/news/story/36551 (accessed January 3, 2011).

Heritage centres in Israel: Depositories of a lost identity?

Hilda Nissimi

General History Department, Bar-Ilan University, Ramat-Gan, Israel

This article explores the role of communal museums as constructors of identity and as political agents in Israeli society. Their avowed target is to act as realms of memory and through that function they provide focal points for the construction of ethnic entities. As the Israeli heritage centres declare communities according to non-Jewish political borders they provide the basis for new identities. As educational centres outside the hegemonic culture they vie for a re-formulation of that culture. For that they glorify the community's past based on its history in the Diaspora, but also very much on Zionist accomplishments.

Introduction

The converging relationship between museums and identity formation is a growing subject, primarily on the theoretical level, but also regarding particular cases. National archives and museums are considered realms of memory striving to tell the story of nations, and these facilities are important in the construction of group identity. Museums are in fact the sites where the collective is on symbolic display.[1] In the context of Israel the emergence of heritage centres-cum-museums of communities from various designated origins, each dedicated to a particular group, each representing a particular identity, might be the proof that Israeli identity broke up into 'several nations'.[2] Each of these centres relates to a geographical area and is a 'relational construct that establishes boundaries by which a community comes to know itself as distinct from another'.[3] As such, each of these centres is the symbolic expression of an ethnic entity, replacing the national as locus of primary identification.

This paper is based on the assumption that 'the essence of a museum lies in its being a collection of artefacts ... and other devices, museums make statements – provide meanings – for their audiences'.[4] Namely, the most important ability of any museum is to use objects and other sensory media to make an implicit thesis.[5] Most Israeli heritage centres claim a role of memorial to lost experiences and to almost forgotten identities. The centres are aspiring to present meaningful collections about their heritage. As such they are commemorative centres for a past that recedes ever faster and cannot be resumed. Thus, communal museums perform the role of archives of fading memories. Therefore, in the context of this article the terms heritage centre and museum will be used interchangeably.

In this article I explore the role of these centres as depositories of (lost) identity and their role as focal points for the construction of ethnic entities. The museums and heritage centres that are examined are of all sizes, some of them quite impressive, others no more than a website.[6] All will be treated as texts to be read and de-constructed. They are regarded according to the subject matters they have chosen and to their presentation methods, as well as to their statements of policy and their goals and objectives.

The melting pot reaction – arresting the fleeting moment

As far back as the 1950s accepted wisdom in Israel, as elsewhere, expected immigrants to assimilate into the receiving society. This expectation was encapsulated in the notion of the state as a 'melting pot'.[7] The persistent inability of some immigrants to 'melt' away was expected to be temporary or blamed on insufficient efforts on their part or by the receiving society.[8] Like many other countries Israel also gave up these expectations of the immigrants. Common wisdom has changed and the popular backlash against the pressures on the immigrants to assimilate by relinquishing their original culture was starting to have political effect. In any case, the late 1970s are considered in Israel a watershed that brought about the de-monopolization of dominant culture; some would even claim that they mark the break-up of a unitary Israeli identity.[9] The proliferation of heritage centres could easily be interpreted as part of this process, as the appearance, or indeed the resurgence, of ethnic identities of immigrant groups and their offspring in Israel.[10]

In fact, the first communal museum was built long before that. When the Museum of Italian Jews was founded in 1952 it was an extraordinary establishment singling out one particular community. It was created with the intention of salvaging Jewish artefacts from Italy from communities that were liquidated during World War II. In a way, the building of the new centre could be seen as part of the commemoration urge after the Holocaust. However, the young state was then making its first and very hesitant steps in Holocaust commemoration and the general attitude towards the survivors and their memories was rather ambivalent. It was moving between compassion and criticism, between commemoration of heroism and condemnation of the Holocaust experience of the survivors, as part of exilic history.[11] Whether commemorative or celebrative, the Italian Museum was the first museum dedicated to one specific diasporic community, and thus an act of celebrating its particularity.[12]

It took two decades, until the 1970s, for new attempts to be made to follow its example. The first was another European museum: a small German heritage museum started by Yisrael Shiloni in Nehariya in 1971. Then two new associations were founded with the intention of building heritage centres: one for the Jews of Aleppo and another for the Jews of Iraq; both centres were opened in the 1980s. The Italian centre was also refurbished in 1982.[13] The Memorial Museum of Hungarian Speaking Jewry was also founded in the 1980s although it opened only in 1990. It is probably significant that none of these communities belonged to the dominant culture,[14] but it is no less significant that since then many other communities have built their own centres, or expressed a wish do so, even if in some cases all they managed to do was to build virtual centres by constructing websites announcing such intentions.[15]

The proliferation of heritage museums fits well into the process of diversification of the dominant culture in Israel.[16] All communal heritage centres – European and non-European – bewail the effects of the 'melting pot'. To be sure, the unitary national identity which was the goal of the process is accepted as a laudable target. And yet at the same time the effacement of the heritage of entire communities is lamented and is blamed on the national educational system. It has inculcated new myths, customs and memories while erasing all else. Thus, so the lament goes, the second generation of Israeli-born or even the first generation of Israeli-educated children 'forgot' their heritage.

The heritage centres place themselves as a reaction to this process – albeit, judging by the note of desperation in their goal declarations, it is a reaction that came too late. Most of the communal museums display a sense of urgency for the preservation and commemoration of their community's history before and after immigration to Israel. It is most poignantly put by the Turkish Heritage Centre. Although the ostensible intention of the centre is to revive the roots of a generation that is already Israeli and to create a living focal point for the community, the dread of the inevitable demise of the world that was left behind is ringing along with the drive for commemoration:

> When the state was founded it was important to create an 'Israeli', with one language – Hebrew, one culture – Israeli, and to abandon as soon as possible the culture which they brought when they immigrated to the Land. In those days, apparently it was an important task to construct Israeli identity.
>
> Now that I am already Israeli ... it was important that I know my roots, and on my journey to recover my roots I found out that there is no information in the internet about Turkish Jewry, no centre that commemorates/eternalises its story, no institution that creates social and cultural activity for people of Turkish origin.[17]

But it is already imbued with the tragic knowledge that as a community their days are numbered: 'When all those who immigrated to Israel, to build it and settle in it, will pass away in the fullness of time, it will be the centre that will tell their stories and honour their memory.'[18] Thus, it is only the memory that can be saved. A meeting of Israeli MPs of Yemenite or partly Yemenite extraction to form a lobby for the preservation of Yemenite heritage expressed the same feeling of anxiety for a disappearance of the heritage with the passing away of the immigrant generation.[19]

Even the Babylonian Jewry Heritage Centre, which believes that 'it isn't quite too late yet', displays the awareness of an ever receding world in its warning: 'oral traditions, if you don't hurry to write them down, and if you don't record them, tomorrow may be too late'.[20] It is quite clear that only the memory of these traditions can still be carried over the abyss of forgetfulness. Only the community of Aleppo is an exception to the entire group, and the note of desperation is completely absent from its goal-setting.

The European centres are driven by an equal sense of urgency. The Museum of the German Speaking Jews demonstrates the sense of urgency in the title of the film that introduces the viewer to the founding of the museum: 'To Arrest the Fleeting Moment'.[21] The Memorial Museum of Hungarian Speaking Jewry is driven by a similar pressure even if it is expressed in a more optimistic note. The young generation that grew up in Israel was detached and estranged from its parents' cultural heritage in the Diaspora. Yet the founders of the museum felt that in 'the past few years there is a trend to bridge the estrangement, to conserve and to emphasise the special values of the communities that Israeli society is composed of'. And yet they do not seem to put their hope in the longevity of an 'immigrant' community.

In all cases the associations or individuals that founded the centres declared their intention to utilise the centres for the preservation of the identities of these communities. But they also affirm that their aim is to give their community a 'proper place in the pages of history'. The heritage centres are therefore *lieux de mémoire* that present themselves as places that collect what would otherwise be discarded and forgotten.[22]

As such, they emphasize not continuity but discontinuity; like any *lieu de mémoire*, 'they create a factitious past to illustrate its difference from the present'.[23] The objects presented by the museum quite often retain the names of the donating family. The visitor's expected reaction in such cases would be: 'This is mine!' and create a feeling of belonging and homeliness.[24] But in most cases, especially where the pre-modern nature of the artefact is obvious, the visitor is expected to feel estrangement as a visitor to a foreign land, or relief that her or his life is much more comfortable. The mixture therefore creates a feeling of crisis and discontinuity, as realms of memory often do.

Thus, museums along with archives and several other functions and institutions, all of them *lieux de mémoire*, are 'the boundary stones of another age, illusions of eternity'.[25] The faster society is transformed the more evident is 'the postmodern predicament of memorial culture' and the more futile appears the ability to 'arrest the fleeting moment'.[26]

Gathering memories – constructing *lieux de mémoire*

By compiling collections of artefacts the museums show an obligation to preserve what otherwise would be swept away by change. The willingness or the obligation to remember is, according to Pierre Nora, the basic condition for any retention of the past.[27] Such retention of the past could be conceived as compensation for the loss of the original communal experience, or, as Andrea Huyssen believes, museal memory is 'a way of slowing down modernization', if only by safeguarding a few elements against the amnesia caused by modernization and immigration.[28] Therefore, the heritage centres cannot reverse the processes set in place by the melting-pot policies, but they can compensate for them by re-enacting some of the scenes, re-presenting some of the objects that have been used in the past.

The centres are founded on research and the collection of information, as well as documents. The Babylonian museum was preceded by a series of gatherings of community members who became informants and informed basic research into the history of the Iraqi community. In July 1975 the association for building the centre held several conventions during which they gathered together 100 informants with researchers and doctoral students. Likewise, the addition of a new diorama was preceded in this centre by research and the gathering of information.[29] Similarly, in the Libyan Jewry Centre in Bat-Yam, Or-Shalom, that is still under construction the founder is dedicating much of his time to gathering information on past experiences, on holidays or on various cultural activities and disseminating it for a token price among community members. Among the subjects on which the centre has already gathered and published information were Zionist songs composed by children before the independence of the State of Israel, the lamentation of the 9th of Av, the cantillations of the *Selihot* (penitential prayers during the month of Elul, before the Jewish New Year), and folklore.[30] The Yemenite association E'ele betamar (after the name of the first modern immigration from Yemen to the land of Israel in 1832) boasts of gathering several life stories and their publication.[31]

Many of the centres include research divisions and host, organise or at least publicise on a regular basis workshops and conferences on subjects of interest to them. The Hungarian Jewry Centre, for example, holds a yearly conference on Herzl Memorial Day on subjects such as Hungarian Zionism, the Hungarian Holocaust and Hungarian culture. In general, the invitations are sent out to second-generation families who have shown an interest in the museum.[32] For one of those gatherings the audience was asked why the museum and its mission of conservation of heritage are important. The general answer was that they wanted to preserve values and a sense of belonging. The museum team hoped the meaning of these values could be clarified in further meetings.[33]

One of the targets of the research is to bring to light the experience of immigration to Israel. Usually it is in self-celebratory terms showing the important part the immigrants played in the building of the state. This is most evident in the Museum of the German Speaking Jews in Tefen, which was founded with the express purpose of showing the contribution of the German-speaking immigrants to the State of Israel.[34] The connection between the heritage centres and research helps them establish their credentials as presenting a 'real past', just like the use of dioramas helps them to convey a 'real' picture of that past.[35]

All the heritage centres present among their goals the intention of creating a place for depositing artefacts and for gathering information about their communities. Only a few of the immigrants, especially during Israel's first decades, left memoirs or written materials that could reflect their experiences.[36] In as much as these centres become focal points for the gathering of these informants and information, they allow the independent voice of the immigrant a hearing that would otherwise be almost absent. Yet, in most cases, these centres do not house an impressive database of first-hand testimonies.[37] Many of the centres, however, play a role in the dissemination of research to the public in organised conferences that emphasise their community.[38]

The gathering of artefacts for the construction of the centres is usually an on-going process, even after the construction of the centre. The Babylonian Museum in its periodical has a section that regularly reports new donations to the museum. Often the artefacts are sent in to commemorate a deceased family member, a possibility also utilised in other museums.[39] The Babylonian Centre also allows community members to dedicate an honorary placard through a donation to the centre.[40] The Hungarian Centre prepares a small information leaflet which includes reports of new and interesting acquisitions.[41] These acts allow each of these centres to represent both a communal and a more intimate, family-oriented memorial and through that become a sacred place.

Two main subjects are apparent among the heritage centres' collections. The most prominent and recurrent subject these centres present is Jewish religious life. In fact, some of the smaller centres, for example, the Centre of the Jews of Cochin in Nevatim, display their artefacts within synagogues. But many other heritage centres, like the Italian Museum, the Babylonian Centre, the Moroccan Museum in Jerusalem and even the Libyan Centre in Bat-Yam (which is still under construction) display reconstructions of different scale synagogues from their country of origin.[42] The centres also present, and in some cases re-publish religious tractates.[43] In most centres, however, religious life is presented through the collecting and display of religious artefacts from both the private sphere and public spheres. These include such items as kiddush goblets (for the festive blessing said before the meal on the Sabbath and on religious holidays), candelabra and various embroidered artefacts. From the public sphere they display Scrolls of Torah in their embroidered garments or ornamented encasements, and these are often the most impressive items the centres hold. The Museum of Italian Jewish Art also presents Torah arks and special, heavily and impressively embroidered, ornamental curtains. Religious artefacts are the main means for presenting the cycle of the year showing particular customs not only for Shabbat and the high holidays, but also the cycle of life: from birth to burial.

The other major subject represented in all heritage centres is the community's ties with the Land of Israel and more specifically with Zionism, presenting Zionist zeal or Zionist ideas. Although it has been surmised that the very appearance of communal heritage centres expresses the break-up of Israeli collective identity, it does not entail a demise of Zionism as the central ethos of the Jewish population of Israel. All the centres parade with great pride their Zionist activities and represent their community's story within the Zionist framework of history: the story of the Jewish people is a story that begins in the Land of Israel and ends in the State of Israel.[44] The identification of Jewish nationalism with Zionism and with the State of Israel is absolute. The only deviation from the Zionist narrative is their emphasis on the period of Exile with pride and oftentimes with longing. They proudly uphold their contacts with diasporic communities, although those communities have no presentation or representation in the display.[45]

Furthermore, the centres present themselves as the last monuments of commemoration to communities that were washed away in the boiling melting-pot. In truth, of course, living communities do exist outside Israel, such as Jewish communities in Turkey and in Hungary. On the other hand, even when the historic communities have ceased to exist in their land of origin, they survive as diasporic communities in other countries in the West and not only Israel. The Babylonian Museum is very proud of its connection with Iraqi Jewish communities outside Israel – but the visitor to the museum is completely oblivious of their existence.[46] It is an existence which, if admitted, would contradict the sense of urgency expressed by the museum and even more so the salience of the Zionist solution.

By disregarding their communities outside Israel, the centres' expression of the Zionist ideal, an ideal that names the State of Israel as the only end-point for a Jewish journey, expresses the Zionist negation of the period of Exile.[47] In accepting the centrality of the state, the heritage centres adopt the phraseology that goes with it: they accept the terms of Exile and Diaspora as opposites of homeland and sovereignty. And yet the museums challenge the negation of the Exile by showing that their communities prospered during Exile. They are closer to the theological view of Exile which found various merits in the period of Exile. Indeed, theological thought, although never ridding itself of the apologetic strain, presented the period of Exile and Jewish existence in the Diaspora as having deep intrinsic value, turning a challenge into an asset.[48] Although from a different point of view the heritage centres also appreciate the exilic period as an opportunity for demonstrating Jewish merit in the midst of suffering. Thus, contrary to the expectations of thinkers like Raz Krakozkin, who argue that by presenting lost traditions the united national ethos would fall, the heritage centres present a positive view of the period of Exile while retaining a Zionist outlook.[49]

Indeed, Zionist negation of Exile also involved a break with tradition because Zionism rebelled against the religious tradition which it identified with political passivism and acquiescence to diasporic conditions. The heritage centres follow a Zionist secular view by presenting their community's glory in terms of culture, and especially by Zionist activity. At the same time they continue tradition by articulating cultural and artistic achievements through the presentation of religious objects.

This interpretation of Jewish history could therefore fit neatly within a view of a Diaspora nationalism, which recognises the various communities as parts of a greater whole which are 'bound together by shared historical memories associated with a specific territory which they regard as "homeland"'.[50] Yet representing the community without its global branches also positions the community as part of the nation *in* Israel and the museum as an actor in local identity construction, rather than a focal point for an international self-sustained diasporic community.

The centres show exhibits that represent the longstanding connection with the land of Israel – sometimes only historical maps, as in the heritage centre of the Libyan community in Or-Yehuda and in the Babylonian Centre.[51] The Memorial Museum of Hungarian Speaking Jewry shows longstanding ties with the land of Israel starting with non-Zionist ties, represented by a flat stone plate that testifies to the amounts of money donated by five Hungarian Jews to a Yeshiva in Safed. For the modern period they parade their ties with the Zionist movement as they declare on the museum's website: 'Hungarian Jewry have a part in the renaissance of the Jewish People in its land, since Theodor Herzl, the prophet of the Jewish State came from Hungary, and many settlements were founded by Jews from Hungary'. Pictures of Theodor Herzl and his family make good this declaration as well as a piece in a newspaper that announces the foundation of Petah-Tiqwa and many other articles which present and represent Zionist activity in Hungary itself.[52] The German Heritage Museum emphasizes the immigrants' contribution and their elite status in the State of Israel.[53] This is emphasized even more in the tiny Dona Gracia Museum in Tiberias. Dedicated to the commemoration of Dona Gracia Mendes (1510–1569) and the Ladino heritage, the museum is not expected to display Zionist activity. And yet the museum presents Dona Garcia's experiment to found a 'Proto-Zionist' autonomy: 'her dream was to set up Tiberias as a national home for the persecuted Jews. Thus, she foresaw the vision of the Return to Zion 350 years before the first Zionist Congress'.[54]

Although dependent on informants and on donations in general the artefacts in all the centres are expected to exude a richness of cultural life. They are expected to include religion, but to incorporate as wide a range as possible, reflecting the different professions and statuses community members occupied. And yet most communal heritage centres prefer objects that impress with the richness of the creativity invested in them and the affluence of the original user. It is therefore clear that artefacts are presented with the intention of enhancing the glory of the community.

But even very mundane artefacts are raised to a status of importance and given a licence to eternal life as they are set in the museum, a place accepted as a shrine of knowledge and culture.[55] Informants bring in the items that they saw as connected to their private life – sometimes mere ephemera. This could include kitchen ware, school books, toys, documents and pictures. They may never have thought of them as edifying, and they find out now that they are considered worthy of museum presentation. They find out that their knowledge, expertise and life experiences are worth telling. By elevating their objects to the level of museum exhibits, the symbol of high culture, they are allowed to feel that their life experience and their knowledge of it is also elevated.[56] They are presented as objects that bring to life the home country, before immigration and sometimes long before that. Value, as Bourdieu argues, 'is accrued by an object according to its insertion according to a classification legitimated by an institutional signatory'.[57] From mere memorabilia they are raised to the importance of History, with a capital H. Even where it is obvious that an item donated was of high emotional or pecuniary value, it is quite obvious that the centre would keep the item's value and even enhance it. The item is donated because its owners feel that its time of direct usefulness is over. By presenting these artefacts, the past and through it the community are being objectified as part of the knowledge of the public, and as part of the 'history of the Nation'.

Imagined communities – empowered entities

Heritage centres are normally the handiwork of one dedicated person, who has worked selflessly to preserve and almost resurrect a lost heritage and by her or his efforts the museum can be presented as non-political, universally credited institution.[58] Thus the heritage museums' claim to be part of the necessary knowledge of the general public and an objective player in the field of public education is further enhanced. The same conception would see the archive as the place where society preserves the documents which are not in use any more – an objective collection without edge or politics.

According to Lyotard, who characterises our postmodern age with narrative and therefore with forgetfulness, museums are conceived as transmitters. Lyotard sees narrative as legitimated by repetition; it becomes immemorial without a chronological sequence thereby forgoing memory altogether. However, Lyotard counterposes the museum to narrative and sees it as a storage place of the past. Thus, according to Lyotard, museums are places for storing the past and objectifying it as 'science' as opposed to narrative that consumes the past.[59]

It is, however, impossible to see the heritage centres as objective places, as depositories of a past community, or as its 'mere' memorials. The collection of items in both archives and museums is a political decision. It is, in fact, a cluster of decisions: what to preserve and what to consign to forgetfulness, how to categorise them and how to present them to the visitors; together they constitute questions of information, and knowledge or memory which inform the present as well as the future of society.

As *lieux de mémoire* these centres present idealised entities. The great disputes of the past about secularisation processes, about absorption in the general society are mostly silenced. In the Hungarian Speaking Jewry Museum the different communities and the feuds that plagued them are muted. The Neologs, the Status-Quo and the Orthodox, all the different and deeply differing Jewish communities, are all finally at peace and united with each other as 'Hungarian Jews', at least as far as the item labels are concerned.[60] Likewise, the Babylonian Centre makes no mention of the communists or any other non-Zionist segment of the community.[61] The invitation to the visitor to come to the Italian Jewish Art Museum makes it clear why: 'come and see for yourself the full glory of those lauded days'.[62]

The past is conveyed to the visitor exclusively by those chapters which can evoke the glory of the community. In spite of the wish to present a 'real' past, hardships are rarely shown. In the Babylonian Centre, before closing that part of the museum for refurbishment, they used to show pictures from the mass immigration of the early 1950s and of the immigrants living in tents. In this case, although the hardship is admitted it is not presented as criticism of the absorption process. The detrimental effect of discrimination of the Iraqi immigrants in the transit camps and their redirection to agricultural settlements are presented to the visitor as a heroic experience that 'granted them their place in Israeli society'.[63] One of the most hurtful episodes for many immigrants was their disinfection upon landing. The Babylonian Museum shows a picture of the DDT container and thus alludes to the painful experience, but the explanation is straightforward and unemotional within the context of care for the immigrants upon arrival.[64] The small Yemenite Centre in Rosh-Ha'ayin boasts the ownership of a film about the Yemenite children who disappeared during the 1950s, a point of contention between Yemenite Jews and the State of Israel. However, that film is far from being the centrepiece of the museum. In fact, some of its visitors may miss it entirely. Random visitors are shown another film: a highly celebratory film prepared by

Beit Hatefuzot. They emphasise their contribution to the growth of the State of Israel, not their complaints against it.

However, these are imagined communities in the sense that Benedict Anderson refers to the nation – as an imagined brotherhood that constitutes a political entity. And yet these centres are building imagined communities in even a deeper sense. In most cases, the Jewish communities which are presented are an amalgamation of Jews in imagined political entities. To give but one example: the planned Romanian Jewry Centre promises to represent the history of Jewish communities starting with the Romanian principalities during the fifteenth to the eighteenth centuries. Not only does this present a Romanian nationalist view that constructs a Romanian primordial nation, it also proposes Romanian boundaries that include Bukovina, Bessarabia, Transnistria and Transylvania. These regions were part of Romania only for a short duration during the period between the two world wars.[65] Until this period, some of these principalities (Moldova and Walachia) were under the Ottoman Empire, under the Russian empire (part of Moldova), and under the Austrian and later Austro-Hungarian Empire (Transylvania), disregarding other changes of hands. In fact, these areas are at least theoretically represented by other heritage centres in Israel: the Turkish Jewry Museum is supposed to represent Ottoman Jewry of all periods; The Museum of the German Speaking Jews is supposed to include Bukovina, and the Hungarian Museum promises to include Transylvania.[66] This simple example points to two conclusions. The communities these centres claim to commemorate as authentic experiences are imagined communities, and they are imagined along contours and boundaries that enhance their past importance.

The centres are usually based on extensive research, but they do not present a self-reflective picture, and they are not interested in a critical view. Although the museums provide a view of a past that they admit is no more, it is not history in the academic sense. Pierre Nora calls history a reconstruction of the past that is no more with mediation and distance being the essence of history and the contrast of memory. But then Nora conceives of history as a secular intellectual operation that calls for analysis and criticism.[67] The communal centres do not intend either. They were not driven by an academic detachment, and although deeply convinced that they are to reveal a truth, it is a truth that requires building rather than deconstructing. These centres intend to build memories rather than disintegrate them.

In some respects these heritage centres remind one of the saints' shrines in several peripheral Israeli townships. These are alternative mechanisms for commemoration of the past and the preservation of heritage of the groups that have not built such museums or centres. Traditional communities, such as the Mashhadis, have found that synagogues and museums can fulfil similar objectives. Within the Moroccan community, the pilgrimage to saints' sanctuaries developed around the same time as the first community centres appeared. In the southern development town of Netivot the gravesite of the Rabi Abuhazeira (Baba Sali) is one of the most important pilgrimage sites in Israel. It provides a focal point of veneration for the Zadik (righteous one) in ways that are similar to or reminiscent of practices of Jews and Muslims in Morocco. The site's architecture replicates the building style from the region where the Baba Sali was born in Morocco; thus they commemorate not only the Zadik but also the geographical environment from where he and his community came. It is a site that glorifies the community's ties with its past and with its land of origin. It is possible to read the creation of these sanctified sites as symbolic realms within real space, in between place, not quite 'here' and not really 'there', a 'hybrid space'.[68] Similarly, the heritage centres aim to recreate a space of 'there' and 'then' in the present time and space.

Such practice contradicts what we expect from museums, as halls of knowledge and science.[69] Indeed, as the heritage centres often call their establishments 'museums' they intend to bank on the notion of scientific objectivity and cultural eminence. But at no point do they try to present a chronological, numbered past. The Libyan Museum in Or-Yehuda, for instance, represents a 2000-year-history in a few maps. It is obvious that the intention is what Lyotard would call 'narrative', not 'science'.

In fact, these heritage museums conform better to what Lyotard thinks of avant-garde artists: that they have disqualified reality by using the museum to 'subordinate thought to the gaze and to turn it away from the unpresentable'.[70] Perhaps it is permissible to use that as metaphor in the sense of seeing the communal museum not as a way of presenting what used to exist, and not as concretizing a past or as its depository. Rather, it could be read as a construction of a picture of a past that has never been. The picture is not of things gone by, restored and stored away, but it is rather a depiction of a new idea of what the present should or could have been like if the past had been as represented in the museum. Indeed, the objects in the museums serve as means to subordinate thought and research, and preconceived prejudice, to the gaze of the visitor.

The fact that the communities represented by these museums are 'imagined', in the sense that they are not historical entities, does not make them any less real. Museums which are built by communities empower communities, or minorities that feel underrepresented in the public sphere by building a collective memory of the past and by disseminating that particular idea of the past. Once presented in the museum, the objects are given a meaning and a context. Only within the museum do the objects become a representation of a past, a heritage, a culture – and through all these, they become a presentation of an identity. One of the visitors to the Babylonian Museum was impressed by the fact that even facts that she knew became concrete through the objects in the museum.[71]

A communal centre, as a mnemonic device, can empower a communal identity, but it can also create a new one. By its very existence, by creating new memories among its visitors, it will create new social boundaries.[72] Hence, the centre becomes not only a custodian of the fleeting moment and the heir to the communal past, it also becomes the essence of the communal 'home'. The empowerment stems from the new collective memory that is constructed, and through the sense of responsibility from having achieved the target, and from building social and economic networks.[73]

The situation of the museum as the new 'home' is best expressed by bringing to these centres family celebrations of birthdays and even rites of passage. The Hungarian Museum reports family celebrations on the one hand but also offers workshops for the second generation for whom the museum is a replacement of connection to the large families that were lost during the Holocaust, especially after the parents have passed away.[74] The Babylonian Centre boasts of a 70-year-old birthday celebration.[75] The Libyan guestbook attests to exciting and moving family gatherings in the museum which made the visitor 'proud to be Tripolitanian' (sic).[76] The Italian Jewish Art Museum invites families to celebrate the Bar-Mitzvah there, offering a special programme for such an event.[77] Being celebrated within the precincts of the museum, these parties create a piece of 'performance art' which enhances the general claim of the museum as custodian and as 'home'. While it gives the participants the illusion of a re-enactment of an imagined past, it creates a hybrid space and time. But as each museum is open to all, not necessarily to those who were born in that particular Diaspora, such parties blur the very borderlines which the museum in its exhibition sets out to define, while still enhancing a feeling of worth and full life of the community that was supposedly re-enacted.[78]

Having collected, registered and presented what the community brought in, these museums represent communities to which they are intimately connected. Thus, museums in general, as recreational pastimes and as educational institutions, are brought closer to publics that may have felt alienated because they found no correlation between their cultural experiences and the exhibitions.[79] Indeed, a similar effect is achieved when a national museum presents a certain community in a special exhibition. But in that case, when a community comes to visit, and the visit is limited to the special exhibition, the outcome is one that emphasises the alienation from the museum culture and not integration.[80]

A communal museum is also an expression which is not performed by the hegemonic group, or at least not by the establishment. It is therefore the opportunity to vie for counter-hegemony. For communal centres this means that their presentation of the Diaspora as the source of their glory is not an alternative Zionism, and certainly not an alternative to Zionism. But it is rather a demand for a change in the power balance in the present Zionist state on the basis of past glory and achievements. Within this context presentation of Zionist zeal is their credential for partaking in present identity politics.

By providing new interpretations of the period of the Diaspora from the point of view of the particular group, the group is brought to centre stage. All the centres want to make their community 'seen' by the general public. They prepare special programmes for pupils, and they hope to attract the public at large.[81] In some of the museums this need to make the community present and to make it visible is expressed literally by giving it a face. In the Yemenite Museum in Rosh Ha'ayin the visitor first encounters faces of Yemenite brides, in the Libyan Museum in Or-Yehuda a row of pictures – without names is providing a virtual set of anonymous hosts and hostesses. The curator put them there, as 'faces that tell without words'.[82] The Babylonian Centre prefers the metaphor of 'voice'. In a short history of the museum it is claimed that it has been founded 'as part of the awakening of the immigrants from Eastern-Countries [namely Muslim countries] in order to have a voice in Israeli society'.[83]

Furthermore, new educational relationships are fashioned. One of the visitors to the Babylonian website excitedly wrote in the guestbook: 'This is just an incredible insightful educational quality website. I am so happy to have found it.'[84] The Libyan Museum in Or-Yehuda expects to show its visitors that their lack of knowledge is a disadvantage that needs to be rectified. It is especially cognisant in the fact that the pictures and objects lack labels. The curator explained it with the wish to have the visitor's undivided attention on the object. However, at the same time the outcome is also a much greater need for a guide to educate the visitor with the meaning of what is on view.[85] The same curator boasted of success when a visitor admitted that she learned of the rich culture of the community only through her visit to the museum, then hurried to bring 'a bus full of friends' so that they could learn as well. By teaching non-European Jewish history to the public, they become instructors and providers of information competing with the formal education provided by the establishment.[86]

National agenda

The need to become visible suggests that the centres are acts of protest against the exclusion of the non-European Jews from Israeli culture.[87] Some even thought that they expressed 'an explosion of ethnic self-identity'.[88] However, as we have seen, European Jews also lament their lost heritage in very similar terms and also build heritage centres.[89]

Admittedly, only the non-European Jewish museums are directed against cultural stigma and only their centres carry as their main message the unity of Israeli Jewish ethnicity.[90] At the very least they expect greater understanding and respect of the differing segments of society. Certainly, that is the role of heritage museums in a multi-cultural society.[91] But actually the non-European heritage centres call for a united entity, with a united culture, on the basis of a united ethnicity and a history unified by their interpretation.[92] That is one of the reasons for the emphasis on the period of Exile in all the heritage centres. The period that challenges the unity of the Jewish people by creating what might be sub-ethnicities is utilised in the heritage centres to show the unity of the Jewish people.

That period is utilized to highlight religious faithfulness and to express the nationalist activity within or outside the Zionist movement. But it also shows how the group's particular history is part of the 'greater story'. This is best exemplified by the Babylonian Centre, which appropriates national history into its own group's annals. At the entrance the visitor encounters the declaration that:

> For over a thousand years the Babylonian Jewry led all the diasporas of Israel ... through the great Talmudic Colleges of Neharda'a, Sura and Pumbdita who preserved the spiritual ember of the Jewish People and through the exilarch that symbolised Jewish autonomy ... this Museum shows some of the glory of the Babylonian Jewry since they have sworn 'If I forget thee, O Jerusalem, let my right hand forget her cunning' until they immigrated to the state of Israel.[93]

In fact, Mordechai Ben-Porat, one of the founders of the Babylonian Museum, made very clear that the centre is not a nucleus for a sub-ethnic organization. The heritage is not intended to be preserved as an isolated culture, but rather it is hoped to be amalgamated within the general culture. The expectation is that 'in ten years time, when the heritage will be part of the society of Israel, may be there will be no need to found heritage centres'.[94] Indeed, in trying to bring the Babylonian heritage to the forefront of Israeli culture there is no intention of challenging the Zionist ethos, but rather to see that ethos fully implemented in their way. The Yemenite Centre in Rosh-Ha'ayin also saw the centre as a chance to disseminate Yemenite values as 'a spiritual property of all the communities and tribes of Israel'.[95]

Thus, the centres strive to achieve visibility and recognition for their communities within the scope of a more sensitive Zionism and not through its breakdown. Jewish history according to the perception of these heritage centres has not come to a tragic end through the exile of the Jewish people from Eretz Israel. Rather, it is this period which affords each community the opportunity to show its particularity and through it to shine. It is this period which gives each community the legitimation to be different, and thereby to deviate from the Israeli 'central' ethos – be that in its musical culture, or in its attitude to family, or in its attitude to religion, or in its preference for a certain language, besides Hebrew.

Two of the museums of European Jews – for German speaking and Hungarian speaking – are slightly different in carrying an additional agenda. Both call for further secularisation and a liberal interpretation of Jewish nationalism in Israel. The thrust for secularisation is particularly obvious in the German Centre. Its attitude to religion is well represented by a few of the least impressive looking religious artefacts one could imagine, arranged as an odd assortment: a Kiddush goblet, a case for scented spices, family pictures, a Passover-Seder plate, *Juden Porzellan*, a picture of Moses Mendelssohn, a basket for Matzoth and two oil lamps for Shabbat.[96] This and another case of religious artefacts is engulfed by the sound of lament music, the *Kadish* – the prayer said over the deceased. The voice is coming from a small computer screen which shows in a running slide-show synagogues burnt down during *Kristallnacht* and virtually reconstructed at the Darmstadt Technical University in Germany.[97] The burnt synagogues are lamented but consigned to a never returning past; they are reconstructed virtually as an act of atonement and not as a revival. On the other hand, the museum presents the deep commitment of the German Jews to the enlightenment and their profoundly embedded contribution in German civil society but does not show the shattering conclusion of that ideal in the Holocaust.

The German speaking museum interprets 'being a Yeke' (originally a mildly derogatory term for German Jew) as the 'framework of all the universal cultural values that they brought from Germany: enlightenment, modernism, criticalness, Liberalism'. They commend themselves for infusing these into the Israeli culture while combating a list of evils: 'statism' (*mamlakhtiyut*), diasporism (*galutiyut*, derogatory term for behaviour that lacks dignity and proper appreciation for European 'high-culture'), East Europeanism (again a derogatory term, this time meaning East European Jews who lack the attributes of the Yeke and are therefore, not dignified) and Orientalism (meaning the culture of non-European Jews, which also means all of the above, in addition to avowing non-European culture; especially music). Besides the Orientalism that imbues these targets, it is a wish-list that boils down to an aspiration for a more Westernised, more secularised but still Zionist Israel.[98]

Although the Hungarian version is more subdued, the tendency is similar. The curator, son of the founders, sees the mission of the museum as not to create a Hungarian preserve; quite the opposite. He hopes the visitors will come 'and see our past ... more in the sense of finding out what of it is significant and relevant'. And he sees the main message the museum should send out as 'how we kept in touch [with Jewishness] with or without the religious circle'.[99] Since the museum allows about a third of its space for commemorating the Holocaust it might also be seen as providing another 'holy site', a place of pilgrimage to Israeli civil religion. It stands in stark contrast to the marginalisation of the Holocaust in the German Museum.[100]

The few ultra-orthodox heritage centres only accentuate the political goal of the heritage centres.[101] They do not avow Zionism like the others, and they deal with religious tractates and the rabbinic leaders. But they are apparently part of the growing ultra-orthodox involvement in the Israeli public sphere: in the workforce, in the army and in politics.[102] In this sense the museums are an attempt at influencing Israeli culture by providing an alternative, by showing the way back to its former religious glory.

Conclusion

Eileen Hooper-Greenhill said that 'reality is produced, maintained, repaired and transformed. This view proposes that "reality" has no finite identity, but is brought into existence, is *produced*, through communication'.[103] And she believes museums can play an important part in changing reality if only they can move away successfully from their modernist roots. Indeed, the picture this article is conveying shows that museums play a part in a postmodernist world whether they change their policy or not. They produce a place that claims to represent the past of an immigrant group, and thereby create a forum for constructing a community in the present. The end-target is to influence the aspirations of the Israeli society as a whole for the future.[104]

All the heritage centres play identity politics by providing realms of memory. As memory agents they enhance identities and change them. As the Israeli heritage centres present communities according to imaginary political entities they provide the basis for new identities. When they provide education about communities that were outside the hegemonic culture they vie for a re-formulation of that culture. Indeed, they all, even the European centres, try to reverse to some extent the melting-pot policies and re-enhance some of the cultural and perhaps ethnic identity of their groups. For that they create a vision of greatness that is based on the history of the Diaspora period, but also very much on Zionist accomplishments.

They also challenge national politics, not because they reject the Zionist ethos, but rather because they accept it. The idea I am trying to convey here is similar to Bourdieu's analysis of the interaction between orthodox art and avant-guardists – a competition over the legitimate view of the world. This competition is constrained by the actual wish of the avant-guardists to move their objects to a higher value stratum without displacing others. Likewise, the communal centres, one and all, do not wish to displace the 'orthodox' Zionist institutions, but rather to move into the same 'value strata' as them. Put more simply, they do not wish to erase the Zionist ethos, only to have *their* view of Zionism equally endorsed.[105]

Notes

1. Stuart Hall, "Culture, Community, Nation," in *Representing the Nation: A Reader. Histories, Heritage, and Museums*, ed. David Boswell and Jessica Evans (New York: Routledge, 1999), 38.
2. Shlomo Ben-Ami, "Israeli Identity as an Identity of an Immigrant Society," in *Religion and Nationalism in Israel and in the Middle East*, ed. Neri Horowitz [in Hebrew] (Tel Aviv: Am Oved, 2002), 227.
3. Barbara Black, *On Exhibit: The Victorians and their Museums* (Charlottesville: University Press of Virginia, 2000).
4. Cited in Ghislaine Lawrence, "Object Lessons in the Museum Medium," in *Objects of Knowledge*, ed. Susan Pierce (London: Athlone Press, 1990), 103.
5. Elaine Heuman Gurian, "What is the Object of this Exercise? A Meandering Exploration of the Many Meanings of Objects in Museums," in *Reinventing the Museum. Historical and Contemporary Perspectives on the Paradigm*, ed. Gail Anderson (Lanham, MD: Altamira Press, 2004), 282.
6. The websites announce the forthcoming museum and include statements of intentions. As such they are pertinent to the subject of this study.
7. Of course, this wasn't an Israeli peculiarity. The United States held similar ideas about the 'absorption' of immigrants. Charles Hirshman, Philip Kasinitz and Josh DeWind, "Introduction to Part II: Immigrant Adaptation, Assimilation, and Incorporation," in *The Handbook of International Migration: The American Experience*, ed. Charles Hirshman, Philip Kasinitz and Josh DeWind (New York: Russell Sage Foundation, 1999), 127.
8. Michael R. Weisser, *A Brotherhood of Memory. Jewish Landsmanschaft in the New World* (New York: Basic Books, 1985), 279–83. Similarly see S.N. Eisebstadt, "The Oriental Jews

in Israel A Report on a Preliminary Study in Culture-Contacts," *Jewish Social Studies* 12 (1950): 199–222.

9. One of the prominent protagonists of this analysis is Shmuel Noah Eisenstadt, "The Struggle over the Symbols of Collective Identity on its Limits in the Post-Revolutionary Israeli Society," in *Zionism: Contemporary Debate, Attitudes and Ideologies*, ed. Pinhas Ginosar and Avi Bareli [in Hebrew] (Beer Sheva: Ben-Gurion University Press, 1996), 2–19, 28. Interestingly, this process is almost simultaneous with the emergence of African American museums in the US, Edmund Barry Gaither, "'Hey! That's Mine': Thoughts on Pluralism and American Museums," *Reinventing the Museum* (see note 5), 113.

10. Ruth Kark and Noam Perry, "Museums and Multi-Culturalism in Israel" [in Hebrew], *Horizons in Geography* 70 (2008): 111, http://geography.huji.ac.il/.upload/RuthPub/Num%20135%20Museams%20and%20Multicaulturalism%20in%20Israel.pdf (accessed August 7, 2011).

11. Hanna Yablonka, "The Law for Punishment of the Nazis and their Collaborators: Legislation, Implementation and Attitudes" [in Hebrew], *Cathedra* 82 (December 1996): 136, and also Yechiam Weitz, "The Law for Punishment of the Nazis and their Collaborators as Image and Reflection of Public Opinion" [in Hebrew], *Cathedra* 82 (December 1996): 153–64. See also Mooli Brog, "A Memorial for the Fighters and Commemoration of the Victims: Efforts by the Va'ad Haleumi to Establish Yad Vashem 1846–1949" [in Hebrew], *Cathedra* 119 (March 2006): 87–120.

12. Amnon Raz-Krakozkin, "Exile Within Sovereignty: Toward a Critique of the 'Negation of Exile' within Israeli Culture" [in Hebrew], *Theory and Criticism* 4 (Autumn 1993): 24.

13. But, it keeps to a custom that is neither Sephardic nor Ashkenazi, called the 'Roman Custom'.

14. A comparison between two other centres exists – which takes for granted the ethnic protest. Shelly Shenhav-Keller, "Ethnicity, Identity and Collective Memory in Two Ethnic Heritage Centers in Israel, AIS 2010 – Toronto," 9, http://www.aisisraelstudies.org/papers/AIS2010_Shenhav_Keller.pdf (accessed August 10, 2011). Likewise, Esther Meir-Glitzenstein, "Zionist Identity and Jewish-Arab Identity in the Collective Memory of Iraqi Immigrants in Israel," *Alpaim* 27 (2004): 173–252, focuses on the Babylonian centre which also emphasizes the duality of the professed Zionism of the centre and its protest against ethnic marginalization. However, this research disregards the European centres and the similarities with these centres. For a comparison between the history of modernisation of German, Hungarian and Iraqi Jews and the implication of the processing of their memories into historical writing in Israel: Guy Miron, "Between Berlin and Baghdad – Iraqi Jewish History and the Challenge of Integrated Jewish Historiography" [in Hebrew], *Zion* 71 (2006): 73–98.

15. See the websites of the Romanian, Al-Ghariba and Tunisian communities: The Romanian Jewish Community Museum – About the Museum, http://www.amirorg.com/apage/16258.php (accessed April 3, 2012); El Ghriba Jerusalem – Cultural Centre for the Heritage of Tunisian Jews in Jerusalem [in Hebrew], http://elghribajerusalem.com/about (accessed April 3, 2012); and Tunisian Jews, http://www.amit4u.net/home/doc.aspx?mCatID=9757 (accessed April 3, 2012).

16. Ariella Azoulay, "With Open Doors: Museums of History and the Israeli Public Space" [in Hebrew], *Theory and Criticism* 4 (Autumn 1993): 87–8.

17. The Heritage Centre for the Turkish Community in Israel, Eyal Peretz, "Letter from the Chairman," http://www.arkadash.org/site/index.asp?depart_id=99510&lat=en (accessed August 15, 2012).

18. "Background" [in Hebrew], http://www.arkadash.org/99510/המרכז-למורשת-יהדות-טורקיה (accessed March 24, 2011).

19. Yemenite MPs for the Preservation of Yemenite Heritage [in Hebrew], http://rotter.net/cgi-bin/forum/dcboard.cgi?az=show_thread&forum=gil&om=5316&omm=35&viewmode; Ranit Nahum Halevi, "A New Group in the Knesset: Yemenite MKs Come Together to Preserve Yemenite Heritage" [in Hebrew], NEWS 1, March 4, 2004, http://www.news1.co.il/archive/001-D-41664-00.html?tag=8-15-07 (accessed March 27, 2011).

20. Ya'akov Manzur, "Welcome at the Beit Hahayal 10 Sept. 1987" [in Hebrew], *Neharde'a* 6 (Passover 1998): 25; Ruth 'Atar, "Report on Events in the Babylonian Jewry Heritage Center during 1988–1989" [in Hebrew], *Neharde'a* 7 (1990): 41.

21. "To Arrest the Fleeting Moment" [in Hebrew only] (1991) is among the movies that are viewed in the museum and can also be purchased, http://www.omuseums.org.il/museum/sitePage.aspx?pageID=339&Place=1 (accessed August 15, 2012).
22. Eyal Peretz founder of the association Arkadash and the heritage centre, in a video "Arkadash, the Turkish Community in Israel" [in Hebrew], http://www.arkadash.org/ (accessed September 1, 2011).
23. Daniel J. Sherman, "Objects of Memory: History and Narrative in French War Museums," *French Historical Studies* 19, no. 1 (Spring 1995): 49–50 is based on Pierre Nora, "Between Memory and History: Les Lieux de Memoir," *Representations* 2, no. 6 (Spring 1989): 12: 'it is the nostalgic dimension of these devotional institutions that makes them seem beleaguered and cold – they mark the rituals of a society without ritual'.
24. Teddy Kollek, "Museums and National Spirit" [in Hebrew], *Studio* 15 (1990): 42.
25. Nora, "Between Memory and History," 12.
26. Johannes von Moltke, "Identities on Display: Jewishness and the Representational Politics of the Museum," in *Jews and Other Differences: The New Jewish Cultural Studies*, ed. Jonathan Boyarin and Daniel Boyarin (Minneapolis: University of Minnesota Press, 1997), 81.
27. Nora, "Between Memory and History," 16.
28. Andreas Huyssen, "Monument and Memory in a Postmodern Age," in *Holocaust Memorials. The Art of Memory in History*, ed. James E. Young (Munich and New York: Prestel, 1994), 10.
29. Ruth 'Atar, "A Dream and its Realization. The History of the Heritage of Babylonian Jewry 1971–1988" [in Hebrew], an unpublished essay, the Babylonian Jewry Heritage Centre, 23. See also Yehuda Avishur, "The First Convention for the Documentation of Babylonian Jewry's Heritage" [in Hebrew], *Neharde'a* 8 (December 1990): 2. For the new Diorama: Zvi Yehuda, "The Store of the Spices Seller – the 'Atar' – Design and Research" [in Hebrew], *Neharde'a* 11 (February–March 1993): 13.
30. Interview with the founder and curator of the Bat-Yam Libyan Centre, Pedahzur Ben'atiya, July 25, 2011, and in e-mail to the author, August 1, 2011. On December 27, 2005 the Or-Shalom centre initiated a series of community meetings. The gathering of the Khoms community was filmed and documented. "News of the Website" [in Hebrew]; Or-Shalom Centre, http://www.or-shalom.org.il/news.asp?PageId=2&article_main_id (accessed July 23, 2012).
31. http://www.eelebetamar.co.il/hebrew//Default.aspx (accessed March 27, 2011).
32. On the website, along with a call to help the museum in its efforts in gathering information and artefacts one can also find an invitation to register and to receive information about the museum's activities, "Appeal to Visitors and Websurfer," http://www.hjm.org.il/?leftframe=menueng.html&mainframe=/main.aspx/En (accessed March 3, 2014).
33. The Memorial Museum of Hungarian Speaking Jewry, "Website Archive for Information leaflets – Echoes from the Herzl Day 2007," http://www.hjm.org.il/ (accessed August 8, 2012).
34. Stef Wertheimer, "Foreword" [in Hebrew], *The Museum of the German Speaking Jews – The Yeke Heritage Centre*, ed. and curator Ruti Ofek (Tefen: Open Museum and Association of Israelis of Central European Origin, 2011), 8.
35. Ludmila Jordanova, "Objects of Knowledge: A Historical Perspective on Museums," in *The New Museology*, ed. Peter Vergo (1989) (Trowbridge: Redwoodbooks, 2000), 22–41, see esp. 34–6.
36. There are very few articles online by Or-Shalom Centre on the immigration experience: http://www.or-shalom.org.il/article_2.asp?article_main_id=1&article_topic_id=68&article_topic_name=עליה וקליטה; Research is picking up the subject, but not much has been published yet; see for instance Esther Meir-Glitzenstein, "Iraqi Immigrants and the Israeli Establishment – the Struggle for Integration" [in Hebrew], *Age of Zionism*, ed. Anita Shapira, Jehuda Reinharz and Jacob Harris (Jerusalem: Zalman Shazar Centre, 2000), 271–95. another example can be found in a book about Yemenite immigrants, where only four of the 18 articles (those by Yael Katzir, Yosef Halevi, Dina Greitzer and Rachel Sharabi) bring out the immigrant's experience: Bat Zion and Araki Klurman, eds., *Yemenite Immigrants in the Land of Israel: Yemenite Jews – History, Society, Culture* (Jerusalem: Ben Zvi Institute, 2006).

37. Of the kind conducted by CIJOH (Centre for Iranian Jewish Oral History) in the USA: http://www.homasarshar.com/cijoh/oralhistory/index.htm (accessed March 25, 2011).
38. For instance on August 15, 2012 the yearly memorial conference for the founder of the Association for the Cultivation of Society and Culture (of Yemenite Jewry) in memory of Ovadya Shalom held a study day on the religious literature and on Yemenite immigrants in Israel: http://www.teman.org.il/ni-0053.php (accessed July 23, 2012).
39. "In memory of Reuven Sa'id a razor for shaving," *Neharde'a* 30: 10. Similarly in the Hungarian centre some of the artefacts were dedicated to the memory of family members murdered during the Holocaust; an example is the book of birth registrations from Beled donated by Dr Willy Hoffman-Hirsch: http://www.hjm.org.il/pritim/default.aspx [page in Hebrew] (accessed July 23, 201)2.
40. Orly Bahar, "Donations to the Museum during 2007–2008," *Neharde'a* 30 (June 2009): 10–14.
41. One of the most recent and most impressive acquisitions for the Memorial Museum of Hungarian Speaking Jewry, information sheet no. 39, April 2012, announces the discovery of the diary of Szálasi Ferenc, leader of the Arrow Cross Party and prime minister of Hungary October 15, 1944–April 1945.
42. "Cochin Jewish Heritage Center," http://kochinculture.beer-sheva.gonegev.co.il/english.asp (accessed August 6, 2012).
43. Even the Museum for Italian Jewish Art that is dedicated to arks and religious objects from the Renaissance and Baroque periods distributes to visitors at no extra charge the book Elia Samuel Hartom, *The Life of the People of Israel* (1954) [in Hebrew], a new extended edition edited by his son Rabbi Menachem Emanuel Hartom (Jerusalem: Kedem, 1989), which presents the particularities of their religious customs.
44. The room that deals with the Zionist and Israeli chapters in the Babylonian Jewry Heritage Centre is temporarily closed due to reorganization upon the addition of a new room.
45. For one example out of many: on the contribution of the Babylonian Heritage Centre for the foundation of the international association of Iraqi Jews see Zvi Gabai, "The Foundation of the International Organization of Iraqi Jews" [in Hebrew], *Neharde'a* 29 (October–November 1987), http://www.babylonjewry.org.il/new/hebrew/nehardea/29/7.htm (accessed September 4, 2011). Avi Pedahzur from the Libyan Museum also talked about the connection to the Rome community: interview, June 21, 2011, Or Yehuda.
46. The only heritage centre that refers to expatriates outside Israel is the German Speaking Heritage Centre, but even there it does not refer to communities outside Israel and not after the foundation of the state. The Babylonian Centre is supposed to include expatriates outside Israel after the current refurbishment is completed. Esther Meir-Glitzenstein, "Facing the Past" [in Hebrew], *Neharde'a* 29 (1987), http://www.babylonjewry.org.il/new/hebrew/nehardea/29/25.htm (accessed August 18, 2011).
47. In common Zionist phraseology, the period when the Jewish people were scattered in diasporas was the period of exile (Galut) from the homeland, when the history of the people came to halt. Only during the 1970s and 1980s did the Zionist negation of Diaspora weaken, and Western Liberal diasporas came to be accepted as part of normal modern Jewish existence. Danny Gutwein, "Criticism of 'Diaspora Negation' and the Privatization of Private Consciousness in Israel," posted March 19, 2011, http://danigutwein.wordpress.com/2011/03/19/44/#_ftn1 (accessed May 26, 2013).
48. Raz-Krakozkin, "Exile within Sovereignty," 23–55. Yet, contrary to Raz-Krakozkin's thesis, theological affirmation of the Diaspora never entirely rid itself of the negative challenge that initiated it: Joel E. Rembaum, "The Development of a Jewish Exegetical Tradition regarding Isaiah 53," *The Harvard Theological Review* 75, no. 3 (July 1982): 292. An example of the importance of the Christian challenge in the disputation of Majorka: Ora Limor, "Polemical Varieties: Religious Disputations in 13th Century Spain," *Iberia Judaica II* (2010): 73, 74. One of the modern reactions to this challenge is: Eliezer Berkovits, *Faith after the Holocaust* [in Hebrew] (Jerusalem: Shalem, 2006), 107.
49. Amnon Raz-Krakozkin, "Exile Within Sovereignty: Toward a Critique of the 'Negation of Exile' within Israeli Culture – Second Part" [in Hebrew], *Theory and Criticism* 5 (Autumn 1994): 113–32. See also, following Raz-Krakozkin, Sara Chinski, "'Eyes Wide Shut': The Symptomatic Acquired Albinism in the Field of Israeli Art" [in Hebrew], *Theory and Criticism* 20 (Spring 2002): 61, 77. Raz-Krakozkin expects a healing of the relationship with

the Palestinians would follow a more positive and affirmative attitude towards the Exile. Admittedly, the centres follow Zionist practice by omitting any mention of the Palestinian problem – except for the German Speaking Museum which mentions the Brit-Shalom two-nation state idea.

50. A.D. Smith, "Zionism and Diaspora Nationalism," *Israel Affairs* 2, no. 2 (1995): 5. See also Yaron Zur, "Diaspora Nationalism and Serious Crisis in the Diasporas," in *Vision and Revision. A Hundred Years of Zionist Historiography*, ed. Yehi'am Weitz (Jerusalem: Shazar Centre, 1997), 171–92.
51. See short video on website. The video represents faithfully the version that guides tell visitors in the museum: http://www.livluv.org.il/?CategoryID=123 (accessed July 30, 2012).
52. The Memorial Museum of Hungarian Speaking Jewry, "About the Exhibition – the Ties with the Land of Israel" [the Hebrew site], http://www.hjm.org.il/ (accessed July 31, 2012).
53. The Association of Israelis of Central European Origin is the co-founder of the German Speaking Jewish Heritage Centre. On the website the goals of the centre are presented: http://www.irgun-jeckes.org/?CategoryID=201&ArticleID=85 (accessed August 6, 2012).
54. The museum is part of the Dona Gracia Hotel in Tiberius: "The Dona Gracia Medal" [in Hebrew], http://www.donagracia.com/pages/he/mdlyit-donh-grtzih.php (accessed August 6, 2012). In the Babylonian Jewry Heritage Centre the section dealing with the Israeli chapter of the community's history is currently being refurbished.
55. Charles Saumarez Smith, "Museums, Artefacts, and Meanings," in *The New Museology* (see note 35), 6; Jordanova, "Objects of Knowledge," 92.
56. Anthony Alan Shelton, "In the Lair of the Monkey: Notes towards a Post-Modernist Museography," in *Objects of Knowledge* (see note 4), 97–8, although he speaks of works of art, the same is true of ethnographic museums, even if to a lesser extent. See also in African American museums, Gaither, "'Hey! That's Mine,'" 114–15; Gurian, "What is the Object of this Exercise?," 273.
57. Bourdieu is discussing art, but it works for all museum objects. Shelton, "In the Lair of the Monkey," 83.
58. Azoulay, "With Open Doors," 84.
59. Fredric Jameson, "Foreword" to Jean-François Lyotard, *The Postmodern Condition: A Report on Knowledge*, trans. Geoff Bennington and Brian Massumi (Manchester: Manchester University Press, 1979), xii.
60. On the differences within the Hungarian community between the different areas see Sari Reuven, "The Centre of Jews in Slovakia and the Jewish Council in Hungary: Similarities and Differences" [in Hebrew], *The Path of Memory* 36 (2000): 49–54; Kinga Fromovitz, "The Religious Movements in Hungarian Jewry (Orthodoxy, Neology, and Status Quo-Ante) 1868/9–1950: Socio-economic Demographic and Organizational Characteristics" [in Hebrew], PhD Thesis, Bar-Ilan University 2002.
61. Meir-Glitzenstein, "Zionist Identity," 188–96. Yosef Meir claimed that communists and other non-Zionists were left out for pragmatic reasons Yosef Meir, "Research on the Heritage Center of Babylonian Jewry" [in Hebrew], *Neharde'a* 28 (2006): 10–12.
62. The U. Nahon Museum of Italian Jewish Art is presented on several websites with those very words. Among others see Michael-Israel, a multi-language database for Cultural heritage in Europe, U. Nahon Museum of Italian Jewish Art [the Hebrew site]. The English site does not have the same invitation: http://www.michael-culture.org.il/pub-mpf/document.html?totaldocs=7&base=dcollection&id=IL-DC-eab759a4&querybase=dcollection&pagename=results.html&from1=browsing_place.xml&val1=browsing.fspacecov.italy&qid=miKl-q&hppage=20&curlang=he (accessed March 24, 2011); likewise, a brochure that reports the activity of the Allepo Jews Centre, "Events to Disseminate the Heritage of Allepo Jews 1985–2005," http://www.aleppojews.com/binhanhalat/index.html (accessed March 24, 2011). The Centre for the Research of Yemenite Jewry in the name of Ovadiah Shalom also calls for raising the prestige of 'Yemenite culture and heritage', "The Research of Yemenite Jewry, Events – Conferences and Congresses," http://www.teman.org.il/seminars.php (accessed August 28, 2011).
63. Meir-Glitzenstein, "Zionist Identity," 194; on the socio-economic detrimental effect see Shlomo Svirski, *Orientals and Ashkenazim in Israel. The Ethnic Division of Labour* [in Hebrew] (Haifa: Mahbarot Lemehkqr uleviqoret, 1981), 50–56, and Deborah Bernstein,

"Temporary Encampments in the 1950s" [in Hebrew], *Magazine for Research and Criticism* 5 (1980): 19–21.

64. The museum is undergoing refurbishment and many of the pictures are stored away – including those about the tent-townships, but the museum preserves its original set-up in several picture albums which have been kindly shown to me by the museum's curator, Ms 'Idit Sharoni. However, the DDT container and its inscription are currently presented. Due to the addition of a new wing the whole Israeli chapter is being removed and remodelled.
65. The United Organization of Jews from Romania, Richard Armon, "The Rationale for Establishing the Museum of Romanian Aliya," http://www.amirorg.com/len/apage/62018.php (accessed August 6, 2012). Transylvania is indeed included within Romania, yet the dominant language is Hungarian and the sovereignty of the region is contested by the Hungarian government. On the construction of Romanian nationalism see Wim van Meurs, "Carving a Moldavian Identity out of History," *Nationalities Papers* 26, no. 1 (March 1998): 39–56. On the first stirrings of Romanian nationalism in the late eighteenth century see Vlad Georgescu, *The Romanians a History*, trans. Alexandra Bley-Vroman (Columbus: Ohio State University, 1989), 118–21.
66. The website of Arkadash, the Turkish Jewry's Centre, provides a history of Turkish Jewry which precedes the Ottoman empire, then identifies with it, then succeeds it, http://www.arkadash.org/99510/%D7%9E%D7%91%D7%95%D7%90-%D7%94%D7%99%D7%A1%D7%98%D7%95%D7%A8%D7%99 (accessed August 6, 2012). The German Speaking Heritage Centre – according to the website of the Association of Israelis of Central European Origin – 'unites expatriates from Germany, Austria and other regions of Central Europe influenced by German culture'. In fact, in the museum and in the catalogue that was published people are included who were born in Hungary, in Romania and in Poland: http://www.irgun-jeckes.org/?CategoryID=201&ArticleID=85 (accessed August 6, 2012), and see Ofek, *The Museum of the German Speaking Jews* (see note 34), 69–71, 76–9, 83–4. The Memorial Museum of Hungarian Speaking Jewry represents expatriates from: Transylvania, Slovakia, Carpatho-Russia (Russia), Bachka (Croatia), Banat (Hungary, Serbia, Romania) and Burgenland (Austria), "About the Museum," http://www.hjm.org.il/ (accessed August 6, 2012).
67. Nora, "Between Memory and History," 8–9.
68. Eyal Ben-Ari and Yoram Bilu, "Saints' Sanctuaries in Israeli Development Town: On Mechanism of Urban Transformation," *Urban Anthropology* 16, no. 2 (1987): 243–72; The term 'hybrid space' is used by Haim Yacobi, "From State Imposed Urban Planning to Israeli Diasporic Place. The Case of Netivot and the Grave of Baba Sali," *Jewish Topographies: Visions of Space, Traditions of Place*, ed. Julia Brauch, Anna Lipphardt and Alexandra Nocke, (Aldershot: Ashgate, 2008), 77; Erez Zfadia and Haim Yacobi, "Periphery, Architecture and Diasporic Sense of Place," in *Rethinking Israeli Space: Periphery and Identity* (New York: Routledge, 2011), 30.
69. Shelton, "In the Lair of the Monkey," 92–3.
70. Jean-François Lyotard, "What is Postmodernism?," in *The Postmodern Condition*, 79.
71. Haya and David Goren (Dangur) writing to Pnina Shaham, December 8, 2010 [in Hebrew], *Nehrde'a* 31 (Autumn 2010): 69.
72. Elizabeth Crooke, *Museums and Community: Ideas, Issues and Challenges* (Abingdon and New York: Routledge, 2007), 11–15, 30–45.
73. Local museums help to consolidate a community, ibid., 3–4, 17–18.
74. The Memorial Museum of Hungarian Speaking Jewry, "Website archive for information leaflets – Echoes from the Herzl Day 2007," http://www.hjm.org.il/ (accessed August 8, 2012).
75. The Memorial Museum of Hungarian Speaking Jewry, Information Leaflet, 34 (September 2008); Haya and David Goren (Dangur) writing to Pnina, December 8, 2010.
76. Libyan Jews Museum Or-Yehuda, Guestbook, June 14, 2011, although it is worth noting that the visitor did not take on the encompassing Libyan identity the museum is propagating and retained the original more particular identity.
77. Italian Jewish Art Museum, Handout leaflet.
78. Eavry sees these parties as the continuation of community life as it has been lived as opposed to the exhibition which he reads as 'anachronistic and frozen episodes' giving the

parties an aura of authenticity – thus overlooking the 'unauthentic' environment, Yuval Eavry, "Hafla fi El Museum" [in Hebrew], *Block* 6 (2008): 77.
79. Gaither, "'Hey! That's Mine,'" 117.
80. Chinski, "'Eyes Wide Shut,'" 58, 71.
81. Mordechai Ben-Porat, "The Babylonian Heritage Center" [in Hebrew], *Neharde'a* 1 (Autumn 1979): 5; the centres boast of seminars for national and district inspectors from all educational movements, for teachers, and cultural events' organisers from schools, and for groups from the IDF, see 'Atar, "Report," 40, 41. A list of subjects and plans for guided activity in the Museum of Libyan Jews. In the Information Leaflets of the Or-Yehuda Municipality 1998 [in Hebrew], 7, http://storage.cet.ac.il/CetForums/Storage/MessageFiles/242/11313/Forum11313M1I0.doc (accessed August 18, 2011), The Memorial Museum of Hungarian Speaking Jewry carries eight different plans: "Plans for Children and Youth" [in Hebrew], http://www.hjm.org.il/ (accessed August 19, 2012); The German Speaking Jews Museum also carries various activity plans for children and grownups "Guided Activity Plans" [in Hebrew], http://www.iparks.co.il/museum/sitePage.aspx?pageID=344&Place=1 (accessed September 1, 2011).
82. Avi Pedazur, Libyan Museum's curator, guide to a tour, June 21, 2011.
83. Cited in 'Atar, "A Dream," 2.
84. Lisa Rabinovitz on the Guest Book of the Babylonian Jewry Centre, http://www.babylonjewry.org.il/new/hebrew/index.html (accessed August 8, 2012).
85. Crooke, *Museums and Community*, 39, following Bourdieu, and the new theories about the new 'active audience' that made the move to conceptualise museum visitors as active in the construction of their own knowledge do not apply. We can see that all the heritage centres make use of the educational establishment, expecting schools to bring pupils to be educated in the museum, as a 'captive audience'. About the new theories of learning and communication in museums, see Eileen Hooper-Greenhill, "Museum Learners as Active Postmodernists: Contextualizing Constructivism," in *Educational Role of the Museum*, ed. Eileen Hooper-Greenhill (1994) (London: Routledge, 2001), 67–72.
86. Cited in Moltke, "Identities on Display," 82.
87. Kark and Perry, "Museums and Multi-Culturalism," 111.
88. Azoulay, "With Open Doors," 87–8. Shenhav-Keller about the Libyan and Babylonian Museums in Or Yehuda, Shenhav-Keller, "Ethnicity, Identity and Collective Memory," 9 .
89. The Memorial Museum of Hungarian Speaking Jewry, About the Museum [in Hebrew], http://www.hjm.org.il/ (accessed August 19, 2012). The German Speaking Jews' Museum celebrates more the success of transplanting the German Jewish culture but it also tells of the struggle against the melting-pot: David Witzthum, "Life Stories," *The Museum of the German Speaking Jews* (see note 34), 33. The Italian Jewish Museum is the only one that doesn't mention the melting-pot policy.
90. Meir-Glitzenstein, "Zionist Identity," 183–4.
91. George F. MacDonald, the director of the Canadian Museum of Civilization Quebec from 1983 to 1998, saw the role of communal museums in a multi-cultural society as helping disseminate inter-cultural understanding and respect, George F. MacDonald, "Museums and the National Spirit" [in Hebrew], *Studio* 15 (1990): 48–9. See also: L. Forgan, "Heritage has the Power to Connect People and give them a Sense of Identity," *Museums Journal* 108, no. 11 (November 2008): 19.
92. European ascendency is accepted without protest; see the editor of the Babylonian Jewry's organ: Eliya Agassi, "Dear Readers," *Neharde'a* 4 (Spring 1982): 3. He wishes to see concepts like 'full equality in all spheres of life', including the search for roots. Sociological research shows that people of Oriental/Muslim countries accept the unified national myth and do not undermine the Western self-perception of Israeli society, Efi Ya'ar, "Continuity and Change in Israeli Society: The Test of the Melting Pot" [in Hebrew], in *Generations, Spaces, Identities: Contemporary View on the Israeli Society and Culture – to Shmuel Eisenstadt on his Eightieth Birthday*, ed. H. Herzog, T. Kowhai and S. Zernike (Tel Aviv: Van Leer, 2007), 96, 98.
93. Placard at the entrance to the Babylonian Jews Heritage Museum.
94. Mordechai Ben-Porat, "Opening and Greetings at the Opening Show in Habima Hall Tel-Aviv 21 April 1987 and in Beit Hahayal in Tel Aviv 10 Sept. 1987" [in Hebrew], *Neharde'a* 6 (Passover 1988): 25.

95. Cited in the agreement of the associations, persons and institutions that act for the dissemination and preservation of Yemenite Jewry's Heritage and the Rosh-Ha'yin Municipality on January 19, 1997; the agreement is in the Museum of Yemenite Jewry in Rosh-Ha'ayin. Similarly in an interview with Naftali Simhi, the present curator of the Yemnite Museum, with the author, June 27, 2011, Rosh Ha'ayin. Also Ben-Porat, "Opening and Greetings," 25; Glitzenstein-Meir, "Iraqi Immigrants and the Israeli," 295; elsewhere Meir-Glitzenstein, "Zionist Identity," 187–8, sees the demand for equality and the acceptance of the Zionist ethos as contradictory, however, can also be an inclusionary reading of it.
96. P.W. Hartmann, "Judenporzellan," *Das grosse Kunstlexikon*, BeyArs.Com, http://www.beyars.com/kunstlexikon/lexikon_4521.html (accessed April 24, 2012). For contrast to the simple style of the religious objects in the German Speaking Museum see Vivian B. Mann, "A Court Jew's Silver Cup," *Metropolitan Museum Journal* 43 (2008): 131–40. For Israel see the catalogue of a recent exhibition of Persian Jews: Lights and Shadows: The Story of Iran and the Jews, Exhibition, main curator Hagai Segev (Tel Aviv: Beit Hatfutsot Museum of the Jewish People, 2010).
97. Zeller Ursula, *Synagogen in Deutschland: eine virtuelle Rekonstruktion* (Darmstadt: Technische Universität, 2004), see also: Technical University Darmstadt, "Synagogues in Germany – A Virtual Reconstruction," http://www.cad.architektur.tu-darmstadt.de/synagogen/inter/en_menu.html (accessed April 24, 2012).
98. Witzthum, "Life Stories," 32–3. The Orientalist theme is prevalent in the museum and its catalogue. On Orientalism among German Jews against East European Jews see Noah Isenberg, "To Pray Like a Dervis: Orientalist Discourse in Arnold Zweig's 'The Face of East European Jewry,'" in *Orientalism and the Jews*, ed. Ivan Davidson and Derek J. Penslar (Waltham, MA: Brandeis University Press, 2005), 94–124; and Steven Ascheim, *Brothers and Strangers: The East European Jew in German and German Jewish Consciousness, 1880–1923* (Madison: University of Wisconsin, 1982).
99. Roni Lustig in an interview with the author, July 13, 2011, Safed; see also Nahum Halevi, "A New Group in the Knesset."
100. Yael Padan, "RePlacing Memory," in *Constructing a Sense of Place: Architecture and Zionist Discourse*, ed. Haim Yacobi (Aldershot: Ashgate, 2004), 260. The Libyan museum in Or-Yehuda also provides a special space for the commemoration of the Holocaust.
101. The Yemenite Jews have a small museum in Benei Beraq that folds up and unfolds for groups of visitors, see http://www.nosachteiman.co.il/?CategoryID=876 (accessed August 19, 2012), and another small museum for German Jews 'Institute of the Ashkenazi Heritage', see Hayim Revir, "Wake-up Ashkenazis! How One Man Changed the Mistaken Image of the Small and Glorious Yekke Community in the Land of Israel" [in Hebrew], *Family*, March 26, 2006, 44–6. Similarly, the North African community (Maghreb) have an Institute for the Research of the Communities and the Spiritual Heritage of the Jews of the Maghreb: Morocco, Tunis, Libya.
102. Different research shows different trends for the Ultra-Orthodox community; a general review of the differing opinions and trends is Eliezer Ben Rafael and Lior Ben-Chaim, *Jewish Identities in a Multi-Modern Age* [Hebrew] (Ra'anana: Open University Press, 2006), 205–12, 217–23, 245.
103. Eileen Hooper-Greenhill, *Museums and the Interpretation of Visual Culture* (London: Routedge, 2000), 72.
104. Gurian, "What is the Object of this Exercise?," 282.
105. Shelton, "In the Lair of the Monkey," 85.

Means of transport and storage: suitcases and other containers for the memory of migration and displacement

Joachim Schlör

Department of History, University of Southampton, UK

Several exhibitions in recent years – in the 'Deutsches Auswandererhaus' Bremerhaven and other museums in Germany, the United Kingdom, Australia, and the United States – have used suitcases (and 'the suitcase') as a central symbol and metaphor for the migration process. Based on a variety of examples, the article discusses the idea and the use of memory containers – and their function as archives – in the context of emigration, transmigration, and immigration. Suitcases are the most obvious material objects relating to these processes and the connected cultural practices. They are concrete objects, but beyond that they have been used as symbols and metaphors for the experience of travel and of dislocation. Suitcases often contained, and therefore are connected to, other items of memory storage: photographs and personal documents (letters, diaries about the migration experience – documents that have been termed, in a different context, 'Schreibakte auf der Schwelle' – acts of writing on the threshold); manuscripts, farewell letters (written on the boat, in border stations, in port cities), memorial and yizkor books, songs and poems, self-drawn maps which show the stations of the journey. An analysis of such 'things' – material objects which often carried an emotional value – and their representation in museums and exhibitions opens up a wide and rich field of research for the ethnography of migration.

'They will all tell you about the train station, no matter whom you ask, they all talk about the train station, and when I do that, I am 13 years old again.' For Ada Brodsky, this train station was Berlin's Anhalter Bahnhof, October 1938, the place and the time she left Germany, and her parents, behind. Christian Staas, in a portrait of Ada Brodsky for the German weekly *Die Zeit*, writes:

> When Ada Brodsky boards the ship 'Gerusalemme' in Trieste, she only carries her violin and a suitcase. In the suitcase, under her clothes, the blue shorts and blouses, there are books, especially poetry, especially Rilke. After eight days the ship reaches the shores of Palestine and the recently opened port of Tel-Aviv. A scary arrival: Ada's suitcase was lost. ... She arrived in the children's village Ben Shemen, founded by Siegfried Lehmann. A month later Ada's luggage arrived. 'Finally, the books! A piece of Germany. Of a lost Germany.'[1]

In the context of our discussions on Jewish migration and the archive, I would like to present some thoughts about the one material object which is most closely connected

---

This article was originally published with errors. This version has been corrected. Please see Erratum (http://dx.doi.org/10.1080/1462169X.2014.922364).

to the process – and the cultural practice – of migration: the suitcase (in connection with other such containers). This object, container, travel companion, and witness, plays a central role in many stories, testimonies as well as literary treatments, about migration and displacement. The suitcase, with its contents, is at the same time an authentic material object that tells – if we manage to make it speak – the history of an emigration. It has become the symbol of loss and of rescue; a book that once started out quite simply, as a personal memoir, Shaun Tan's *The Arrival*, can now be bought in luxury collector's editions – and in the form of a suitcase.[2] In both functions, suitcases are widely and very frequently used, in history museums as well as in art exhibitions: 'Those who have visited contemporary art exhibitions over the past decade have become accustomed to seeing a plethora of suitcases within art gallery installations', says Irit Rogoff.[3] In her *Terra Infirma. Geography's Visual Culture*, Rogoff uses 'Luggage' – along with 'Subjects/places/spaces', 'Mapping', 'Borders', and 'Bodies' – as one of the five central analytical categories for a work that sets up 'an exploration of links between ... the dislocation of subjects, the disruption of collective narratives and of languages in the field of vision'.[4] With her work, we move around (as might be apt for the topic we are researching) in the in-between-ness of academic fields: Migration Studies, Cultural Studies, Visual Culture, Material Culture, Museology, the study of place and space in History and Sociology. Rogoff herself mentions the names of Henri Lefèbvre, Neil Smith, Rosalynn Deutsche, Iain Chambers, Sara Suleri, and Anton Shammas as inspirations for her work, and more names come to mind, such as James Clifford, Homi Bhabha, Edward Soja, to name but a few. What brings these people, sociologists, historians, art historians, but also writers of fiction, and their work together, is a common interest in the spatial dimension of culture, in travel and migration, in the flux and hybridity of travel and migration experiences, in material objects, but also in the literary representation of such experiences.

Or I could have just said: They are all interested in suitcases. When I asked a colleague at the University of Tübingen to put me in touch with one of his students who had published an article – more on that below – in an exhibition catalogue on 'Reisebegleiter', travel companions, Bernhard Tschofen provided me with a contact but also added, 'I already see an international network of suitcase studies emerge'. This could indeed be an interesting enterprise:

> Like many other important terms, such as 'exile', 'diaspora', 'migration' or 'hybridity', the suitcase has become the signifier of mobility, displacement, duality, and the overwrought emotional climates in which these circulate ... Luggage, with its double inscription of concrete material belongings and of travel and movement away from the naturalized anchorings of those belongings ..., is one of the main metaphors of 'sadness at leaving'.[5]

Ethnographic research is mostly interested in the 'concrete material' aspect, but the metaphorical aspect connected to luggage is important as well. Jan Hinrichsen, the student mentioned above, brings these two aspects very convincingly together.[6] There has been, he writes, a massive rise in 'migration-related' themes and exhibitions in museums big and small, from the opening of the Cité nationale de l'histoire de l'immigration in Paris to local exhibitions such as 'Heimat im Koffer' 2008 in the South German city of Ulm. Is there also, Hinrichsen asks, a new consciousness for the substantial and permanent processes of wandering, and how does the study of 'memory containers' help us to interpret such changes in memory culture?[7] In his overview for the German context, suitcases were used very explicitly in this context for the first time in 1981.

The huge and very impressive exhibition on 'Prussia' exhibited 'raw wooden boxes, the luggage of emigrants stored on the ships, as a personal legacy';[8] three years later the Vienna-based AEIOU project, Austria's 'Network of Knowledge', used suitcases as part of an installation/staging of the emigration of Jewish intellectuals. In both cases the message seemed to be: 'These pieces of luggage have been there' (*sind dabeigewesen*), this provides them with an auratic quality – especially when the suitcase is covered with signs (from hotels, shipping lines etc.) that confirm this character of a witness.

Suitcases are containers for personal belongings; they are, in the language of museums, 'biographical objects'. They have an intimate side to them and offer a space of restriction or confinement since they allow you only to take what fits inside. A suitcase is a shell, an envelope, a cover that contains things but also meaning: traces of its own and of its owner's movements and history are inscribed on as well as in it. It is mobile and can be taken along, it is a medium that creates a relationship between places, it draws maps – changing geographies of migration – it is set in a continuous in-between-ness and does not completely belong to a 'here' or a 'there'. It makes the fugitive and the volatile tangible and concrete, it holds 'the things of a life' together and creates a kind of order among them.[9] The acts of packing and unpacking a suitcase can be seen as a dealing with one's own past and future – another in-between-ness – and as a moment of considering experiences and expectations. The suitcase is a marker for biographical stages, it holds other things and the stories they tell together, it produces and relates knowledge about migration; it is, in a way, an archive: quite a lot for such a small object! Hinrichsen presents three different categories:

- The *original suitcase* that has 'been there' (*der dabeigewesene Originalkoffer*) as an authentic object that has material support in the de facto world (*dinglicher Rückhalt im Tatsächlichen*); this is usually one specific example, a suitcase with a name;
- The *anonymous symbolic suitcase* as a signifier and visualizer for the meanings that inhabit the material object 'suitcase' and show what it is that brings places into contact with each other; this is often represented by a collection, a greater number of suitcases, often shown in connection to a train compartment or a ship's gangway;
- The *idea of the suitcase*, the staging of suitcases in museums and art installations or the use of suitcases in classrooms; this is mostly represented by artificial 'suitcase' images or replacements.

Together they offer a system of signs meant to uncover the meaning(s) of migration and displacement, especially the implication of a 'home': once owned, then lost. In most migration narratives, the suitcase stands for the possibility to carry parts of this old, lost *Heimat* to a new place where it helps to create a new home: *Heimat* as a transportable item. In ways that need to be carefully explored, the suitcase represents the alchemical process of transformation that is involved in migration. For this reason, the suitcase is such an evocative object – it stands for the need, and the possibility, to change, it somehow represents change itself.

In extreme cases of forced displacement, this needs to be added, the leftover suitcases have become the visual expression of something that is hard to imagine or to express in words, for example in the thousands of suitcases stored, and partly exhibited, at the Auschwitz Museum – this is not part of the migration narrative, but rather a symbol for the ultimate transformation of personhood into objecthood, of death. We will discuss one example, and the question of ownership, towards the end of this paper.

Migration in the museum

I would suggest, in general terms, that we not just cooperate with museums of migration, but integrate them, their exhibitions and exhibits, and the rationale behind them, *as sources* into our own research on migration and the archive.[10] The following part discusses some examples to highlight how museums in the United Kingdom, the United States, Australia, and Germany 'sell' their ideas. One of the most important elements of this product placement (especially online) seems to be the *authentic* place where a museum has been established: London's Museum of Immigration at 19 Princelet Street in Spitalfields

> is a magical unrestored Huguenot master silk weaver's home, whose shabby frontage conceals a rare surviving synagogue built over its garden. We are working to save the building and to create a permanent exhibition where you can discover the stories of waves of newcomers – Huguenots, Irish, Jews, Bengali and Somali peoples among many others – who have shaped this area and this nation.

Authenticity is the first key element to be noted. Apart from the permanent exhibition there is also a site-specific exhibit called 'Suitcases and Sanctuary', it 'explores the history of the waves of immigration that shaped Spitalfields, seen through the eyes of today's children. It is the story of one area, the story of London, and the story of the making of multicultural Britain'.[11] The suitcases here symbolize the continuity of immigration in 'waves of newcomers'. In Melbourne, the Immigration Museum uses suitcases to take a closer look at individual experiences, it tries to bring together memories and memorabilia in order to explore

> stories of *real people from all over the world* who have migrated to Victoria. Located in the Old Customs House in the heart of the city, the museum re-creates the real-life stories of coming to Australia with a rich mix of moving images, personal and community voices, memories and memorabilia. From the reasons for making the journey, to the moment of arrival in a new country, and the impact on indigenous communities, these stories are sometimes sad, sometimes funny, but always engaging. The result is a thought-provoking and moving experience.[12]

After authenticity of place, the emphasis on the museum's capability to translate a large narrative into individual (and recognizable) experiences is the second key element to be noted.

- This personal, individual approach is still more important in the approach of the Museum of the City of New York which presents 'Images of Immigration', photographs of individual immigrants:

The images assembled here portray immigrants who came to and lived in New York during the operation of Castle Garden and Ellis Island. Between 1880 and 1924, the great waves of immigration to and through New York inspired many photographers and illustrators to depict the arrival of these newcomers and to document their new lives in the metropolis. Drawn from the unparalleled collections of the Museum of the City of New

York, these images present a broad overview of *how immigrants arrived* and started to settle in New York City between 1855 and 1955.[13]

The importance of the cultural practices related to emigration and immigration is the third key notion we can note: the museums attempt to make the 'how' of arrival, the cultural practice, visible and translatable to the public: by showing photographs or installations of immigrants carrying their suitcases.

- Bremerhaven's Deutsches Auswandererhaus, opened in 2005, again advertises itself as an authentic setting of emigration from Germany:

Between 1830 and 1974 more than 7 million people emigrated overseas via Bremerhaven. *Located at the historical setting* of the old and new ports, the GERMAN EMIGRATION CENTER is Europe's biggest 'Erlebnismuseum' [adventure museum]. Visitors of the exhibition experience *hautnah* (first hand) what it means to emigrate.

The authenticity of the place is now seemingly transferred to the visitors; they are invited to imitate the cultural practice of migrating and to identify with the emigrants' life stories: 'Selected biographies of emigrants accompany visitors through the exhibition and illustrate motives, conditions, and consequences of emigration'. As a result, the promise continues, 'the GERMAN EMIGRATION CENTER combines knowledge and excitement, recreation and pleasure'.[14]

- Recreation and pleasure might not be what a visitor first expects from such a place – but the competing institution in nearby Hamburg, Ballinstadt, 'Port of Dreams', founded in 2007, stresses the fun factor even more pronouncedly:

'I find the idea quite exciting to travel to America and to live there. Wouldn't you like that, too?' This question is posed by ten-year-old Heinz from Essen, where he saw the light of day in 1897. Heinz is one of nine puppets that, in historical costumes, get the visitors of Ballinstadt in the mood for a trip to America. ... Then they can immerse themselves in all phases of the emigration process, from the departure to arrival in New York and the perspectives of the New World. ... These areas of the exhibition are accompanied by interactive stations where *visitors can experience their very individual emigration history*.[15]

Of course these visitors usually do not have their individual emigration history but they are invited to construct one for themselves.

- Finally, the use of suitcases (and similar, or related, material objects) allows the museums to present a widening of our perspective on exile and emigration and a continuation of the narrative up to the present day – and, indeed, to an integration of the real life-stories of contemporary immigrants and their children. Experience and identification, and sometimes real, are further key notions to be noted. 'Berlin: A Suitcase Full of Histories' is the title of an exhibition that

presents the life stories of ten persons who have decided to move their main place of residence from Ankara or São Paulo, from Kirow or Pointe Noire to [Berlin's districts of] Charlottenburg-Wilmersdorf. You and your pupils can travel with Reşit Mirioğlu from Antakye to Berlin-Schönefeld [airport] and experience his arrival in the foreign country. Dine with Mohammad El-Tayeh-Sewiti on his first day in Germany – in a Lebanese restaurant that reminds him of his home. Listen to the desires expressed by In-Sun Kim who comes to Germany as a nurse apprentice. Be present when Yulia Delamere rides on the S-Bahn and meets her future husband. And cheer for Bedriye Yagcı's daughter who plays football in a boys' team.[16]

How do we read such documents? How do museums and memorials in centres of emigration, transmigration, and immigration present – and represent – the migration experience? Obviously there is a certain lingo of museum advertisements (especially in the case of Ballinstadt) which maybe should not be taken too seriously. But I find it interesting how the process and experience of migration is being turned into an 'adventure', an 'excitement', and more than that, into something that today's visitors should try – and even wish – to relive and be a part of.

A first step in our analysis of containers for the memory of migration and displacement experiences could thus be based on a close reading of such documents. These texts, mainly intended to attract visitors and to publicize the museums, are also sources for a study into the shifting images of historical events and experiences; they are, themselves, means of memory storage and examples for a new representation of both the places and the messages they would like to deliver. The extracts show how such institutions do 'place' migration experiences in their historical and social contexts but, in contrast to most memoirs and testimonies of former migrants, there is a strong emphasis on the individual experience and the excitement of it all.

Many of these museums and exhibitions which cover a wide range of very different migration experiences across time and space from the late nineteenth century up to the present day, make use, not too surprisingly, of the most obvious material object relating to migration: suitcases in many forms and arrangements support the message and serve as educational tools, especially in the pedagogical work with children who learn about the migration experiences of their families and neighbours. 'What Would You Take and What Would You Leave?', for example, is an exercise for children across the UK who are encouraged

> to imagine that they are leaving their home to live abroad. Working together, each pair should select 10 items that they would take with them. The children should write or draw these items in the suitcase. After they have done this, the class can make a list of things that they value that they have had to leave behind.[17]

Similarly, the Australian Migration Heritage Center of New South Wales in an exhibition gave useful hints about the role of the suitcase during – but also, important in our context, *long after* – the migration period, under the title 'Caring for your belongings: Caring for your migration heritage items & family memorabilia', thus encouraging recent immigrants to keep their suitcases (or maybe donate them to the museum) as symbols and metaphors of their experience.[18] The 'Auswanderer-Ausstellung' (emigration exhibit) on a museum ship in the port of Hamburg (a precursor to Ballinstadt) was announced with the following text:

> More than five million people have left Europe, between 1850 and 1934, by ship via the port of Hamburg. They endured tremendous exertions in order to make their dream of a life in the New World come true. The exhibition 'A Suitcase full of Hope' on the museum ship Cap San Diego, at the boarding bridge in St. Pauli [St. Pauli Landungsbrücken] gives an insight into the longings and anxieties of the immigrants.[19]

The use of words such as 'anxiety' is quite rare in sources like this. And it is the very notion of the suitcase that seems to be able to contain and express such feelings – but is this really the case? Cataldo Perri in his play *Bastimenti. Träume und Schimären zwischen Tarantella und Tango*, about Italian emigration to Argentina, is sceptical:

> Will this lousy cardboard suitcase be strong enough to guard my dreams? Will it be strong enough to conserve the smells and the sun of my country? Will it be strong enough to preserve the smell of my house, or will this smell also get lost and mixed up with the anonymous smells of the world?[20]

Suitcases are symbols and metaphors loaded with (too) many meanings. A historical workshop in Berlin started a project in 2005, 'Ein Koffer für Berlin': 'We plan an exhibition of still-existing suitcases belonging to emigrants all over the world, suitcases with which they had to leave Germany in the Nazi era'.[21] To add even more symbolic value, the initiative emphasized that all those who donated a suitcase could then say that, in a variation of Marlene Dietrich's song, they again have a suitcase in Berlin, 'einen Koffer in Berlin'. It seems that such an identificatory offer was too difficult for the public to accept (and too light-heartedly put), so it is maybe not too astonishing that this project has not been very successful.[22]

The presentation of migration processes and experiences in museums of cultural history has already found academic attention.[23] An interesting development of recent years seems to be the growing interest in a cooperation between museums and archives on the one hand and researchers of migration on the other.[24] A conference on Migration and the Archive – 'Inventur Migration' – has taken place in Oberhausen, Germany, in June 2009:

> Archives and museums contain important testimonies for the history of migration. But many collections have not yet been completely registered or researched and their historical importance remains undiscovered. ... What kind of sources do we have, and how is migration history passed down and documented (*überliefert*)? ... The results of this conference shall be used for the conceptualization of a stock register on migration in the coming years.[25]

A second conference on 'Stadt – Museum – Migration' (City – Museum – Migration), organized by the *Network Migration in Europe*, took place on 19–21 October, 2009, at the Industriemuseum Zeche Zollern:

> Migration and integration have become key topics of the contemporary intellectual and political debate. In the framework of this debate, the question of cultural and cultural-political representations of migrants has become ever more important. Museums as places of historical narrative and interpretation have now the task of adequately representing migration and cultural diversity in a society of immigration.[26]

A second analytical step in our attempt to understand the presentation of migration memories, based on this relatively recent development, takes this self-reflection into account. In contrast to the overly excited language of the emigration museum advertisements quoted above, the critical reflection of underlying concepts and future plans reveals the need for a deeper understanding of the complexities of migration and displacement experiences. It becomes clear that a suitcase – or even an assemblage of suitcases – cannot tell or represent the whole story. Several researchers therefore pointed to the need to go 'beyond the suitcase'. Sabine Hess (Munich) and Kerstin

Poehls (Berlin) convened a workshop, 'Beyond the Suitcase: Representations of Migration and Europe and the Role of Museums', at the 15th Nordic Migration Research Conference 2010 in Malmö. Papers referred to 'The Art of Governing Migration? Anthropological Approaches to Studying and Representing the New European Border Regime' (Sabine Hess), 'Approaches to Migration in the City Museums of Antwerp' (Leen Beyers and others), or 'No Ideas but in Things? On the Contested Role of Objects in Museal Representations of Migration' (Kerstin Poehls). In a call for papers for yet another conference in 2010, in Maynooth, Ireland, 'What Crisis? Representations of Migration, Europe and the Role of Museums', the organizers formulated the following questions:

> Images of migrant bodies circulate in the media all over Europe, but in whose interest? A number of European countries have recently sought to revise a national self-image to incorporate their histories of (im-)migration and now reflect this image inside their museum spaces. When migration becomes the topic of an exhibition, the ethics of representation come to the fore: Who is talking about whom? Who are the audience; and what kind of story about migration, Europe and its state is being told? What are the critical/ ambivalent relationships between museal space and migrants? How are migration museums, state policy, migrant rights groups, aesthetic practices, and imaginaries of the migrants' past and present linked?[27]

Most of the research presented, and the papers referred to, have been connected to contemporary processes of migration and the idea and concept of Europe. Debates evolved around the relationship between museums and state policy on migration. Are migration museums (unintentionally) part of a strategy that enforces the boundaries of the 'Fortress Europe'; do they contribute to a distinction between 'good' and 'bad' migrations? Legal or illegal, assimilable or not; indeed, what are political categories to judge migration processes? And how does the use of suitcases illustrate or even support such judgements?

In a report on the 'Suitcase Project' organized by The International Child and Youth Care Network, Glynis Clacherty describes 'the voices of children who participated in an innovative psychosocial support project that has focused on artwork done on and inside a set of old suitcases'. Children from Rwanda, Burundi, the Democratic Republic of the Congo, Ethiopia, and Angola reacted to the notion of the suitcase with accounts of their own experiences, anxieties, and hopes:

- 'I am going to always take this suitcase with me. I want to go to Australia and I will take this suitcase for my interview because it tells my history.'
- 'This suitcase is a good memory. I want to keep it for my children so they will know what I have done and where I have been with this suitcase, my life.'
- 'I remember when I left my country there were many people waiting at the bus and there was a pile of suitcases. My suitcase reminds me of that time when we were all pushing to get on the bus and we were afraid and we wanted to get away because of the war.'
- 'We made these suitcases for some of the people out there. There are rich people out there who live large – they don't know how poor people, like refugees, live. They don't know – they got to know.'[28]

In general, the idea seems to be that a suitcase, from any place or period, presented in a museum, 'will become an object of collective history and can contribute to an overcoming of the historical amnesia ("*Geschichtslosigkeit*") of the migrants which itself has historical reasons'.[29] How can migration, then, be exhibited in museums without turning the migrant into an object? In this context, we need to develop 'methodological approaches that allow for a fruitful exchange between historical research and contemporary theoretical perspectives'.[30] It will also be fruitful to discuss uses and images of the suitcase in the context of other means (and dimensions) of memory storage.

Memory storage and the in-between-ness of migration and displacement experiences

After having discussed the presentation of suitcases in migration museums and the necessity of critical self-reflection in the framework of Migration Studies, I would now like to turn to what Hinrichsen has termed the 'anonymous symbolic suitcase as a signifier and visualizer for the meanings that inhabit the material object', and I suggest that we discuss this in the context of space and place in Migration Studies.[31] An analysis of the suitcase and its uses allows us, hopefully, to discuss the relation between the meaning of material objects and the spatial dimension of the migration narratives. In recent years, the study of Jewish history and culture and the study of Jewish/non-Jewish relations have both been influenced by a 'spatial turn'.[32] A number of studies have brought the notions of space and place and of 'Jewish topographies' to the forefront of research and publication.[33] An important area in this context is the study of displacement: *research into migration*.[34] Research on place-identity, on the other hand, deals with the relationship between different Jewish communities and the place(s) relevant to them: this can include forms of settlement, histories of communities, but also research about the 'place' of a given community or individuals in their relation with Jews and non-Jews: *research into integration*. Too often these two research areas have been treated in isolation; the question of memory storage might be able to bring them together. Notions of 'staying', 'belonging', and 'keeping', all closely connected to the idea of a secure place, a *Heimat*, are also intimately bound to the formation of archives, museums, and other forms of memory storage. In migration processes, terms such as 'moving', 'longing', and 'taking along/leaving behind' can also be connected to the question of the preservation of memory – but under different circumstances, namely in movement. James Clifford, in his groundbreaking book *Routes*, has shown how 'physical displacement' and the 'creation of space' through the act of travelling involve 'obtaining knowledge and/or having an experience (exciting, edifying, pleasurable, estranging, broadening)'.[35] Knowledge and experience acquired in the process of travel – of movement – will be (and have been) stored in memory and expressed in text, or sometimes also in maps such as Fritz Freudenheim's drawing 'Von der alten Heimat zu der neuen Heimat', kept in the archives of Berlin's Jewish Museum.[36]

In Diaspora communities there is a common knowledge about both individual and general migration experiences, and they often create, based on this knowledge, depositories such as archives, museums, memorial books or regular events to make them available to future generations or even to other groups with similar experiences. The very notion of 'Diaspora', used to describe the Jewish (and later also the Armenian and Greek) dispersion 'now shares meanings with a larger semantic domain that includes words like immigrant, expatriate, refugee, guest-worker, exile community, overseas community, ethnic community', and today it also refers to many more different groups and their experiences of displacement.[37] Often the documents preserved in those depositories point us to the political dimension of a relationship of power between those who carry the suitcases and those who inspect and control them.[38]

The figure of 'the migrant' (standing, with a suitcase, on a railway station platform or at Southampton's Town Quay) has been interpreted as a representative figure whose experiences – the loss of a homeland, the breaking of ties, the threat of an impermanent existence, but also positive effects of mobility – are those that, in an age of globalization, individuals and societies at large must expect to face. Edward Soja's reflections on 'Thirdspace' have been used in order to try and understand what happens when processes and cultural practices such as (forced or unforced) migrations put people in a position where they have to 'deal with' (leave, arrive at, live in, get used to, remember) more than one place. Gilles Deleuze and Felix Guattari have provided us with the term 'Movement-Image(s)', and I would argue that for migration research the interesting area lies in the tension between a 'topography of the unknown' on the one hand and the idea of home, homeland, and *Heimat* on the other.[39] With Edward Soja we can argue that spatial thinking, or what has been called the geographical imagination, needs to integrate both the concrete material forms which can be mapped, analysed, and explained, *and* the mental constructs, ideas about and representations of space and its social significance, that are harder to grasp.[40] The study of suitcases in the context of an analysis of the spatial dimensions of migration history will involve an examination of both the material object and its representation (in many forms). In the field of Jewish Studies, important theoretical groundwork can be found in Jonathan Boyarin's *Remapping Memory: The Politics of TimeSpace* as well as in Charlotte Fonrobert's and Vered Shemtov's close analysis of 'Jewish conceptions and practices of space'.[41]

Based on these theoretical foundations, a third step in our analysis of memory containers will be to place the suitcase and the cultural situations and practices connected to its use during the migration process in the larger context of in-between-ness. Like the ship, which Michel Foucault has called 'the heterotopia par excellence' ('a floating piece of space, a place without a place, that exists by itself, that is closed in on itself and at the same time is given over to the infinity of the sea'[42]), the suitcase is both concrete and abstract – this produces a certain tension between the concrete or factual experiences of a migration journey and the experience noted in many migration testimonies of an in-between-ness in time and space, a sphere of suspended reality. In practical terms: can a museum or an art exhibition express the core feelings related to such an experience, for example by showing an arrangement of suitcases?

> As a symbol, then, the suitcase is double-edged, ambivalent in the extreme: on the one hand, it evokes travel, displacement, emigration, exile and transience; on the other, it is that part of home that travels with us, a reminder of belonging and stability, the world of things we collect around us, the promise of continuity in the midst of change, of order restored. The suitcase is a portable heterotopia, an 'other space' that is always there and here at the same time, a home away from home, but also offering the endless possibility of new departures, whether desired or forced.[43]

Suitcases are just one embodiment of such 'signifiers and visualizers'. If we try to go 'beyond the suitcase',[44] it might be helpful for a moment to consider other means of transport and storage relevant for the migration experience and to regard them as containers of the migration experience: music (the songs of emigration and immigration), film (as a medium of mobility), and material objects ('Dinge' related to the experience of exile and displacement). In a talk at Stanford University (celebrating the work of Steven Zipperstein as Head of Jewish Studies), Barbara Mann, in an aside remark, stated that 'memory, as bi-product of exile, leads to song'. 'Migrating melodies' indeed contain musical traditions and relate to their movement across national and language boundaries. Music and migration is one of the research areas which have already attracted scholarly attention, although Shirli Glbert rightly states that 'the larger question of the relationship between music and memory has been relatively underexplored in historical, musicological and ethnomusicological writing'.[45] Music, clearly, is more easily transportable than other media of memory storage:

> It is a well-known fact that music and musicians have always been mobile, constantly in touch with other musical environments and traditions. Research into the numerous transformations of musical practice caused by those migrations proves to be inspiring for musicologists. Traces of migrations can be discovered in music, in the ways it is played and composed, and those traces can sometimes unveil unusual stories.[46]

CD collections such as 'Voice of the People' document songs of exile and emigration, with Volume 4, 'Farewell My Own Dear Native Land', dedicated mainly to the Irish migration to the United States. ('It is to be expected that the Irish dominate this CD. If the Irish had the lion's share of emigration songs, they also had the lion's share of emigration.'[47]) In Italy we can find an impressive number of collections and documentaries on 'i canti dell'emigrazione' and a high level of reflection about their impact on collective memories in – and outside of – the country:

> Emigration has indeed been, and still is today, a multi-determined social phenomenon in the lives of millions of men and women and in the history of many countries .... Whoever left a country and a family, alone or in a group, in order to improve his own life conditions as well those of the people who remained behind, lived through sentiments of sadness, of nostalgia, of melancholy, and of hope, sentiments which authors, many of them unknown, have expressed in texts, oftentimes in poetry and in the regional dialects of their home. These texts, together with their simple melodies, form the popular songs of emigration.[48]

For the Jewish experience there is, as far as I know, no migration-related equivalent to Mark Slobin's *Tenement Songs*, a collection of songs that commemorate and express the processes of arrival and settlement in the US, especially on New York's Lower East Side.[49] Still, teachers have been using music and songs in order to awaken children's interest in the history of emigration and immigration, such as 'Brivele der Mamen' by Solomon Shmulowitz as an example of a song that tells about saying goodbye; 'Amol in a Tsayt' by Weiner Lazar as a song about poverty, desperation and the need to fight for one's rights; 'Vos is gevorn fun mayn shtetele?' as an example of the nostalgia and longing for a lost home; or 'Give me your tired, your poor' as a celebration of the American experience.[50] There is still a wide range of sources to collect as far as the topic of 'music and migration' is concerned. 'Auswandererlieder' are a classical topic of German ethnomusicographical tradition, and Hamburg University is home to a research group on Exilmusik.[51] Music can be a form of storage of the migration experience, an apt and adequate one even, since it reflects the flux and hybridity inherent to the migration movement. This is also true for film as a source and as a medium, and 'suitcase studies' – if they ever exist – can profit from research in both areas. Ulrich Meurer and Maria Oikonomou, in the introduction to their edited volume *Auswanderung und Exil im internationalen Kino*, write:

> Flight from persecution, expulsion, or unforced migration – all three cases can be analyzed in connection with the medium of film. On the one hand, the experiences of homelessness ('Unbehaustheit'), of being on the way, of being a stranger constitute an essential part of

the modern condition, and on the other hand departure, travel, and arrival can be understood as phases of a basic category of movement. Situation and milieu, action and change of place describe both the essence of the migration experience and the dominant elements of a film narrative ... The cinema seems to prefer motives and topics of mobility.[52]

Such an approach manages to connect the study of media with broader concepts on mobility and travel – and the creation of 'thirdspaces' throughout the migration experience. To conclude this section, mention should be made of a renewed interest in material objects (another area of possible cooperation between researchers and museum practitioners) as witnesses and containers of the migration experience. Eugene Halton and Mihaly Csikszentmihalyi have given us new insight into the meaning of things: their project, 'The Meanings of Things: Domestic Symbols and the Self' investigated 'the ways people carve meaning out of their domestic environment'. What happens when the domestic environment, the home, is threatened, destroyed, dissolved? What happens to the things? What happens to the meaning we are used to attach to them? These questions have been discussed in the framework of travel and tourism research,[53] but more recently also in the context of research on exile and displacement. Participants of the Gesellschaft für Exilforschung's yearly conference in Hamburg, in March 2013, were invited to discuss 'Dinge des Exils' – material objects that migrants could take along or were forced to leave behind, objects that concentrated within themselves memories of lost homes, of displacement and in-between-ness in different cultural contexts.[54]

Who owns the memory in the suitcase?

In a paper called 'Take down Mezuzahs, Remove Name-Plates. The Emigration of Material Objects from Germany to Palestine' I looked at the 'things' and the lists of things that a German-Jewish family took along – or left behind – when they left Germany for Palestine in 1936:

> In his own person the emigrant is experiencing a double sense of not belonging, of being a stranger: as a German, a German Jew who has to leave his country, but also as a future resident of a country that wants to become a state. The historical situation is crystallised, symbolised in the things he takes with him and those he leaves behind, and in the lists of them that he draws up. The things become embodiments of conditions and circumstances – bearers of memories, of hopes.[55]

So far this paper has discussed mostly successful migration processes and their presentation, or even celebration, in museums. But there are more extreme, and more painful examples, and they should be integrated when we discuss the question of the ownership of memory. Else Ury was a successful writer of children's stories in the years of the Weimar Republic, her 'Nesthäkchen' novels are still popular today. The fact that she has been a victim of the Holocaust had long been forgotten.[56] Between 1905 and 1939, Else Ury lived on Berlin's Kantstrasse 30. From 1939 on she was forced to live in a 'Judenhaus' in Moabit from where, on 6 January 1943, she was brought to the 'Deportationsstelle' in Große Hamburger Straße 26 and deported to Auschwitz. In an article for the *Jüdische Zeitung*, Ingrid Jüttens reports how shocked she was when she learned about the fate of her childhood hero, and she comments, playing on the title of Marlene Dietrich's famous song 'Ich hab' noch einen Koffer in Berlin: "*Else Ury hatte keinen Koffer mehr in Berlin*. Her last suitcase, bearing the inscription 'Else Sara Ury

Berlin – Solinger-Str. 10', was discovered in the Auschwitz Memorial in 1995 in Auschwitz and is today stored in the Auschwitz Museum.[57] A second story related to this memorial has been reported in *The Sunday Times* of 13 August 2006 as a 'Battle over a Suitcase from Auschwitz':

> Most people who found a faded suitcase in the attic would probably consider it worthless, but for Michel Levi-Leleu, the Frenchman claiming the relic, it is beyond price.
>
> He last saw the suitcase on April 10, 1943. It was in the hands of Pierre Levi-Leleu, his father, when he left his wife, daughter and son in a safe house in Savoy as he tried to find another refuge.
>
> He was arrested in Avignon and taken by the Nazis to the Auschwitz-Birkenau concentration camp in occupied Poland. ... 'They must have allowed him to take the suitcase with him when he was deported.' ... His family never knew the suitcase had been recovered, or that it had turned up as an exhibit at the Auschwitz Holocaust museum in southern Poland.

The suitcase had been on display at the Auschwitz memorial since 1947. It came to Paris as part of an exhibition, borrowed by the Fondation Memorial de la Shoah in September 2005. Lévi-Leleu said: 'I could not believe it when I saw it [...]. I looked at a small tag attached to the suitcase and could even see my father's name on it, together with a printed inscription reading "86 Boul. Vilette, Paris" (his original address).' The son asked the organizers of the exhibition to hand over the suitcase, they refused, and legal proceedings started in Paris, where in the meantime an agreement has been reached. For the museum, 'these items', suitcases that still bear the names of their owners, 'are concrete proof that real people who can be identified and portrayed died in the camp'.

'Memorials can take different forms', writes Hanan Nermut in a contribution to the Association for Jewish Refugees journal:

> In my case, it is my clothes hanger. It has lived quietly in my wardrobe for many, many years, among all the wire and plastic hangers. This one – for me a very special one – is made of wood with a faded pink silk cover with black lettering saying: Richard Brill, Praha 1, Celetna ul. 18.

The object functions as a container of family-related memories, it helps to recall faces and voices, it has been a witness to historical events, it is, Nermut says, 'only a tiny object, but for me it has always been my private symbol and memorial'.[58] The clothes hanger has become a symbol for the family history, and at the same time a personal means of memory storage. With this example in mind – and the idea that there must be thousands of similar objects connected to as many family histories and migration experiences – I think it would make sense to connect the emerging 'Suitcase Studies' to the study of other containers in which individual and collective experiences of migration have been stored. Suitcases represent a kind of thirdspace or in-between space in which the transformation of self and home 'takes place'. The material object used in the actual act of migration often contained other items of memory storage: photographs and personal documents (letters, diaries about the migration experience – documents that have been termed, in a different context, 'Schreibakte auf der Schwelle', acts of writing on the threshold[59]) – manuscripts, farewell letters (written on the boat, in border stations, in port cities), memorial and yizkor books, songs and poems, but also material objects which often carried an emotional value – a wide and rich field of research for the ethnography of migration.[60] Further research could investigate, on the basis of specific examples, how the individual and the collective memories *store, modify and process* the event and the experience of migration – and how these practices reflect and maybe alter perceptions of places as well: hometowns, cities of transmigration, train stations, ports: everywhere migrants needed, used, and later remembered their suitcases.

Notes

1. Christian Staas, "Letzte Zuflucht. Die Geschichte der jüdischen Auswanderung nach Palästina," *Die Zeit*, February 19, 2009, http://www.zeit.de/zeit-geschichte/2008/04/auswanderung-palaestina (my translation).
2. The book presents 'a migrant story told as a series of wordless images that might seem to come from a long forgotten time. ... With nothing more than a suitcase and a handful of currency, the immigrant must find a place to live, food to eat and some kind of gainful employment'. See http://www.shauntan.net/books/the-arrival.html (accessed January 28, 2012).
3. Irit Rogoff, *Terra Infirma. Geography's Visual Culture* (Milton Park, NY: Routledge 2000), 36.
4. Ibid., 1.
5. Ibid., 36–7.
6. Jan Hinrichsen, "Der Koffer im Museum. Ein Metasymbol für Migration," in *Reisebegleiter*, ed. Claudia Selheim (Nürnberg: Begleitband zur Ausstellung im Germanischen Nationalmuseum, 2010); see also his unpublished MA thesis "Ausgestellter Zwischen-Raum. Musealisierte Koffer als Symbol des 20. Jahrhunderts. Eine Untersuchung im Kontext von Flucht, Vertreibung und Migration" (MA diss., Eberhard Karls Universität Tübingen, Ludwig-Uhland-Institut für Empirische Kulturwissenschaft, 2010).
7. Cf. Joachim Schlör, "'Alte Wege, die wir wandern'. Vagabondage in Repräsentationen des Jüdischen," in *Das Figurativ der Vagondage. Kulturanalysen mobiler Lebensweisen*, ed. Johanna Rolshoven and Maria Maierhofer (Bielefeld: Transcript, 2010), 143–62.
8. The 'Preußen-Ausstellung' of 1981 was curated by Reinhard Rürup, a veteran of German-Jewish history, and my own Doktorvater Gottfried Korff.
9. For the materiality of suitcases and their 'constructedness' as material objects, see Andrea Mihm, *Packend... Eine Kulturgeschichte des Reisekoffers* (Marburg: Jonas Verlag, 2001); Andrea Mihm, *Alle Koffer fliegen hoch! Von der Hartschale zum Weichgepäck; die Ge-schichte der Reisebegleiter* (Berlin: Westermann Kommunikation, 1993).
10. For Australia, a promising PhD dissertation is in preparation. Eureka Henrich's article "Suitcases and Stories: Objects of Migration in Museum Exhibits," *International Journal of the Inclusive Museum* 3, no. 4 (2010): 71–82, http://www.ma2010.com.au/docs/ma2010_henrich.pdf, is part of her thesis, supervised by Dr Grace Karskens at the University of New South Wales. Entitled "Whose Stories are we Telling? Exhibitions of Migration History in Australian Museums, 1986 – 2001," this is a cross-institutional comparative history of immigration exhibitions over the past three decades.
11. http://www.19princeletstreet.org.uk/ (accessed December 4, 2009).
12. http://museumvictoria.com.au/immigrationmuseum/about-us/ (accessed December 4, 2009).

13. http://www.nyc.gov/html/nyc100/html/imm_stories/museum/index.html (accessed December 4, 2009).
14. http://www.dah-bremerhaven.de/english/english.html (accessed January 26, 2012).
15. http://www.ballinstadt.net/BallinStadt_emigration_museum_Hamburg/english_Abenteuer_Auswanderung_Hauptausstellung_im_Auswanderermuseum_BallinStadt_der_Leisurework group_Jens_Nitschke_Erlebnisarchitekt.html (accessed January 26, 2012). The exhibition in Ballinstadt has been heavily criticized because the 'stories' that the puppets tell are not authentic, but rather compiled out of several testimonies in order to create 'typical' stories.
16. http://www.epiz-berlin.de/?Service/Wanderausstellung (accessed December 4, 2009); see also a project http://www.koffer-fuer-berlin.de/text2.htm (accessed January 26, 2012), which refers to the German-Jewish emigration during the 1930s.
17. http://www.migrationmuseum.org/wp-content/uploads/2011/04/100-Images-of-Migration-primary-school-teaching-resource.pdf (accessed January 26, 2012).
18. http://www.migrationheritage.nsw.gov.au/ (accessed December 4, 2009).
19. http://www.ndr.de/kultur/ausstellungen/hamburg/hamburg76.html (accessed December 4, 2009).
20. Cataldo Perri, *Bastimenti*. CD, Squlibri Editore, Roma, 2002.
21. 'Geplant ist eine Ausstellung noch vorhandener Koffer von Emigranten aus aller Welt, mit denen sie während der NS-Zeit Berlin verlassen mussten.'
22. http://www.koffer-fuer-berlin.de/text2.html (accessed December 6, 2009); see also Andrea Mihm, *Packend... Eine Kulturgeschichte des Reisekoffers* and *Alle Koffer fliegen hoch!*
23. Joachim Baur, *Die Musealisierung der Migration. Einwanderungsmuseen und die Inszenierung der multikulturellen Nation* (Bielefeld: Transcript, 2009).
24. Rainer Ohliger has been most active in promoting the idea of a German Migration Museum; see Jan Motte and Rainer Ohliger, "Men and Women with(out) History? Looking for a 'Lieux de Memoire' in Germany's Immigration Society," in *Enlarging European Memory. Migration Movements in Historical Perspective*, ed. Mareike König and Rainer Ohliger (Ostfildern: Thorbecke Verlag, 2006), 147–60.
25. See the programme at http://www.domit.de/pdf/Programm_Inventur_Migration_2009.pdf (accessed December 4, 2009).
26. See the programme at http://www.overseaschineseconfederation.org/events/Conference/STADT.doc (accessed December 4, 2009).
27. "Crisis and Imagination," 11th EASA Biennial Conference, Maynooth/Ireland, August 24–27, 2010, http://www.volkskunde.org/wp/?p=226 (accessed January 28, 2012).
28. "Reading for Child and Youth Care People," The International Child and Youth Care Network 75 (April 2005), http://www.cyc-net.org/cyc-online/cycol-0405-suitcaseproject.html (March 22, 2011).
29. Silke Arnold-de Simine, "Das Museum als Vermittlungsinstanz von Migrationserfahrungen," *German as a Foreign Language* 3 (2008): 55, http://www.gfl-journal.de/3-2008/arnold-de-simine.pdf (accessed January 26, 2012).
30. "Routes, Roads and Landscapes: Aesthetic Practices *en route*, 1750–2015," A KULVER supported research project at the Oslo School of Architecture and Design (Mari Hvattum, Brita Brenna, Beate Elvebakk and Lars Frers), http://routes.no/the-project/ (accessed March 24, 2011).
31. See for the Jewish experience Barbara E. Mann, *Space and Place in Jewish Studies*, Key Words in Jewish Studies, II (New Brunswick, NJ: Rutgers University Press, 2012).
32. See Charlotte Fonrobert's review of three publications connected to the "Makom" project at Potsdam University, "The New Spatial Turn in Jewish Studies," *AJS Review* 33, no. 1 (2009): 155–64.
33. Julia Brauch, Anna Lipphardt, and Alexandra Nocke, eds., *Jewish Topographies: Visions of Space, Traditions of Place*, Heritage, Culture, and Identity Series (London: Ashgate, 2008).
34. Diana Pinto, "Are there Jewish Answers to Europe's Questions?," http://www.paideia-eu.org/PintoAreThereJewishAnswersToEuropesQuestions.pdf (accessed February 23, 2009); Ruth Ellen Gruber, *Virtually Jewish: Reinventing Jewish Culture in Europe* (Berkeley: University of California Press, 2002); see also *Jewish Culture and History* 9, no. 2/3, "Place and Displacements in Jewish History and Memory," (special issue) with sections on "Place, Displacement and Belonging," "Race, Place and Periphery," and "Place, Migration and Memory Works."

35. James Clifford, *Routes. Travel and Translation in the late Twentieth Century* (Cambridge, MA: Harvard University Press, 1997), 66.
36. My research paper "Irgendwo auf der Welt: The Emigration of Jews from Nazi Germany as a Transnational Experience" will be published in a collection on *German Jewry and Transnationalism*, edited by Leslie Morris and Jay Geller. I am also preparing a larger research project on Mapping the Promised Lands that will try to collect and analyze such maps.
37. K. Tölölian, "The Nation State and its Others: In lieu of a Preface," *Diaspora* 1, no. 1 (1991): 5.
38. For a discussion of the act of carrying and its cultural meanings, see the work of an interdisciplinary research group at Mannheim University, 'Homo portans'. Studies in economic and social history as well as a central gender perspective provide information about different aspects of the cultural practice of carrying and transporting objects as a prerequisite for every form of human life, for mobility as well as for stability. See Vanessa Wormer's report about a conference at the Deutsches Hygiene Museum Dresden, May 19–21, 2011, http://hsozkult.geschichte.hu-berlin.de/tagungsberichte/id=3809, and the project homepage http://homo-portans.de/ (accessed January 26, 2012).
39. Gilles Deleuze, "On the Movement-Image," trans. Martin Joughin, *Negotiations: 1972–1990* (New York: Columbia University Press, 1995); Bernhard Waldenfels, *Topographie des Fremden. Studien zur Phänomenologie des Fremden I* (Frankfurt/Main: Suhrkamp, 1997).
40. Edward W. Soja, *Thirdspace, Journeys to Los Angeles and Other Real and. Imagined Places* (Oxford: Blackwell, 1996).
41. Jonathan Boyarin, ed., *Remapping Memory: The Politics of TimeSpace* (Minneapolis: University of Minnesota Press, 1994), Charlotte Fonrobert and Vered Shemtov, "Introduction," *Jewish Social Studies* 11, no. 3, New series (Spring/Summer 2005): 1–8. http://www.muse.jhu.edu/journals/jewish_social_studies/toc/jss11.3.html (accessed December 4, 2009).
42. Michel Foucault, "Of other Spaces" *Diacritics*, 16, no. 1 (Spring, 1986): 22–27.
43. Bridget Elliott and Anthony Purdy, "Man in a Suitcase: Tulse Luper at Compton Verney" (2005), http://www.imageandnarrative.be/inarchive/tulseluper/elliot_purdy.htm (accessed January 28, 2012).
44. See Kerstin Poehl's paper "Beyond the Suitcase: On the Musealization of Migration," presented at the conference "Crossings: The Nexus of Migration and Culture," Queen Mary, University of London, July 1–2, 2010, and her article "Zeigewerke des Zeitgeistes. Migration, ein 'boundary object' im Museum," *Zeitschrift für Volkskunde* 106, no. 2 (2010): 225–46.
45. Shirli Gilbert, "Buried Monuments. Yiddish Songs and Holocaust Memory," *History Workshop Journal* 66, no. 1 (2008): 109; Marie Gibert has organized a conference "Music and Migration" at the Centre for Transnational Studies, University of Southampton, in October 2009.
46. "Editorial," *Musicology*, Belgrade, no. 3 (2003).
47. Fred McCormick, Review of "Voice of the People, Vol. 4," http://www.mustrad.org.uk/vop/654.htm (accessed December 4, 2009).
48. Sergio Piovesan, "I canti dell'emigrazione," http://www.coromarmolada.it/I%20canti%20dell'emigrazione.htm (my translation; accessed December 4, 2009); for Mexican immigration, see Maria Herrera-Sobek, *Northward Bound: The Mexican Immigrant Experience in Ballad and Song* (Bloomington and Indianapolis: Indiana University Press, 1993).
49. Mark Slobin, *Tenement Songs. The Popular Music of the Jewish Immigrants* (Urbana, Chicago and London: The University of Illinois Press, 1982).
50. Seattle's Experience Music Project published an "Elementary Teacher's Guide" to immigration and migration: http://www.empsfm.org/documents/education/13A_Elementary_teacher_guide_English.pdf (accessed December 4, 2009).
51. Arbeitsgruppe Exilmusik, *Lebenswege von Musikerinnen im "Dritten Reich" und im Exil* (Hamburg: von Bockel, 2000); C.D. Krohn et al., eds., *Aspekte der künstlerischen inneren Emigration 1933–1945*, Exilforschung. Ein Internationales Jahrbuch Bd. 10 (München: Edition text+kritik, 1994); Hanns-Werner Heister, Claudia Maurer Zenck, and Peter Petersen, eds., *Musik im Exil. Folgen des Nazismus für die internationale Musikkultur* (Frankfurt am Main: Fischer Taschenbuchverlag, 1993); Horst Weber, ed., *Musik in der Emigration 1933–1945. Verfolgung, Vertreibung, Rückwirkung* (Stuttgart/Weimar: Metzler, 1993);

Habakuk Traber and Emil Weingarten, eds., *Verdrängte Musik. Berliner Komponisten im Exil* (Berlin: Argon, 1987).

52. Ulrich Meurer and Maria Oikonomou, "Fremdbilder – Aspekte geographischer und medialer Bewegung," in *Fremdbilder. Auswanderung und Exil im internationalen Kino* (Bielefeld: Transcript, 2009), 9–33 (my translation).
53. Johannes Moser and Daniella Seidl, eds., *Dinge auf Reisen. Materielle Kultur und Tourismus*, Münchner Beiträge zur Volkskunde, 38 (Münster etc.: Waxmann Verlag, 2009).
54. Doerte Bischoff and Joachim Schlör, eds., *Exilforschung. Ein internationales Jahrbuch*, Band 31/2013: *Dinge des Exils* (München: text + Kritik 2013); see also Peter Jackson, "Commodity Cultures: The Traffic in Things," *Transactions of the Institute of British Geographers* NS 24 (1999): 95–108, and Jane Webster, "Looking for the Material Culture of the Middle Passage", *Journal for Maritime Research* (December 2005), http://www.jmr.nmm.ac.uk/server.php?show=conJmrArticle.209 (accessed December 4, 2009).
55. Joachim Schlör, "'Take down Mezuzah, Remove Name-Plates': The Emigration of Material Objects from Germany to Palestine," in *Jewish Cultural Studies*, vol. 1: *Jewishness: Expression, Identity, and Representation*, ed. Simon J. Bronner (Oxford: The Littmann Library of Jewish Civilization, 2008), 142.
56. See Mariane Brentzel, *Nesthäkchen kommt ins KZ. Eine Annäherung an Else Ury* (Berlin: edition ebersbach, 1993).
57. *Jüdische Zeitung*, February 2008, http://www.j-zeit.de/archiv/artikel.970.html (accessed March 8, 2014).
58. Hana Nermut, "My Private Holocaust Memorial," *AJR Review* (February 2008), http://www.ajr.org.uk/index.cfm/section.journal/issue.Feb08/article=1032 (accessed December 4, 2009).
59. Bernhard Siegert, *Passagiere und Papiere. Schreibakte auf der Schwelle zwischen Spanien und Amerika* (Munich: Wilhelm Fink Verlag, 2006).
60. There are some rare occasions where not only the suitcase as an object has been preserved but also its contents. The regional German daily *Siegener Zeitung* reported that the contents of a suitcase, found at a garage sale or bulk trash and brought to the local archives at Hilchenbach, are now being scrutinized by a local history teacher. She met historian Gideon Greif during a trip to Israel, and he told her that he, as many others, would be interested in every little bit of paper that could help us reconstruct the history of the Holocaust. The small suitcase with the Lloyd label, bears the initials 'C.W.' and belonged to a Jewish lawyer, Dr Curt Waldmann from Breslau. It contains documents and papers relating the story of a man, born in 1883 to a well-established Jewish family, who was married to a non-Jewish wife. Waldmann was banned from his profession and had to work as a street cleaner, his plans to emigrate were unsuccessful, and in February 1945 he took his own life. His widow moved to Hilchenbach as a German refugee from the East and brought the suitcase along. http://www.siegener-zeitung.de/a/398347 (accessed January 26, 2012).

Private archives and public lives: the migrations of Alexander Weissberg and the Polanyi archives

Judith Szapor

Department of History and Classical Studies, McGill University, Montreal, Canada

The archives of the Polanyis, a distinguished family of intellectuals of Hungarian-Jewish origins, are today divided between two continents and three countries. The article traces the history of the family's archives, highlighting the way in which the multiple – and in their respective contents distinct – collections of documents testify to the family's history since the late nineteenth century and the intellectual refugee experience at large. Documents of the family's flight from Hitler's Europe, preserved in the Eva Zeisel Papers, shed light on the details of a little-known episode of the intellectual migration from Nazi-ruled Europe to the United States and help integrate the international network of physics and the Ukrainian Physico-Technological Institute in the Soviet Union in the networks of émigré artists and intellectuals. The article also considers the constructed nature of family archives and the shifting perception of what families consider private or public in their own history and legacy.

Introduction: the archive as biography

Taking their cue from anthropology, historians have recently suggested the biography as a useful metaphor when thinking about archives. This approach is particularly apt when applied to the physical existence of archives, reminding 'us that archives, as objects, are also subjects of history'.[1] Throughout the centuries Jewish archives had been frequently subjected to the destructive forces of history, and archives carried by the refugees from Hitler were no exception. As a result of anti-Semitic legislation in Nazi Germany and the rest of Europe under Fascist and Nazi rule, as well as the bureaucratic requirements of the flight itself, refugees' possessions necessarily included identity documents; but identity was at issue in a broader sense as the documents taken with them served to preserve the identities of individuals and families. In the case of these documentary collections the biography metaphor can be further stretched: along with the refugees, the archive, embodying the legacy of individuals, families, and communities, became a refugee itself.

The size, content, and historical and cultural significance of 'what they saved'[2] may have varied widely, but all refugee archives were similar in one aspect: they have all preserved the documents of the flight itself, thus becoming the imprint of and testament to the process of exile – and rescue – itself. 'When émigrés wrote each other letters', remarked the German writer Carl Zuckmayer, 'especially between the years 1938 and 1945, it always concerned the rescue of friends and colleagues who had not yet escaped mortal danger'.[3] Letters asking for (and, at the other end, relating the difficulties of providing) money, affidavits, visas, fares for the passage, letters announcing safe arrival or the closing of borders and options, became the familiar staple of all refugee archives. If the content and even the style of these letters were largely predetermined by their purpose, the writers and addressees of letters revealed the social and professional status and networks of the refugees, thus providing an extremely valuable source for historians.

American scholars came to realize the significance of the intellectual refugee influx for American life early on.[4] Initiatives such as the Harvard project that resulted in the over 260 essays written on 'My Life in Germany Before and After January 30, 1933' were designed to mine the refugee experience, collecting personal information for scholarly gain.[5] The Harvard project and subsequent scholarly works on the refugee intellectuals fundamentally shifted the boundaries – and understanding – of private experience and its value for public interest and scholarship. The autobiographical essays produced for the Harvard project described deeply personal experiences. Yet, in a marked contrast with previous cohorts of migrants to the United States, their writers were, for the most part, highly educated intellectuals and professionals who were most likely aware of the historical significance of their private experiences. Their testimonies thus illustrated, *avant la lettre*, the personal becoming political and the fluidity of the boundaries between the public and the private.

The documents, photos, and objects Jewish refugees carried with them into emigration were repositories of intimate family lore. They had been carefully selected to preserve a family's legacy and proudest achievements but also had become reminders of lost family members, relatives, and friends. Traumatic memories, survivor's guilt, and the demands of creating a new life combined to relegate these collections to the bottom of drawers or into boxes hidden in closets. It was often left to the second and third generation of Jewish émigrés to reconstruct family histories from these clues. Writers of this genre had come to redefine the boundaries of the private and public, recognizing the historically significant, common émigré narrative in their own personal quest.[6]

My research and the resulting monograph on the Polanyi family benefited immensely from the private Polanyi archive, today called the Eva Zeisel Papers, in New York City.[7] Among other findings, the archive extensively documented the flight of the extended Polanyi family, offering a striking illustration of the process described above: how documents describing a single family's flight transcend their private significance, revealing the common challenges faced by Central European émigré intellectuals, and shedding light on the networks of Central European intellectuals.

The Polanyis' itineraries – leading from Hungary, Germany, Italy, and Austria to Western Europe, Great Britain, the United States, Brazil, and Cuba, among others – mirrored some of the common paths of the Hitler émigrés. In addition to these itineraries, extensively covered in the scholarship on the intellectual migration, the Eva Zeisel Papers in New York also revealed another, less well-trodden path, leading to the Soviet Union and, specifically, to the Ukrainian Physico-Technical Institute (UFTI) in Kharkov (today Kharkiv in Ukraine).[8]

The linchpin between the Polanyis and UFTI in the Soviet Union was the physicist Alexander Weissberg, the first husband of Eva Zeisel – the latter the keeper of the Polanyi family archive after whom the Zeisel Papers have been named. The marriage to Weissberg and the Soviet interlude – to be described below – was a significant episode in the long, legendary, storied life of Eva Zeisel and as such figured prominently in my biography.[9] The story of Weissberg and UFTI illustrated the strength and solidarity of the international network of physicists. It also hinted at the close links between the networks of scientists, intellectuals, and artists, built in interwar Central Europe, and the way these links became instrumental during their forced migration. While their role in the extended Polanyi family's emigration was an important element and as such figured in my account of the family's history, other aspects of Weissberg's life story as well as UFTI's history and place in the history of physics, would have strained the boundaries of a study primarily concerned with Laura Polanyi.

This avenue of scholarly exploration also brought to light some of the dilemmas of dealing with private lives and document collections. What may have been an exciting discovery to the historian, highlighting an important episode in the history of twentieth-century physics and, by extension, the intellectual migration of the 1930s, was an intensely private matter to the Polanyis. Several members of the family had lived in the Soviet Union, most notably Eva Zeisel who spent five years there, 16 months of it in prison. What and how much to reveal of their experiences was a justifiably private decision but also one that has not remained constant since the family's immigration to the United States – and over this time period influenced scholarly access to the documents in the family archive.

In the following I first provide an outline of the history of the multiple Polanyi archives, before turning to the ways in which they provide a window into the history of UFTI, the international network of physics, and the latter's role in the broader intellectual migration from Hitler. All this necessitates a brief introduction to the Polanyis, for neither UFTI's human dimension nor its historical context can be interpreted without the rich and multi-dimensional web of networks whose axis was the Polanyi family.

The Polanyis and the Polanyi archives: a short biography

Fond 212 in the Manuscript Division of the Hungarian National Library designates the Polanyi Collection, containing many thousands of documents.[10] It is among the more popular destinations of the Manuscript Division, especially so with foreign scholars, from Great Britain to Japan. This interest is due to the Polanyi family's prominent place in the Central European intellectual elite. From the legendary Budapest salon of Cecile Wohl, the family's matriarch, to her sons' involvement in left-wing student movements, scores of family members exemplified the Monarchy's assimilated Jewish bourgeoisie and their energetic participation in the progressive intellectual, political, and artistic movements of the *fin de siècle*. Following the failed Hungarian revolutions in 1918–1919, several Polanyis joined the ranks of Hungarian exiles in Austria, Weimar Germany, and Italy and extended the family's networks into Central Europe and Great Britain. Members of the family were related, married to, or maintained close friendships with such prominent intellectuals of the interwar period as Arthur Koestler, Anna Seghers, Georg Lukács, Leopold Szondi, Alfred Adler, Emil Lederer, Paul Lazarsfeld, and Leo Szilárd, to mention but a few.[11]

Most of the visitors to the Polanyi Collection would pursue their scholarly interest in the two Polanyi brothers, the economist Karl (1886–1964) and the physico-chemist turned philosopher Michael (1891–1976). They both left behind their own extensive archives, deposited, respectively, at Concordia University in Montreal and the University of Chicago Library, with most of the documents relating to their working lives and legacies.[12] The Polanyi Collection at the Hungarian National Library in Budapest, however, is the largest and most comprehensive in terms of the family's history, with documents going back to the mid-nineteenth century. This division clearly shows that there had been an organizing principle at work, dividing the papers of this extremely literate family into separate archives and distinguishing between the professional legacies of the two brothers on the one hand and the historical significance and legacy of the family on the other.

Indeed, credit for the collection's existence goes to Laura Polanyi (1882–1959), the elder sister of Karl and Michael, and the family historian in more than one sense. Laura was born in Vienna in 1882 and grew up in Budapest as the eldest of five children born to the railway engineer and entrepreneur Mihály Pollacsek and the salonnière Cecile Wohl. She was the first woman to earn a doctorate in history at Budapest University, in 1908; she was also a feminist and educator.[13] In 1904 Laura married the textile manufacturer Sándor Stricker; the couple lived in Budapest and Vienna with their three children. Laura visited her eldest son, Michael Stricker and her daughter, the designer Eva Stricker (later Zeisel) in the early 1930s when they both worked in the Soviet Union, and stayed with them for extended periods. When Eva was caught up in Stalin's terror and imprisoned, Laura was instrumental in galvanizing the efforts of family and friends to free her daughter. In 1938 she followed her three children and their own families to the safety of the US. Once in the United States, Laura devoted her energies to helping several other members of the extended family escape from Europe. She even managed to revive her professional career as a historian before her death in 1959.

The Polanyis made a remarkable transition from the Central European intellectual elite to the highest reaches of American academia, professions, and the arts: it is no accident that in her book on the *Illustrious Immigrants* Laura Fermi devoted almost three pages to this 'exceptionally talented Hungarian family', as an illustration of 'the Secret of the Hungarians' – that is their extraordinary success in emigration.[14] While Michael Polanyi, already a leading scientist, became a distinguished philosopher in England, and Karl Polanyi would become an influential professor of economics at Columbia University, the next generation's outstanding success story belonged to their niece, Laura's daughter, Eva Zeisel (1906–2011), who became one of the leading designers of the twentieth century.[15]

How did the family's documents, preserved today at the Hungarian National Library, survive such a series of displacements? The archival material itself offers clues that as the responsible eldest sibling and a trained historian, Laura took on the role of the family archivist. Documents she had preserved show her assuming responsibility for collecting evidence attesting to the family's long-standing roots in Austria-Hungary, keeping copies of the correspondence between members of the extended family, and providing documentation when needed.[16] The annals of the refugees from Hitler's Europe contain many examples of document collections and photographs, rescued at great personal risk.[17] Like that of their fellow refugees, the Polanyis' odyssey had its share of tragedies and close escapes. But unlike the German Jewish refugees who were forced to leave everything behind to escape with their lives, the Polanyis benefited from their familial networks in Hungary, left relatively intact until 1939, and Michael Polanyi's established position in Britain from 1933. Judged by its volume, the family archive must have been shipped, rather than carried, to America, along with the furniture, books, and art, including the family portraits by noted Hungarian artists. Still, to assemble, maintain, and transfer such a vast volume of documents was no ordinary feat: the collection contains ample evidence for the Polanyis' roots and their generations' path into the Central European intellectual elite, along with samples of their voluminous correspondence, and documentation of various family members' achievements in a wide range of intellectual and artistic endeavors. In other words, the collection preserved everything the family's future historians would possibly need – Laura Polanyi had a strong sense of her family's significance and a firm curatorial hand in shaping the collection attesting to it.

The papers arrived in New York shortly before Europe became engulfed in the war. They rested more or less undisturbed there until the arrival of the Hungarian literary scholar Erzsébet Vezér in the mid-1970s. Vezér was on a mission to rescue the legacy of the Hungarian *fin de siècle*, a prodigiously fertile but by then largely forgotten period of literary, artistic, and political activity. She traveled to Western Europe and the United States, interviewing Hungarian émigrés, surviving members of Georg Lukács's Sunday Society, avant-garde artists, and psychoanalysts, among others.[18] Vezér also visited Eva Zeisel and between 1976 and 1983 arranged for the transfer of the bulk of the family's document collection to the Hungarian National Library.[19]

In 1994, armed with letters of introduction, I went to New York to interview Eva Zeisel. By then I had already been familiar with the Polanyi Collection in the Hungarian National Library; I had also read Zeisel's extensive profile in *The New Yorker*, at the time the only available outline of the family's history in English.[20] Prompted by Vezér, I also knew of the existence of documents kept by the family, not to be found in the Hungarian National Library collection. Yet it was only near the end of my visit that I realized the full extent of this private archive. And it was only by exploring the many boxes of documents in New York and comparing the two collections that the lines dividing the public and the private archives started to emerge: the documents chronicling the extended family's flight from Europe remained almost without exception in the private archive.

The Polanyis, Alexander Weissberg, and the physicists' network

It was in the correspondence in the New York archive that I found letters relating to Alexander Weissberg; it was a name I had already encountered in the memoirs of Arthur Koestler and Manès Sperber, who both rubbed elbows with the Polanyis in the intellectual and artistic circles of Budapest, Vienna, and Berlin.[21] Alexander Weissberg, Eva Zeisel's first husband, an engineer and physicist, was a member of the international network of physics. As such, he was one of the links through which the Polanyis were connected to the physicists' network, although by no means the only one. Laura's younger brother, Michael Polanyi, had established himself as a member of the 'Hungarian Galaxy' of brilliant scientists, and resided in Berlin from 1920. When Michael Polanyi's niece, Eva Stricker, a ceramicist and designer, moved to Berlin in the summer of 1930, she set up her studio near the famed *Romanisches Café*, the epicenter of left-wing Berlin bohemia. Eva and her brother – Michael Stricker – shared a large two-story apartment and gave 'parties studded with writers, actors, even Nobel Prize winners'.[22] 'I do not know how we collected all these people', Eva Zeisel wrote in her memoirs, 'but there were various nuclei of friends and relatives who brought their friends.'[23] Among the younger physicists Michael Polanyi brought to Eva's parties were Fritz Houtermans (1903–1966), Georg Placzek (1905–1955), Victor Weisskopf (1908–2002), and Alexander Weissberg (1901–1964); in the next few years all of them would develop links to UFTI.[24] Another frequent guest at Eva's parties was the journalist Arthur Koestler, a childhood friend from their days as fellow pupils in Eva's mother Laura's experimental kindergarten in Budapest.[25] The sociologist Hans Zeisel also attended the parties – he would eventually become Eva's second husband. Other guests, mentioned in Eva's memoir, further proved the point that the 'nuclei' or networks of left-wing Central European writers, scientists, social scientists, and artists were connected by multiple ties; not only were they not separated by academic or artistic fields but, as in the Polanyis' case, they were all, so to speak, in the family.

In 1931 Alex Weissberg, a member of the Austrian Communist Party, was recruited to work in the Soviet Union as a foreign specialist at the newly established Ukrainian Physico-Technical Institute in Kharkov (today Kharkiv), then the capital of Soviet Ukraine. A few months later, Eva, driven by curiosity 'to see what was behind the mountain' joined him as his fiancée – an arrangement of convenience in order to receive a visa.[26] They later married and separated soon after, and Eva moved to Leningrad and Moscow to pursue a career as a leading designer in the Soviet porcelain industry. In 1932–1933 Arthur Koestler traveled in the Soviet Union, commissioned by the Comintern to write a book on his travels in the Soviet Union (and personifying the term 'fellow-traveler'); he stayed at the Weissbergs' flat in Kharkov on several occasions. For the following two decades, Koestler remained a crucial witness and participant in his friends' saga.

In the spring of 1936 Eva, then living in Moscow, was arrested, accused of a plot to assassinate Stalin; she subsequently spent 16 months in prison before her release in the autumn of 1937. Meanwhile, Weissberg and his colleague Houtermans were arrested in the spring and winter of 1937, respectively, and spent nearly three years in prison, until they were both handed over to the Gestapo in early 1940. While Weissberg's fate – narrated in detail in Arthur Koestler's memoir, *The Invisible Writing* – was known to Cold War specialists and historians of physics, Eva's story remained subject to her request for privacy. *The Invisible Writing*, the second volume of Koestler's autobiography, was published in 1954; it charted the writer's path from Communism in the early 1930s to crusading anti-Communism by the mid-1940s. In it, Koestler depicted his visits with the Weissbergs, and reported in detail on Alex's subsequent fate, as paradigmatic to his own disenchantment with Communism; yet he mentioned Eva's fate only in passing, along with the hint that she 'was to supply, from her own tragic experience, the background material of a future novel, *Darkness at Noon*'.[27] Unlike Weissberg, Eva was identified only by her first name; and it was well after Koestler's death that she publicly acknowledged the nature of 'her own tragic experience'.

Weissberg too would write an account of his years in the Soviet Union: *The Conspiracy of Silence – The Accused* in the American edition – was among the first detailed eyewitness reports of the Great Terror.[28] It was published in 1951 with an introduction by Koestler; at her request, Eva was mentioned throughout the book under a pseudonym.[29] Eva wrote a short memoir of her prison experience as well. She shared it with a select few but was conflicted about publishing it: according to her daughter, she was 'still traumatized by the memory as well as being afraid that the NKVD would come after her in the U.S.'[30] This changed in 1987, when Eva Zeisel allowed the author of her *New Yorker* profile to quote extensively from the memoir.[31] Interest in Eva Zeisel's oeuvre as a designer revived and publications about her multiplied, and a brief outline of her 'Russian adventure' became part of her standard biography.[32] Shortly after Eva Zeisel's death in December 2011 aged 105, her *Soviet Prison Memoir* was published in an e-book, lovingly edited by her daughter and son-in-law. The centerpiece of the book is the memoir, framed by original documents relating to her case and essays from experts. One of the essays in the volume mentions Weissberg's courageous efforts, along with those of Eva's mother, to free her from prison.[33] But, as is expected from a volume designed to pay tribute to Eva Zeisel, the focus is on the artist; the flip side of the story, including the equally heroic efforts of Eva and Laura Polanyi, two years later, to save Weissberg from Stalin's prison, remain in the shadows.

These efforts, documented by correspondence, today in the Eva Zeisel Papers, represent a missing link, connecting Weissberg's individual fate with the history of UFTI as a way station for the refugee physicists and, in turn, adding a new perspective to the history of the intellectual migration from Hitler's Europe. The correspondence of the Polanyis with members of the international network of physics in their efforts to rescue Weissberg, one of their own, add an important case study to the well-documented solidarity of the community of scientists. It also offers a rarely considered aspect to the history of the intellectual migration: the connection of the network of physicists with other networks of Central European intellectuals before and during their escape from Hitler's and Stalin's Europe.

UFTI and the traveling seminar

The Ukrainian Physico-Technical Institute in Kharkov (today Kharkiv in Ukraine) was founded in 1928 as part of the Soviet expansion of scientific and industrial research. Established as a satellite of the Leningrad Institute of Physics, the leading Soviet academic institution in its field, UFTI soon became important in its own right as a flagship institution of Stalin's First Five-Year Plan.[34] Along with the Leningrad Institute, it was also the institution most closely associated with the short period of relative openness in Soviet–Western academic relations. Between 1928 and 1933, and to a lesser degree until 1935, the Soviet Union recruited so-called foreign experts to ease the tremendous shortage of technical professionals and highly educated skilled workers. Incidentally, after Hitler's rise to power, the Institute became a temporary haven for refugee physicists from Central Europe. UFTI's community of Soviet and foreign scientists, connected by previous friendships and collegial ties established in Berlin and other European centers of physics, created a short-lived scientific idyll, shattered by Stalin's terror. Around 1936 the wave of repression breached the previously protected walls of UFTI; and although some of the foreigners managed to leave in time and found refuge in European countries or the US, many of the Russian and even some of the foreign scientists were arrested. This turn signaled the end of the era in which the Soviet Union was a possible destination for scientists seeking refuge from Hitler's Germany and, eventually, Nazi Europe.

UFTI was little more than a blueprint when foreign physicists and engineers were invited to visit and stay on. By the early 1930s UFTI had the highest percentage of foreigners employed among Soviet academic institutions. In this, previously established connections and serendipity all played a role. Among the directors of newly founded UFTI were a number of young physicists, including Lev Shubnikov (1901–1937), Aleksandr Leipunsky (1903–1972), and Kiril Sinelnikov (1901–1966); all beneficiaries of Rockefeller scholarships, they had been trained at the European hubs of physics, from Copenhagen to Heidelberg and Cambridge. Likewise, Lev Landau (1908–1968), considered the most brilliant young Soviet physicist, had spent the better part of the years 1928 to 1930 abroad on Rockefeller scholarships. All of them built personal ties to members of the 'traveling seminar', the network of physicists first described by Charles Weiner.[35] This short window of relatively open relations with the West in the Soviet Union coincided with the emergence of the new theoretical physics and would enable Soviet physics to progress during the next 20 years of Stalinist dictatorship and international isolation.[36] These professional and personal relationships, formed during their shared apprenticeships between young Soviet and Western physicists, would become the basis for the recruitment of Western physicists to UFTI. After 1933 the 'traveling seminar' turned into a veritable rescue operation and, by settling many of the refugee scientists in the United States, eventually shifted the center of physics from Central Europe to the US.[37] Meanwhile, the coinciding self-inflicted isolation of the Soviet government resulted in severing the ties between Soviet and European physics, thus excluding the Soviet Union from the possible havens for refugee scientists.

Soviet propaganda in Western Europe praising the achievements of the First Five-Year Plan was set against the backdrop of the Great Depression in the West. To young European physicists, the invitation to work at a newly built Soviet institution, and in leading positions no less, must have been highly appealing at a time when academic positions had become increasingly sparse and Hitler began his rise in Germany. The Nazi takeover in January 1933 further raised the currency of UFTI and other Soviet institutions, especially for those who were in immediate danger in Germany because of their Jewish background and/or leftist politics. All this contributed to the high number of foreign experts working at UFTI.

Despite recent accounts of Soviet physics, describing the connections between Soviet and international physics in detail,[38] UFTI does not figure in the scholarship on the European refugees. Grounding the history of UFTI and its contingent of 'foreign experts' in this broader context offers an important corrector to the history of the intellectual migration in the Hitler era, particularly the migration of physics from Europe to the US.

UFTI: a brief history

A general history of UFTI is outside of the scope of this article. What is important to note in this context is that the new institute's scientific leaders were exceptionally young, almost all of them in their late twenties. They were dispatched from Leningrad to a construction site in the Ukrainian steppe on the outskirts of Kharkov, complete with blowing dust storms and water and electricity shortages. Despite its designation as the capital of Soviet Ukraine until 1934, Kharkov and its cultural offerings could hardly be mentioned on the same page with Kiev, the historical Ukrainian capital, let alone Leningrad, the most cultured city of the Soviet Union.

In exchange, the young scientists were entrusted with responsibilities rarely assigned to scholars of their age. UFTI was designed to be a complex for basic and applied physical research: the Soviet government allocated significant funds toward the construction of the site and imported state-of-the-art technology. Despite the tremendous economic and political hurdles, including the 1932 famine inflicted on Ukraine by Stalin's collectivization campaign, some of the departments opened in 1930 even as construction continued through the 1930s. A first-rate low-temperature laboratory, the pride of the Institute, was operational in 1932, and in the same year UFTI undertook the building of a Van de Graaff generator, at the time the largest in the world.[39]

In 1932 Lev Landau was appointed head of UFTI's Theoretical Department as well as a chair of Kharkov University's General Physics Department, and from then on his name became synonymous with theoretical physics in the Soviet Union. By the mid-1930s UFTI became second only to the Leningrad Physico-Technical Institute in terms of scientific output. Consensus among historians of Soviet science is that UFTI was more severely hit by the Great Terror of 1937–1938 than perhaps any other institution in the Soviet sciences.[40] Why was UFTI singled out among the Soviet scientific institutions for such persecution? It is safe to conclude that two factors combined to seal UFTI's fate: first, its close ties to Leningrad, a special target of Stalin's wrath, and, second, the relatively high number of foreigners and Soviet scientists trained abroad employed within its walls, targeted during the period of xenophobic hysteria.

From its first days, while experiencing great difficulties in completing and equipping the sites, the staff of UFTI lived in anticipation of its future greatness. Foreign visitors, a rarity in the Soviet Union in those days, were a staple of UFTI's daily life: Van de Graaff visited twice after 1932 to supervise the installation of the largest generator at the time, and such luminaries of twentieth-century physics as Max Born, Paul Dirac, and Niels Bohr visited, some of them several times. Paul Ehrenfest and Piotr Kapitza both served as scientific advisors to the new institute.[41] Another personal link between the West and Soviet science was represented by Piotr Kapitza (1894–1984). Kapitza's training in Cambridge with Rutherford and his subsequent tenure at the Cavendish Laboratory eventually led to the invitation and extended stays of Leipunsky and Sinelnikov, both future leaders of UFTI, in Cambridge.

At UFTI's founding, some of the appointed leaders of the new institution were still in Western Europe, including the director, Ivan Obreimov (1894–1981), the head of the low-temperature department, Lev Shubnikov, and his wife, the physicist Olga Trapeznikova.[42] These Western tenures, however short, were instrumental in the recruitment of the first Western physicists to work at UFTI.

'Weimar on the Donets'

The first Western physicist hired by UFTI, Walter Elsasser (1904–1991), owed his frustrating nine-month-long stay in Kharkov to the delays of construction that extended the director Obreimov's stay in Berlin. Elsasser worked at the Polytechnic School in Berlin-Charlottenburg as a lowly part-time lab assistant, a job his friend Fritz Houtermans procured for him. He was just about to abandon science when he received an offer he found impossible to refuse. In his memoir, Elsasser described the conversation and his reasons for accepting the offer:

> Some time late in 1929 the telephone rang: 'This is Obreimov. I am in Berlin and would like to see you.' Obreimov was an experimental physicist who had been in Leiden at the same time as I; and since we stayed at the same rooming house, we had become well acquainted. He told me that he had been made director of the Ukrainian Physico-Technical Institute in Kharkov, a large industrial town in the Ukraine. ... Would I be interested in coming to Kharkov for a year as a 'technical specialist' under a suitable contract. Half of my salary would be paid in rubles that could be not taken out of Russia, the other half in marks or any other currency convertible on the world market. The sum he mentioned would have been generous for a reasonably experienced practical engineer; for me it was princely. He also informed me that I was the first non-Russian to be associated with the Institute, so it was a thoroughly experimental and challenging undertaking ... After a short hesitation I agreed. Although it might not be beneficial to my career as a scientist – and ultimately it wasn't – it offered both a new possibility of escaping from Germany and a great adventure. By then, with the large American stock market crash which everybody had heard of, the employment situation in the West was bound to deteriorate.[43]

Elsasser found UFTI little more than a glorified construction site and cut short his stay. Shortly after he left for Germany, two more Western scientists arrived. The first was Alexander Weissberg; he had left an uninspiring position as an assistant instructor at the Berlin-Charlottenburg Polytechnic Institute.[44] Weissberg was introduced to Obreimov by Houtermans, his friend from Vienna and Berlin.[45] Weissberg was assigned a managerial role in the construction of the low-temperature laboratory and his sunny temperament proved to be singularly suited to dealings with Soviet bureaucracy. In addition, he initiated the publication and became editor of the *Physikalische Zeitschrift der Sowietunion*, another sign that – at least in science and for a limited period – the Soviets were intent on opening windows to the West. The journal, published between 1932 and 1937, provided Soviet physicists with a chance to publish in German and English.[46]

In the summer of 1931, Weissberg was back in Vienna on holiday, with the mission to find and hire experimentalists. Friends recommended Martin Ruhemann.[47] The British-born Ruhemann moved to Germany as a young man. His German wife, Barbara, was also a physicist.[48] Ruhemann was no Communist: Weissberg recruited him not because of his political leanings but his excellent reputation as an experimentalist. Ruhemann worked in the low-temperature lab and in 1935 he and Weissberg proposed a plan for a new low-temperature research station, to develop the local nitrogen industry and other branches of the Soviet chemical industry.[49] Between 1935 and 1937, Ruhemann was the prospective scientific director of this large, new development, with Weissberg as director and manager of the construction.[50]

Weissberg's description of Ruhemann's initial reaction to the living and working conditions in Kharkov, followed by his gradual change of heart, is illuminating:

> When he first came to the Soviet Union in 1932 the country was experiencing the worst year since the end of the civil war. At first he and his wife were always on the point of leaving. All they could see was chaos, poverty and hunger. ... He had never thought much about the significance of social revolutions but once in the Soviet Union he grasped what was really at stake and was swept up in a new and larger movement than he had ever known before.[51]

Fritz Houtermans who arrived in 1935 had been a Communist since the 1920s. He was a legendary figure in physicist circles, the subject – and himself a famous raconteur – of countless anecdotes. His eventful personal and professional trajectory in many ways encapsulates the themes of migration and exile. Houtermans was an assistant at the *Technische Hochschule* in Berlin but, as a known Communist, he fled Germany in early 1933 to take up an industrial position in England.[52] He met Leipunsky, the Leningrad nuclear physicist and the new head of the nuclear physics department at UFTI, at Cambridge during 1934–1935; he was one of the last Soviet physicists allowed to go abroad. Leipunsky talked Houtermans into taking a position at UFTI, a decision that, according to the eternally joking Houtermans, was equally influenced by the appeal of the offer and his aversion to English food.[53]

Another Western arrival in 1935, the Hungarian Laszlo Tisza, represented a younger generation. His connections to the physics network, although more recent, were sufficient to get him to Kharkov.[54] Tisza was trained in Gottingen and Leipzig and then, as a young, naïve sympathizer, was jailed in Hungary for Communist activities in 1932–1933. Seeing no prospects in either Hungary or Nazi Germany, he accepted the advice of Edward Teller (1908–2003), his good friend and former schoolmate, and Georg Placzek, both of whom recommended him to Lev Landau.[55] In the summer of 1934, Tisza attended the theoretical conference organized at UFTI and returned in January 1935 as Landau's doctoral student.

Tisza's experience as the only non-Russian member of Landau's handpicked group of students was unique. For the next two and a half years he worked with one of the most charismatic figures of twentieth-century physics. In Tisza's memory, UFTI was preserved in its last hour of glory as a utopian site, whose blissful isolation from the outside world – including the signs of the approaching Terror – was highly conducive to theoretical physics: 'UFTI was a miraculous place. I never encountered anything like it before or after. For me the most important w[ere] Landau and his group. In spite of my altogether different background I got very well integrated. [...] They were totally friendly to foreigners. (This was to change in 1937.)'[56]

Years after my interview with Tisza, he provided a more detailed but equally idyllic picture of life at UFTI: intense scientific life there was accompanied by skiing and swimming trips, parties with dancing and singing, and amateur productions of Chekhov one-act plays. It was 'a golden period during which the life of the Landau group was sheltered from political events going on outside. This splendid isolation was to end in the fall of 1936'.[57]

Weissberg's memoir confirmed the sense of relative safety and protection from the political storm brewing outside the walls of the Institute. He wrote: 'until the beginning of 1935, UFTI was still an oasis of freedom in the desert of Stalinist despotism. ... We lived together in a separate community on the territory of the Institute and we had very little to do with outsiders.'[58]

UFTI's mix of colorful personalities and well-traveled young Soviet and Western physicists recreated the intellectual spirit and camaraderie of Copenhagen and Berlin of the 1920s. Tisza remembered an informal circle whose members transcended national boundaries and socialized outside the Institute. The circle consisted of Western employees of UFTI, including the Weissbergs, the Houtermans (Houtermans's wife, Charlotte Riefenstahl, was a Gottingen-trained PhD in physics), and the Ruhemanns, as well as Landau, Shubnikov and his physicist wife Trapeznikova, and a few other Soviet physicists.[59] Nearly all of them were Jewish but this seemed to carry little significance. Much more important was their shared commitment to science, the Institute, and the Soviet experiment. This social circle predated the Kharkov days and, in many ways, kept alive the cultural openness of Berlin and was reminiscent of the Houtermans' Berlin gatherings from the old days, *'Eine Kleine Nachtphysik'*.[60] Kharkov, although promoted to the capital of Soviet Ukraine, bore very little resemblance to glittering Berlin at the height of the Weimar period. Yet as the news of the Nazi takeover reached Kharkov, the Berlin preserved in the memory of UFTI's 'foreign experts' had increasingly taken on the shape of a mirage.[61] Their small circle, isolated from the outside world but also of shared memories, interests, and values, became the closest substitute to their former world that was crumbling in their absence.

In many respects 1934 was a crucial year for Soviet physicists. It was the time of Landau's last visit, after long delays, to Copenhagen.[62] The winds were changing: in the summer of the same year, Piotr Kapitza, back in Moscow on his annual visit from Cambridge, was forbidden to return.[63] George Gamow, Landau's friend from Leningrad and Copenhagen, read the signs correctly and defected to the West in the same year.[64]

I left the crucial testimony of Viktor Weisskopf to the last; the Viennese physicist visited UFTI twice and, between his six-month stay in 1932 and a shorter visit in 1936, he keenly observed the changes. On his first journey to the Soviet Union, Weisskopf was invited to work with Landau and had old friends already at UFTI, including Weissberg and his wife, Eva, whose parties he had frequented in Berlin.[65] In 1932 Weisskopf was eager to leave Berlin where he felt the political situation becoming too 'disagreeable' for people of leftist leanings. He needed a position to tide him over for only a few months, before he was to take up a Rockefeller fellowship in Copenhagen in the autumn of 1932.[66] His reaction to the heroic project of building socialism in one country was the opposite of Ruhemann's: he had come as a sympathizer but crossed the border to Poland with great relief.

Four years later, in 1936, he returned as a refugee from Germany to consider an offer from Kiev University for a full professorship as well as Kapitza's invitation for a position in his Moscow Institute. Accompanied by Georg Placzek, by then also a refugee in search of a position, they 'left for the USSR without any illusions'. Moreover, Weisskopf added, 'what we found was even more dispiriting that what we had expected. We were instantly and sharply aware of an atmosphere of fear and terror and … quickly convinced that a job in Russia, even under the most generous of terms, would have been most problematic'.[67]

Although in Weisskopf's experience the fear of Moscow in the winter of 1936 had not yet penetrated Kharkov, he found it as a 'sort of a receptacle of refugees, either depression refugees or Nazi refugees'.[68] The Western physicists there were 'either communists, half-communists or non-communists who just went there because it was the only place where you could stay alive'.[69] His comments underline the unintended, added cruelty in the timing of the Great Terror: just when physicists fleeing Hitler's Europe would have needed it the most, a potential escape route to the Soviet Union closed in front of them.

Soon after Weisskopf and Placzek left Kharkov, the Terror struck at full force. Weissberg, one of its survivors and chroniclers, drew up the following balance sheet of UFTI's losses as they stood in May 1938:

> Our Institute had eight departments, each headed by a capable man. And what's the situation now? The head of the laboratory for crystallography, Obreimov, is under arrest, and so is the head of the low-temperatures laboratory, Shubnikov. The head of the second low-temperatures laboratory, Ruhemann, has been deported [expelled from the Soviet Union]. The head of the laboratory for atom-splitting, Leipunsky is under arrest, and so is the head of the x-ray department, Gorsky, the head of the department for theoretical physics, Landau, and the head of the experimental low-temperatures station, myself.[70]

The physicists' network in action

Weissberg was arrested in March 1937 and not heard from again until April 1940 when, after having been transferred from Soviet to German custody and a couple of months in the Gestapo's Lublin prison, he surfaced in German-occupied Cracow. In April 1940 he sent a telegram to the aunt of Eva in Budapest.[71] Eva by then had been released from Soviet prison, divorced Weissberg and married Hans Zeisel, and, along with her mother, husband, and her two brothers and their families, settled in the United States. All of this happened while Weissberg himself had been in Soviet prison, cut off from the outside world. He was similarly unaware of the extraordinary efforts by the Polanyis and the physicists' network to have him released.

In September 1937, upon her release from prison and the Soviet Union, Eva joined her brothers and mother in Vienna. A few months later, in March 1938 she escaped from Nazi Vienna and met up with Koestler in London. The experiences of her captivity and interrogation in Soviet prison found their way into Koestler's *Darkness at Noon*, to be published in 1941. Reciprocating Weissberg's courageous attempts to free her, she mobilized her uncle, Michael Polanyi, to activate the physicists' network, including Albert Einstein, to vouch for Weissberg and Houtermans' innocence and ask for their release.[72] In Paris, Georg Placzek and Koestler prepared a telegram signed by three French Nobel laureates, Joliot Curie, Irene Curie, and Jean Perrin, which was sent to Stalin, protesting at the two physicists' arrest.[73] It will never be possible to determine the exact degree to which these actions influenced the fate of the two physicists; but it can be reasonably assumed that the international attention had at the very least helped to keep them alive. This is not to say that everyone was prepared or able to help: Felix Bloch, the Nobel laureate by then settled in Stanford, was at pains to explain to Eva how his American colleagues, upon learning that the two physicists were Communist Party members, declined all assistance.[74]

In 1940, when Weissberg miraculously emerged, trapped in German-occupied Crakow, his first communication in three years indicated that he had been well aware of his place in the physicists' community: his telegram to the Polanyi relative in Budapest was a cry for help addressed to his colleagues and friends from Berlin and Kharkov: Weisskopf, Placzek, Houtermans, and Ruhemann.[75] Once again, Eva Zeisel launched frantic efforts to mobilize the physicist network, by then spread over the United States, to obtain affidavits, financial support, and a university position which would have guaranteed Weissberg's exemption from the American visa quota or, failing that, a visa to any other country. Weissberg's letters from Crakow reflected his increasing desperation to leave the trap Europe had become. The two years since 1938 made all the difference: the exits from Hitler's Europe were about to close and even if his friends and colleagues declared their willingness 'to go to the outermost edge of the limited possibilities' they were preoccupied with the urgent need to rescue their own family members.[76]

Epilogue and conclusion

Surviving in occupied Poland between 1940 and 1945 Weissberg was cut off from the Polanyis and his physicist friends until 1946, when he miraculously reappeared in Stockholm, as the representative of a Polish commercial company. Always a sharp observer of political developments, he did not like his chances in post-war Poland under Soviet rule. He moved to Paris and in 1951 he published an account of his years in Kharkov and prison. Despite its merits as one of the earliest eyewitness testimonies and analyses of the Gulag – perhaps because Weissberg refused to toe the anti-Communist line – the book sold poorly and received disappointing reviews. Weissberg never returned to physics; he wrote two more books and made his living as a businessman. He died in Paris in 1964.

For his introduction to his good friend's 'rambling, sprawling, spouting whale of a book' Koestler recycled the chapter written about Weissberg and Eva in *The Invisible Writing*.[77] At the time, as was usually the case with Koestler, he was already on to his latest current political mission: to open the West's eyes to the reality of the evils of Communism. Koestler's anti-Communist crusade as one of the leaders of the Congress for Cultural Freedom brought him to the United States; in 1950 he spoke at Carnegie Hall calling for a confrontation with the Soviet Union. Despite her prison experience, Eva preserved her affection for the Soviet people; she could not share or condone her old friend's passionate anti-Communism. As she explained, she had never been a Communist and thus had no reason to atone for it. In her own words, 'a former non-Communist cannot become a former Communist'.[78] Although Zeisel and Koestler mended their friendship in the last years of Koestler's life, this episode must have had added to Eva's ambiguity about the publication – and potential fallout – of her prison memoir.

As for some of the rest of the characters of the Kharkov days, Fritz Houtermans was also extradited to the Gestapo in 1940. He was kept in a Berlin prison until Max von Laue vouched for him, despite his political past and partially Jewish background. Houtermans was allowed to work in nuclear physics during the war in Germany. Independently of Weissberg, he also wrote an undeservedly little-known account of his prison experience in the Soviet Union with his former cellmate, under the pseudonyms F. Beck and W. Godin, titled *Russian Purge and the Extraction of Confession*.[79] Houtermans moved to Switzerland in 1952 where he became professor at Bern University. He died in 1966.

After the arrest of Weissberg and the removal of Landau, Laszlo Tisza appealed to the Hungarian Legation in Moscow for help. He was allowed to leave the Soviet Union and returned to Budapest, only to have to escape anti-Semitic persecution in Hungary just before World War II. He settled in the United States, where he died in 2009 aged 102, as professor emeritus at MIT.

Eva Zeisel returned to Russia in 2000 at the invitation of the Lomonosov Porcelain Factory in St. Petersburg where she had worked as chief of design in the early 1930s. The visit and Zeisel's following retrospective in 2005 at the Hillwood Museum and Garden in Washington DC that showcased her work from the Soviet period helped to exorcise the ghosts of her past. The long-delayed publication of her prison memoir, after her own passing, completed the process but also signaled the complexities and ambiguities of reconciling the personal and historical legacy of a high-profile family.

By exploring the fate of Weissberg and UFTI's other 'foreign experts' in this article I intended to make a case for incorporating this Soviet way station more fully into the history of the international network of physics, and, in turn, for grounding the physicists' network more firmly in the Central European intellectual, literary, and artistic networks and their migration from Hitler's Europe. None of this history could have been written without the inspiration provided by documents in the Eva Zeisel Papers and, indeed, by Zeisel's own fascinating life story – and without the shift that has made these documents, once considered private, increasingly more accessible to historians. The narrative of the migrations of Alexander Weissberg and, by extension, European physics, an important episode of the intellectual migration, would be incomplete if not for the Polanyi archives and their achievement: the preservation of the complex legacy of the family that had created and sustained them.

Acknowledgements

I am grateful to Jean Richards and the late Eva Zeisel for granting access to the family's documents. Eva Zeisel was most generous in sharing her memories with me. The late Laszlo Tisza graciously responded to my inquiries in writing. Thanks are due to Alexei Kojevnikov for access to his unpublished conference paper and for valuable comments on an earlier draft of this article. I also thank the two anonymous readers for their helpful comments.

Funding

Early research for this article was facilitated by a Social Sciences and Humanities Research Council of Canada postdoctoral fellowship, held at the University of Toronto between 2001 and 2003.

Notes

1. John Randolph, "The Bakunin Family Archive," in *Archive Stories; Facts, Fictions, and the Writing of History*, ed. Antoinette Burton (Durham, NC and London: Duke University Press, 2005), 210.
2. Nancy K. Miller, *What They Saved; Pieces of a Jewish Past* (Lincoln, NE and London: University of Nebraska Press, 2011), demonstrates eloquently that archives should be defined more broadly than collections of written documents: her quest for the family past has been sparked by such clues as photos and a lock of hair.
3. Cited in Debórah Dwork and Robert Jan van Pelt, *Flight from the Reich; Refugee Jews, 1933–1946* (New York and London: W.W. Norton, 2009), 254.
4. Maurice R. Davie, *Refugees in America: Report of the Committee for the Study of Recent Immigration from Europe* (New York and London: Harper and Brothers, 1947), and Donald Peterson Kent, *The Refugee Intellectual: The Americanization of the Immigrants of 1933–1941* (New York: Columbia University Press, 1953), are but two of the notable examples.
5. 'Prize competition held in 1940, on theme "My Life in Germany before and after Jan. 30, 1933." Contest was sponsored by Harvard University; judges included faculty members Gordon Allport, Sidney B. Fay, and Edward Y. Hartshorne.' Harry Liebersohn and Dorothee Schneider, *"My Life in Germany Before and After January 30, 1933": A Guide to a Manuscript Collection at Houghton Library, Harvard University*, Transactions of the American Philosophical Society, vol. 91, Pt. 3 (Philadelphia, 2001), contains a useful introductory essay and summaries of the contributions.
6. Helen Epstein, *Where She Came from, A Daughter's Search for Her Mother's History* (New York: Little Brown, 1997), and Daniel Mendelsohn, *The Lost; A Search for Six of the Six Million* (New York: Harper, 2006), are but two examples of this genre.
7. Judith Szapor, *The Hungarian Pocahontas: The Life and Times of Laura Polanyi Stricker, 1882–1959* (Boulder, CO: East European Monographs, distributed by Columbia University Press, 2005). Formerly in the possession of Laura Polanyi and Eva Zeisel, the family archive has passed on to the care of Eva Zeisel's daughter, Jean Richards. It has been named the Eva Zeisel Archives following the death of Eva Zeisel in 2011. This is the designation used in Eva Zeisel, *A Soviet Prison Memoir*, compiled and edited by Jean Richards and Brent C. Brolin with essays by Karen Kettering and Edward P. Gazur, FBI. (retired) (Amazon, Kindle-book, 2012).
8. In the following I will use Kharkov, in keeping with the spelling of the sources cited.
9. Szapor, *The Hungarian Pocahontas*, especially 81–96.
10. Polányi hagyaték [collection], Hungarian National Széchényi Library, Manuscript Division, fond 212.
11. Szapor, *The Hungarian Pocahontas*, especially chapter 1, "Literate Generations," 9–38.
12. Michael Polanyi Papers, University of Chicago Library, Special Collections Research Center; Karl Polanyi Archive, Karl Polanyi Institute Institute of Political Economy, Concordia University, Montreal.
13. Szapor, *The Hungarian Pocahontas*, 53–66.
14. Laura Fermi, *Illustrious Immigrants; The Intellectual Migration from Europe, 1930–41* (Chicago: The University of Chicago Press, 1968), 113. The Polanyi family's success is described on pp.113–15.
15. Lucy Young, *Eva Zeisel* (San Francisco: Chronicle Books, 2003), provides a good overview of the designer's work.
16. Notes of Laura Polanyi on the Polanyi ancestors, no date, Polanyi Collection, Manuscript Collection, Hungarian National Library, fond 212/268 and letter of Laura Polanyi to István Erdös, February 20, 1938, Polanyi Collection, fond 212/77.
17. Dwork and Van Pelt, *Flight from the Reich*, 449.

18. This accomplishment was what earned Vezér the epithet of 'the family historian of the Hungarian progressives'. György Litván, "A magyar progresszió krónikása," in *Sorstársak és kortársak* (Budapest: Noran, 2008), 92–3.
19. The requisition record of fond 212 indicates receipt of the material in two stages, in 1976 and 1982–83; it names Eva Zeisel as the main benefactor of the collection.
20. Susannah Lessard, "Profiles: The Present Moment," *The New Yorker*, April 13, 1987, 36–59.
21. Arthur Koestler, *The Invisible Writing; The Second Volume of an Autobiography: 1932–40*, The Danube Edition (New York: Stein and Day, 1969); Manès Sperber, *The Unheeded Warning, 1918–1933* (New York: Holmes and Meier, 1991).
22. Zeisel, *A Soviet Prison Memoir*.
23. Ibid.
24. Weisskopf was born in Vienna, Weissberg in Krakow, and Placzek in Brunn/Brno, all part of Austria-Hungary at the time, into assimilated Jewish families. Various sources alternately identify them as 'Austrian', 'Austrian-born', 'Polish-Jewish', or, as in Placzek's case, 'Czech'.
25. Michael Scammel, *Koestler: The Literary and Political Odyssey of a Twentieth-Century Skeptic* (New York: Random House, 2009), did much to right the excessively critical biography of David Cesarini, *Arthur Koestler: The Homeless Mind* (London: Heinemann, 1998). While Scammel interviewed Eva Zeisel and relied on her, then unpublished, memoir, only Scammel made, albeit limited, use of the Polanyi Collection in the Hungarian National Library. Scammel had permission to use the Zeisel–Koestler correspondence but otherwise neither author seems to have had access to the Eva Zeisel Papers.
26. Jean Richards, "Preface," in Zeisel, *A Soviet Prison Memoir*.
27. Koestler, *The Invisible Writing*, 61.
28. Alexander Weissberg, *The Accused; A Personal Story of Imprisonment in Russia* (New York: Simon and Schuster, 1951).
29. Interview with Eva Zeisel, New York, April 1994; Alexander Weissberg to Eva Zeisel, Zurich, May 8, [1950], Eva Zeisel Papers.
30. Jean Richards, "Preface," in Zeisel, *A Soviet Prison Memoir*.
31. Lessard, "Profiles: The Present Moment."
32. Young, *Eva Zeisel*, 13–16.
33. Karen Kettering, "Behind the Scenes," in Zeisel, *A Soviet Prison Memoir*.
34. Iurii Raniuk, Interview with A.I. Akhiezer, American Institute for Physics, Niels Bohr Library and Archives, Oral History Collection.
35. Charles Weiner, "A New Site for the Seminar: The Refugees and American Physics in the Thirties," in *The Intellectual Migration: Europe and America, 1930–1960*, ed. Donald Fleming and Bernard Bailyn (Cambridge, MA: Belknap Press of Harvard University Press, 1993), 190–234.
36. Alexei B. Kojevnikov, *Stalin's Great Science; The Times and Adventures of Soviet Physicists* (London: Imperial College Press, 2004), 85.
37. Weiner, "A New Site for the Seminar," 217–28. In his foundational article, Weiner did not include any of the Soviet institutions where European refugee physicists found a temporary refuge.
38. Loren Graham, *Science in Russia and the Soviet Union* (Cambridge and New York: Cambridge University Press, 1993); Kojevnikov, *Stalin's Great Science*.
39. Oleksandr Bakai and Yurii Raniuk, *History of Physics Research in Ukraine*, chap. 3: "Between the Two World Wars," http://www.cam.org/~ahryck/ukugmtl/bakai01.html#III (accessed August 31, 2012).
40. A. Kojevnikov, *The Roots of Soviet Physics in the 1930s: The Rise and Tragedy of the Kharkov Physico-Technical Institute*, presented at the 18th International Congress of History of Science, Hamburg, August 1989, p.3, unpublished conference paper, courtesy of A. Kojevnikov; Loren Graham, *Science in Russia and the Soviet Union*, 210.
41. Bakai and Raniuk, *History of Physics Research in Ukraine*.
42. Ibid.
43. Walter M. Elsasser, *Memoirs of a Physicist in the Atomic Age* (New York: Science History Publications, 1978), 106.
44. Arthur Koestler, "Preface," to Alexander Weissberg, *The Accused*, trans. E. Fitzgerald (New York: Simon and Schuster, 1951), ix.
45. Weissberg, *The Accused*, 465.

46. According to Weissberg (ibid., 184), Leipunsky, as a Soviet citizen and party member, put his name on the masthead.
47. Ibid., 67.
48. In his memoir Max Born mentions a 'Professor Ruhemann, a chemist, of German origin' he met at Cambridge before World War I – he may have been Martin Ruhemann's father. M. Born, *My Life; Recollections of a Nobel Laureate* (London: Taylor & Francis, 1978), 117.
49. Weissberg, *The Accused*, 68.
50. Ibid., and my interview with Laszlo Tisza, December 2002.
51. Ibid., 69.
52. An overview of his life was published by I.B. Khriplovich, "The Eventful Life of Fritz Houtermans," *Physics Today* (July 1992): 29–37.
53. Weissberg, *The Accused*, n.15, 363; and Khriplovich, "The Eventful Life of Fritz Houtermans," 29.
54. Interview with Laszlo Tisza, December 2002; Laszlo Tisza, "Adventures of a Theoretical Physicist, Part I: Europe," *Physics in Perspective* 11 (2009): 46 and 71–4.
55. The irony in Teller, the future 'father of the hydrogen bomb' and Ronald Reagan's advisor on 'Star Wars' recommending Tisza for a position in the Soviet Union is inescapable – but it is also an indication of UFTI and Landau's standing in the physicist community.
56. Interview with Laszlo Tisza, December 2002.
57. Tisza, "Adventures of a Theoretical Physicist, Part I: Europe," 81 and 83.
58. Weissberg, *The Accused*, 157–8.
59. Interview with Tisza, December 2002.
60. Victor Weisskopf, *The Joy of Insight; Passions of a Physicist* (New York: Basic Books, 1991), 52.
61. Koestler provides a characteristically trenchant description of receiving news of the burning of the Reichstag in the midst of a friendly card game at the Weissbergs' flat. Koestler, *The Invisible Writing*, 182–3.
62. Hendrik Casimir, *Haphazard Reality; Half a Century of Science* (New York: Harper and Row, 1983), 116.
63. For the details of the Kapitza case, see L. Badash, *Kapitza, Rutherford and the Kremlin* (New Haven, CT: Yale University Press, 1985), and W. Boag, P.E. Rubinin, and D. Shonberg, eds., *Kapitza in Cambridge and Moscow: Life and Letters of a Russian Physicist* (New York: Elsevier, 1990).
64. Charles Weiner's interview with George Gamow, AIP, Niels Bohr Library and Archives, Oral History Collection.
65. Weisskopf, *The Joy of Insight*, 44–5, 52–8.
66. Ibid., 52–3.
67. Ibid., 101.
68. Charles Weiner, interview with Viktor Weisskopf, AIP, Niels Bohr Library and Archives, Oral History Collection.
69. Ibid.
70. Weissberg, *The Accused*, 364.
71. Letter of Irma Strausz to Laura Polanyi, April 11, 1940, Eva Zeisel Archives.
72. A copy of Einstein's telegram is in the Eva Zeisel Papers. It is published in the Appendix of Szapor, "From Budapest to New York: The Odyssey of the Polanyis," *Hungarian Studies Review* XXX, no. 1 (Spring 2003): 29–60.
73. Koestler's account in *Invisible Writing*, 501, and Placzek's letter to Eva Zeisel, Paris, April 1, 1938, Eva Zeisel Papers, give slightly different versions of the process, each emphasizing their own contribution.
74. Felix Bloch to Eva Zeisel, Stanford, June 9, 1938, Eva Zeisel Papers.
75. Irma Strausz to Eva Zeisel, April 11, 1940, Eva Zeisel Papers.
76. Georg Placzek to Eva Zeisel, Ithaca, July 21, 1940, Eva Zeisel Papers.
77. Koestler, "Preface," in Weissberg, *The Accused*, vii–xix. The characterization of Weissberg's memoir is on page xiii.
78. Zeisel, *A Soviet Prison Memoir*.
79. F. Beck and W. Godin, *Russian Purge and the Extraction of Confession* (London: Hurst and Blackett, 1951).

The making of a South African Jewish activist: the Yiddish diary of Ray Alexander Simons, Latvia, 1927

Veronica Belling

The Kaplan Centre, University of Cape Town, Cape Town, South Africa

This article explores the contents of a Yiddish diary, written in 1927 in Latvia by Jewish Communist and trade unionist Ray Alexander Simons, which accompanied her on her immigration to South Africa in 1929, to avoid arrest on account of her activities in an underground Communist cell in Riga. In the context of her autobiography, 'All My Life and All My Strength', written when she was in her eighties, and completed by various hands, the examination will consider how the diary, written when she was 14 years old, supplements the more impersonal account of the autobiography, enhancing our understanding of Simons' single-minded dedication to the workers' struggle and to the liberation of the Black peoples in South Africa.

The Communist Party of South Africa, formed in 1920, enjoyed disproportionate Jewish patronage from its very beginnings, when the Party was imported by English-speaking British immigrants and by Yiddish-speaking Eastern European Jews. Before its establishment, former members of the Bund, the Jewish Workers' Party in Eastern Europe, supported the International Socialist League (ISL), a forerunner of the Communist Party that had a 'Yiddish Speaking Group'. The ISL was a major player in the founding of the united Communist Party of South Africa, which duly became an affiliated section of the Communist International.[1]

Of the many Jews who arrived in South Africa imbued with socialist ideologies of various stripes, Rochel Esther Alexandrovich, known in South Africa as Ray Alexander, stands out for arriving as a fully formed Communist at the tender age of 15. Born in 1913 in the town of Varaklan in Latvia, where during the interwar years the Social Democratic Party held sway,[2] Ray and her sisters were attracted to Marxism at an early age, a fact which she attributes to her home as much as her school. By the age of 14 Ray had joined a youth movement that was slightly left of the Bund. When Ray moved to Riga to study dressmaking, she was immediately recruited into a Communist cell. After a narrow escape from arrest after attending an illegal meeting, her mother arranged for her to immigrate to South Africa. Before her immigration to 'a capitalist country', where it was certain that the Communist Party would one day be banned, her unit saw to it that she should receive training in conducting activities underground. Thus by the time she left Latvia she was already a fully fledged agitator.[3]

Ray left Varaklan on 17 October 1929 and arrived in Cape Town on 6 November, just a day before the anniversary of the Russian Revolution. Initially devastated that there was to be no form of celebration to mark the anniversary of the Russian Revolution, she realized that she had a mission to fulfil in Cape Town. This was to organize the workers because South Africa 'was virgin soil'. Within five days, on 11 November 1929, she had joined the Communist Party of South Africa. In January 1931, she was elected chair of the Cape Town District Committee of the Communist Party.[4]

Ray's main focus, however, was the trade union movement. She worked for the Commercial Workers' Union, followed by the Non-European Railway and Harbour Workers' Union. But it is with the Food and Canning Workers' Union (FCWU), a multi-racial union which she founded in 1941, and with the multi-racial Federation of South African Women (FEDSAW) which she co-founded in 1954, that her legacy lies. After the passage of the 1950 Suppression of Communism Act, in 1953, Ray was served with the first of a series of banning orders.[5] On the day in April 1954 that she was due to take up her seat as one of the three native representatives in South Africa's white parliament, she was issued with a banning order forbidding her to enter the premises.

Ray Alexander married Jack Simons (b. 1907) in 1941, a lecturer in Native Law and Administration at the University of Cape Town and a fellow Communist. He was detained in 1960 and some five years later when he was banned from teaching at the university the couple went into exile. They initially went briefly to Zambia and then to England, where Jack received a fellowship at Manchester University and Ray studied Labour Relations, Russian and German. They returned to Zambia at the end of 1967 where they set up a home for themselves, one where their three children could visit.

Ray and Jack Simons co-authored a number of booklets and pamphlets in addition to the pioneering work *Class and Colour in South Africa, 1850–1950*, an analysis of the effect of class and race on South Africa's socio-political landscape.

While in exile Ray worked for the International Labour Organization and the banned African National Congress (ANC) and continued her work in the trade union movement by serving on the Congress of South African Trade Unions (SACTU). Jack was appointed first Reader and later Professor of Sociology at the University of Zambia. With the unbanning of the ANC and other liberation organizations in 1990 the Simons were able to return to South Africa to rejoin their three children, Mary, Tanya and Johan, after an absence of 25 years.[6]

Today Ray remains honoured for her contributions to organizations such as the Communist Party, the ANC, the Unions, FEDSAW and the New Women's Movement. In 2004 the ANC's National Executive Committee bestowed upon her its greatest honour of Isithwalande (literally translated it means 'the one who wears the plumes of the rare bird'). She is only the third woman to receive this award, whose previous 18 recipients include Chief Albert Luthuli, Father Trevor Huddleston and Yusuf Dadoo in 1955; Lilian Negoyi in 1982; and Nelson Mandela and Helen Joseph in 1992.

Ray Simons died on 12 September 2004 at the age of 91. On 6 November 2010 the Ray Alexander Simons Memory Centre and Heritage Square in Guguletho, an African township adjacent to Cape Town, was launched by Deputy President of South Africa, Kgalema Mothlante.[7]

Archival sources

Ray and Jack Simons amassed a mammoth collection of archival papers at their home in Lusaka in Zambia. In 1987, when approached to donate their papers to the

University of Cape Town Libraries, they agreed in principle, but only at such a time when South Africa was liberated. In the meantime, to save their vast collection from destruction by the encroachment of white ants and by damp, a section was sent to the Nordiska Afrikaininstitut in Sweden for sorting and microfilming, on the understanding that the originals would be transferred to UCT Libraries with the dawn of democracy. Less than a year after South Africa's first democratic election in February 1995, the Simons collection was launched at a ceremony at the University's Centre for African Studies.[8] This initial handover was followed by the gradual transfer of those papers that had not been taken to Sweden and that had been brought from Lusaka with Jack and Ray on their return in 1990.

After the death of Jack Simons in 1995, Ray became increasingly occupied with the sorting of her papers for the purposes of writing her autobiography.[9] In October 1997, following a bad bout of sciatica, she appealed to the Manuscripts and Archives department for assistance with the sorting of the papers at her home. It was during this period that a small collection of papers in Yiddish, that Ray had brought along with her on her hurried emigration from Latvia to Cape Town and which she had lovingly preserved for all those years, found their way to UCT Libraries.[10] Among these papers were two diaries: the first being the subject of this article, and the second a poetry diary or commonplace book, dated 1928, in which the 15-year-old Ray had copied out her favourite Yiddish poems. These include leading Yiddish poets, such as Shimon Frug, Shin Anski, Mani Leib, Avraham Reisen, Leib Halper, Yehoash, David Einhorn, as well as the group known collectively as the Sweatshop or Proletarian poets: Morris Rosenfeld, Morris Winchevsky and Dovid Edelstadt, whose poem, *Mayn tsevo'e* (My Testament), captures Ray's lifelong commitment to the workers' struggle.

O guter fraynt ven ikh vel shtorbn	Oh good friend if I should die
Trogt tsu mayn keyver unzer fon-	Bring our flag to my graveside
Di fraye fon mit royte farbn	Freedom's flag all coloured red
Beshprits mit blut fun arbetsman!	Soaked in the blood the workers shed
Un dort unter dem fon dem roytn	And under the red flag over there
Zingt mir mayn lid mayn fraye lid!	My song of freedom I wish to hear
Mayn lid in kamf vos klingt vi keytn	My song of struggle ringing out like chains
Fun dem farshklaftn Krist un Yid.[11]	Of enslaved Jews and Christians

Other items include two autograph books belonging to Ray's oldest sister Gessy, and to her youngest sister Minnie, that are inscribed with verses in Yiddish, German and Russian, illustrating the sisters' budding socialist fervour. There is also a book of poems, *Kaylekhdike vokhn* (*Week In, Week Out*), by the Soviet Yiddish poet, Izi Kharik (1898–1937) published in Minsk in 1933, that is inscribed by Ray to her mother, 31 October 1944. Kharik was one of the Soviet poets killed in Stalin's purges of Jewish intellectuals and writers in 1937.[12] These few Yiddish items occupy precisely one folder in this huge collection of 456 boxes, containing material relating to the African National Congress, the South African Communist Party and the trade unions.

The diary

There is no consensus about the nature of the diary as a genre. It has been characterized as 'a capacious hold-all'[13] that falls somewhere between autobiography and letter writing. It is generally agreed that it is united by three elements: its commitment to the day-to-day recording of events, to the first-person narrative, and by its special relationship to privacy, intimacy and secrecy.[14] According to Philippe Lejeune, the main distinguishing feature between a diary and an autobiography is the fact that the autobiography is retrospective.[15] It is precisely because of its retrospective character – because it is personally authored after the fact – that the Yiddish linguist and scholar Max Weinreich (1894–1969), citing the psychologist Charlotte Buhler, felt that the diary was a more reliable source than the autobiography.[16]

Ray's diary is contained in an exercise book consisting of 60 pages, written in a cramped and at times virtually illegible hand. As a day-to-day record of events it is extremely brief as it spans only nine days, from 22 to 31 December 1927. It is written in Yiddish, the language of the East European Jews and Ray's mother tongue that is written in Hebrew script. The pronunciation follows the Lithuanian dialect while the spelling of the Hebrew words adheres to the Soviet Yiddish orthography.[17]

At the time of writing, 14-year-old Ray, or Rokhl, as she was known then, and her nine-year-old sister Minnie (b. 1918), were the only siblings of the eight children who were still living at home with their mother. Their father had died four years before in 1923. Her half-sisters Anna and Tanya, and older sisters Gessie (b.1903) and Dora (b. 1909), were living in Riga and her sister Mary (1905–1926), had passed away from a botched appendectomy only a year before, while her brother Iser (b. 1904) had recently immigrated to South Africa. Ray had completed the schooling available to her in Varaklan, and was waiting to go to Riga, where she would be studying dressmaking at the vocational school of ORT, the Society for Handicraft and Agricultural Work among the Jews of Russia, established in 1905.[18] Meanwhile she took sole responsibility for the housework and the cooking, while at the same time looking after her younger sister Minnie. In addition she was doing the books for the bakery that her mother operated from their home in order to support the family after her father died.

Although the period of time covered by the diary is extremely brief, its record of the events of the day is extremely detailed, providing an intimate glimpse into the nature and rhythm of day-to-day Jewish life in a small town in Eastern Europe. Ray records the events of the day from the minute that she wakes up in the morning to the moment that she falls asleep at night. The diary was written during December when the weather was very severe with wind and snow storms abounding. Ray bundles herself up in a large shawl, jacket and snow boots to protect herself against the cold outside in the street, and inside she and her mother sit next to, or climb on to the stove to keep warm. Her day is punctuated by attending to her own personal hygiene (no simple matter with no running water), tidying and cleaning the house, washing her clothes, cooking, washing up and feeding the animals. She constantly needs to go out to buy provisions or to make or collect payments for the bakery. Customers arrive to buy bread at all hours of the day; peasants arrive with wood for the oven or to clean the samovar. She meets her friends in the street, or pops into their homes, and they arrive unannounced to visit her at her home. Writing and receiving letters to and from family members living in another city or in South Africa is another regular feature of the daily routine that is very typical of the period that was characterized by large-scale Jewish emigration from Eastern Europe.[19]

Autobiographical section of the diary

The diary is preceded by a summary of her life up to that point. This section has been consciously fashioned to reflect the most significant events that have shaped her world view. Written under the influence of leftist politics, much like the Soviet diaries examined by Jochin Hellbeck, this brief autobiography served as a means 'of self-construction and self-fashioning within an ideological mould'.[20] The contents closely resemble the autobiographies of Jewish youths in Poland, that were elicited by the YIVO, the Yidisher Visnshaftlekhe Institut – the Yiddish Scientific Institute, in Vilna in the 1930s, a selection of which were published in English translation in the collection *Awakening Lives* in 2002.[21]

It is significant that Ray starts the diary on her fourteenth birthday, 22 December 1927, clearly indicating it to be a milestone in her life, her political coming of age. As the YIVO autobiography contest was directed at youths between the ages of 16 and 22, based on the premise that they only became interested in political youth movements at the age of 17,[22] Ray was clearly politically precocious having joined the political youth movement, *Kultur-Lige* (Culture League), a socialist organization slightly to the left of the Bund,[23] at the age of just 14. Established in Riga in 1922 (as a branch of the original organization established in Kiev in 1918), branches of the *Kultur-Lige* operated in all of the Latvian towns that had sufficient Jewish numbers, sponsoring clubs, libraries, and drama and music circles. *Kultur-Lige* was the heir to the *Arbeiter Heim*, an organization that existed between 1920 and 1923, to which her older half-sisters Anna and Tanya had belonged.[24]

This section has to be read in the context of Ray's published autobiography, *All My Life and All My Strength*, where 20 pages are devoted to this period of her life. While it is clear that Ray has utilized her diary in the writing of her autobiography, she has omitted the more painful and intimate aspects of her life. Thus, although the autobiography contains a more comprehensive overview of this period, it does not convey the wealth of personal details as well as the emotionalism of the teenage diary, elements that serve to deepen our insight into the underlying reasons why Ray followed the particular path that she did.

This illustrates how the transition from the diary, written in Yiddish in Varaklan at the age of 14, to the autobiography, written in English in Cape Town in her twilight years, archives Jewish migration, tracking Ray's journey from the trials and tribulations of Jewish life in Latvia to her more comfortable life in Cape Town. Simultaneously it demonstrates how her Latvian Jewish socialist politics were transferred to the workers' struggle and to the liberation of the oppressed Black peoples of South Africa.

Death of her father and sister

Among the elements omitted from the autobiography, death and dying loom large. Whereas in the autobiography, the death of her father is mentioned only in passing, in the diary her father's collapse in Ray's presence and her reaction to his death and burial is dramatically depicted. Ray's emotional reactions are emphasized by the use of repetition and exclamation marks – 'Tate!!!!!!!!!!!' – 'Father!!!!!!!!!!'. After his death she describes just how miserable she and her sister Dora felt when they used to come home after school to a silent house, instead of to the tumult of the boys studying at their father's *kheyder*.[25]

Moreover, there is a discrepancy in the date of her father's death between the diary and the autobiography, the result of Ray's failing memory towards the end of her life. While in the autobiography it is recorded as 1925, when she was 13 years old, in the diary it is recorded as December 1923, when Ray was just 11.[26] The date in the diary is confirmed on her father's tombstone in the cemetery in Latvia (3 Tevet 5684 – Tuesday, 11 December 1923), proving the accuracy of the diary.[27] This intimate encounter with death at the age of just 11, along with the customary visit to the cemetery on the eve of the Day of Atonement, caused her to experience terrifying nightmares, followed by an extended period of feeling unwell that culminated in the onset of her menses.[28]

The death of her beloved older sister, Mary, in 1926 was not witnessed as intimately, as Mary was living in Riga when she died. Nonetheless Ray is bereft at the loss of her beloved confidante, eight years her senior, who features frequently in the diary.[29] Ray was shocked by her death at such a young age and at the illusory nature of life. She writes: '*Akh, mentsh du mentsh ot shteystu, geyst, ligst, un blaybst lign oyf eybik!!*' / 'O man, man, no sooner do you stand up, you walk, you lie down and remain lying down eternally!!'[30]

It is a pity that Ray decided to exclude these painful early impressions from the autobiography, which suffers from the general absence of reflection, feelings or emotion. However like the date of her father's death, her memory of these events, that were still very raw and fresh at the age of just 14, had faded. The death that is uppermost in her mind in the autobiography is that of Jack, her beloved husband of 54 years. In a rare and touching display of emotion in the autobiography, she describes how they renewed their marriage vows on his deathbed.[31]

Poverty

Also omitted from the autobiography is any description of the poverty, deprivation and suffering of her early years, which are accentuated in the diary. Varaklan, the small town where the family was living, was situated in the Rezekne (Rezhitse) Province, part of the Latgale region, the largest and the poorest of the three provinces (that included Courland and Livonia), that constituted Latvia. According to the *YIVO Encyclopedia of the Jews of Eastern Europe*, 18.5% of the Jewish population of approximately 62,000 (12.8% of the total population) of Latgale required welfare in 1898.[32]

Ray attributes the struggles of the family during those years to her father's inability to earn a living, the result of the restrictive legislation placed on the Jews of Latvia. Their situation improved somewhat when her father opened a *kheyder* – a religious elementary school for boys in their home. She describes her mother as old beyond her years, the result of constant worry about their economic situation. As children they were dressed in second-hand clothes that were often threadbare, but spotlessly clean.[33] She also describes a time when she and her sister Dveyre (Dora) went to school hungry[34] – and another occasion when, as a result of having no shoes to wear, she became ill and when she and her sister were transferred to a school for poor children where they were provided with food and clothing. She writes:

Gedenk ikh genoy nisht vi fun nisht hobn vos ontsuton oyf mayne fis. Farkil ikh zikh un ver krank. Di mame trogt mir arayn bay Iser Levin, a dokter, Avrams a brider un ikh ver gezunt. Do hot zikh geshafen a min shul far oreme kinder. Dortn vu ikh iz fri'er gegangen geyen di mer farmeglekhe iber hoyft balebatishe kinder un ikh mit di shvester Meri – Dveyre iz dan geven in Birzh – geyen far 3 vi'orst. Un shul lere bakumen mir dortn zeyer veynik. Nor esn git men undz un kleydung.[35]

And I don't remember anything about not having what to wear on my feet. My mother took me to Iser Levin, a doctor, Avram's brother, and I recovered. There was a type of school for poor children. The school that I was attending before, was for the wealthier and mainly the *balebatishe* (householders') children, and I with my sister Mary – (my sister) Dveyre was in Birzh at the time – walked 3 verst (Russian miles). And we very seldom had lessons there. They only provided us with food and clothing.

It is possible that Ray was simply too proud to include these painful but revealing recollections in her autobiography. She might also have wished to avoid embarrassing her children by her family having been forced to accept charity. Whatever her reasons, there can be no doubt that these experiences would have sensitized Ray to the plight of those in straightened circumstances, and influenced her decision to dedicate her life to the cause of the oppressed and the downtrodden.[36]

Jewish identity and politics

For the Jewish historian, however, the most significant aspect of the diary of this budding Communist and trade unionist is that it documents in a way not possible in the autobiography the transfer of her allegiance from Judaism to Bundism to Communism. Ray was not only politically but also academically precocious. She studied in the Yiddish medium, favoured by the Bund that held sway among the Jews of Varaklan. She was registered early for the Committee school,[37] at the age of five,[38] and was soon put up to the second class, where in addition to the Hebrew Pentateuch, that was taught in the first year, Russian was taught as well.[39]

In her autobiography, Ray relates that she learnt her human values from her home, where she was inspired by the Jewish biblical heroines, Rachel, Ruth and Esther, who were depicted in tapestries hanging in her parents' bedroom.[40] In the diary it is unnecessary for Ray to recount the sources of her Jewishness as it defines her life and her diary.

Her Judaism is clearly evident in the language that she uses – Yiddish – and in the dating of the diary entries that follow the Hebrew as well as the Christian calendar. The first entry is dated as *Di finfte likhtl* ('The fifth candle'), 1927, Ray's birthday.[41] The fifth candle refers to the fifth of the eight candles that are lit on the Jewish festival of Chanukah. Ray's Jewishness is also evident in the strict division of the plates that she is regularly washing up, into those of meat and milk respectively. When she is feeling unwell on the night of the Day of Atonement during the period after her father's death her mother suggests that she recite the '*Sh'ma*' –'Hear O Israel',[42] the Jewish affirmation of faith – in order to obtain some relief.[43]

However, the diary also demonstrates that Ray's faith was already being challenged. As illustrated in the verses inscribed in their autograph books, all the sisters were converted to the cause of the class struggle at an early age. They were influenced by Leib Yoffe, the principal of the school and a close family friend, a Communist, who was also the mayor of Varaklan, whose name is cited both in the diary and in the autobiography, as the main influence on the children of Varaklan.[44]

While in the autobiography the reader is acquainted with various elements in their background that predisposed the sisters to Marxist socialism, such as their father's attendance at a Russian school and their mother's sojourn in Leeds in England,[45] Ray's focus in the diary is on the Varaklan Workers' Society, the *Kultur-Lige*, that she joined against her mother's wishes, at the age of just 14.[46]

Ray participated in the social evenings organized by the club, reciting workers' poems (such as those that that are contained in her poetry diary), and taking part in Yiddish plays. She also joined two study circles: one on political economy that she attended regularly and the other on religion and faith in which she participated less frequently.[47] However, its radical left-wing rhetoric caused the Latvian authorities to close down the *Kultur-Lige* in 1926.[48] Its closure is recorded in the diary, but not in the autobiography, as is the establishment in its stead of a society, known as 'Winchevsky',[49] named after the Yiddish sweatshop poet Morris Winchevsky, two of whose poems, *Di Freyheyts-gayst* ('The Spirit of Freedom') and *Mayn Eynstiger Farlang* ('My Only Desire') – are included in Ray's poetry diary.[50]

At the same time Ray was recruited into an underground Communist cell where she read works by Marx and Plekhanov as well as Bukharin's *Communist Alphabet*. She writes that she gave a lecture to the group on the class system that completely opened the eyes of her comrades to the exploitation of the workers.[51] It would seem that Ray was torn between the two groups and would have preferred to focus all her attention on the underground Communist cell, which was more serious and committed and attracted a more mature audience; however, she felt that it would be unwise to cut herself off from her peers in the more culturally orientated Varaklan Workers Society.[52]

Yet despite her involvement in the Workers' Society and the underground Communist cell, she and her sister Mary still fasted on the Day of Atonement. However she significantly qualifies this fact, saying that she did so '*nit vilndik*' (unwillingly) as she believed that it was '*umzist*' (all in vain). During the day the sisters went for a walk and sang workers' songs, and in the evening they read the *Yugnd Hamer* (Youth Hammer), a Communist sympathizing Yiddish newspaper for the youth.[53] There can be no doubt the sisters would have fasted out of respect for their mother, an observant Jewish woman, who many years later, on first hearing the news that her youngest daughter, Minnie, had married out of the faith, was so devastated that she threatened to 'drown herself in the De Waal reservoir' near their home in Oranjezicht in Cape Town.[54]

Two issues central to Ray's world view in her autobiography are absent from the diary. These are her awareness of racism that she later attributes to hearing the story of *Uncle Tom's Cabin*, by Harriet Beecher Stowe, and her rejection of Zionism.[55] It is possible that this is because neither of these were burning issues to her at that time.

The struggle against the oppression of the Black people only became central to Ray's political agenda once she had taken the decision to immigrate to South Africa. Similarly in the overwhelmingly Zionist South African Jewish community her own early rejection of Zionism would have taken on far greater significance. In her autobiography she recalls a speech that she made at her school in 1926 to celebrate the establishment of the Hebrew University in Jerusalem. On that occasion she declared that one should celebrate the establishment of a university anywhere, not only in Jerusalem, but also in Timbuktu![56] Nonetheless her universalistic views are already evident in the diary in an expression of good wishes, '*Le-khaim*' ('To life'), that she specifically extends to all of humanity – 'I made a *Le-khaim* and said: for the lives of all humankind!!'[57]

Cultural allusions

In addition to her political activities, the diary opens a window into the cultural life of a young Jewish girl in Latvia at that time. The diary is embedded with allusions to the life and culture of the Eastern European Jews, many of which are quite obscure and long forgotten.

Reading is Ray's chief form of recreation and a large section of the diary is devoted to the discussion of the books, periodicals and newspapers that she is reading.[58] This conforms to the findings contained in the aforementioned YIVO autobiographies where the reading of secular literature was the most popular pastime among the youth and the library emerged as a cultural institution of central importance.[59]

Ray was brought up on the Yiddish classics of Peretz and Sholem Aleichem,[60] and in the diary she particularly recalls her enjoyment at reading a story by Mendele Moykher Sforim, the progenitor of modern Yiddish literature.[61] From the library of the *Kultur Lige* she borrowed Yiddish translations of European literature, the product of the post-revolutionary project in Russia to broaden the intellectual vistas of the Jewish population.[62] In this regard her tastes, as reflected in the diary, are extremely sophisticated compared to that of a 14-year-old girl today. She has just finished reading Dostoevsky's first novel, *The House of the Dead*, a harrowing account based on his experiences in a Siberian prison. She quotes the last line of the novel: 'Liberty! New life! Resurrection from the dead! Unspeakable moment!'[63] Later she begins to read the Nobel prize-winning novelist and philosopher Anatole France's *Thaïs*,[64] a novel about a fourth-century Egyptian monk, whose life symbolizes the struggle between the forces of stoicism and epicureanism. Anatole France was particularly popular in Jewish circles because of his support of Alfred Dreyfus, the French Jewish officer falsely condemned for treason in 1897.[65] Other famous European authors that she is reading are the Swedish dramatist Auguste Strindberg and the Russian novelist Maxim Gorky.[66] While she does not read them herself, Ray does on one occasion allude to the sentimental melodramatic Yiddish romances, by writers such as Isaac Meyer Dik and Shomer,[67] that were so popular with the women in Eastern Europe at that time.[68]

Ray was also very interested in medicine and health, and in the autobiography she relates that she had wanted to study medicine, but abandoned that idea because of problems with anti-Semitism in Varaklan where a university had recently been established.[69] She does not mention this ambition in the diary although she does mention going to study Latin with the local Greek Orthodox priest.[70] She discusses numerous articles from the periodical *Folks Gezunt* (The People's Health), published by TOZ, a Polish society established in 1921,[71] closely associated with the OZE, the Society for the Protection of the Health of the Jewish Population, established in 1912 in St Petersburg.[72] Published in Vilna from 1923 to 1937, the monthly and later bi-weekly *Folks Gezunt* was a popular scientific journal for the broad Jewish public.

Ray lauds Edward Jenner, who discovered the smallpox vaccine, and Nicholas Kopernik (Copernicus), the founder of modern medicine. Ray also believed in the importance of breast feeding and considers theories of nutrition and vegetarianism, that associate meat eating with alcoholism and character degeneration.[73] She supports the establishment of special schools for retarded children, so that all the members of society should be productive. These ideas echo the Soviet fear of becoming 'superfluous', not needed by society, in an age where both one's public worth and one's self-esteem were determined above all by the extent of one's usefulness to society.[74]

Her own personal hygiene occupies a central place in the diary, something which is apparently common to similar memoirs of the *shtetl* at that time, relating to the conditions of extreme poverty that existed among the Jewish population.[75] Ray cites 'Ten Commandments for school children!', that she most likely copied out from the journal *Folks Gezunt* that she was reading. But here again her interest coincides with the celebration of strength, health and beauty that was part of the Stalinist world view.[76]

(1) Get up early, get out of bed immediately, wash your hands, face, neck, chest and feet with soap and water. Have your own hand towel, never use a strange one.

(2) Every morning and evening, brush your teeth with a brush, or at least with your finger.

(3) Every day comb your hair out with a thick comb. Boys should wear their hair short. Girls should comb their hair so that it does not fall into their eyes.
(4) Every day clean your clothes and shoes with a brush. See that your clothes are washed. Open the window while you clean.
(5) Wash your hands before you eat, don't eat too quickly and chew the food well. After eating, wash out your mouth with water.
(6) Don't spit on the floor. Don't scratch in your nose or your ears.
(7) Air out your room before you go to sleep and lie in bed.
(8) Bathe yourself at least once a week. Wash your whole body and your hair with water and soap and cut the nails of your hands and feet.
(9) Sit up straight, but not completely rigid, when writing and studying, hold your book or your notebook on the table, don't read when it is dark.
(10) After studying, have a rest. Go for a walk or play in the fresh air. Cleanliness is health![77]

Yiddish theatre and song also feature in her diary. Ray makes much of a performance of the play *Miriam*, the landmark play by the Yiddish playwright Peretz Hirschbein that many of her friends had attended. Ray preferred to save the 40 rubles for the ticket, but saves face by telling her friends that she did not attend because she was ill at the time. Instead she reads the play, which makes a very strong impression on her. The play, which was originally written in Hebrew in 1902, then translated by the author into Yiddish, deals with the fate of a poor Jewish girl, an orphan, who is forced into prostitution. Forced to leave home to find work in Warsaw, she is employed as a seamstress in the cellar of the home of a rich Jewish family. When the son of the family takes a fancy to her, she leaves her job and falls pregnant, hoping against all odds that he will marry her. Instead he tires of her, and, on the eve of giving birth, she goes to his house, only to be pushed down the steps. She has no option but to return to her friends in the cellar, who help her to deliver the baby. Now a fallen woman she is forced to take up a life of prostitution in order to feed herself and her baby.[78] Ray's heart goes out to girls in situations such as these and she weeps bitterly.[79]

One day when Ray is feeling particularly melancholy, she mentions singing various songs to perk up her spirits. One is from the Yiddish play *Ashmeday*. In Jewish legend Ashmeday is the name of the king of the devils, but it is not clear exactly to which play she is referring. Another song is about the Russian revolution of 1905, and a third is about Simon Petlyura, the leader of the Ukrainian government during the Civil War, 1919–1921, and the Zionist revisionist leader Vladimir Jabotinsky,[80] seemingly unlikely bedfellows. The song emanated from an agreement signed in 1921 between Slavinsky, Petlyura's representative in Prague, and Jabotinsky to form a Jewish militia that would accompany Petlyura's putative invasion of the Ukraine, in order to protect the Jewish population from pogroms. This agreement did not materialize and was heavily criticized by most Zionist groups.[81] Ray was reminded of the song by the recently concluded trial where Sholem Schwarzbard, who had assassinated Petlyura in Paris in 1926 in retaliation for his government's complicity in the pogroms against the Jews, had been acquitted, and Petlyura condemned instead.[82] One imagines that Ray would have rejoiced at the vindication of this fearless Jewish avenger of the blood of innocent men, women and children, who was being celebrated throughout the Jewish world, and whom some believed to have acted as an agent of the Bolsheviks.

Conclusion

Whereas Ray's autobiography, *All My Life and All My Strength*, documents the events and personalities that made an impression on her during the course of her long life, the Yiddish diary, written when she was only 14 years old, captures Ray at her political coming of age as she stands on the threshold of her new life. At this point Ray depicts herself as a progressive, determined, confident and accomplished young woman, a budding feminist who plays a leading role in the leftist societies to which she belonged, giving lectures and reciting poems. At the age of just 14 she already knew that she had a mission in life: to liberate the workers!

Unlike the autobiography, which is largely impersonal and non-reflective, the diary recalls a time when, although she is clearly committed to Communism, nonetheless she is still observing her religion and fasting on the Day of Atonement, the holiest day in the Jewish calendar. The diary also reveals the struggles and trials of her childhood, including her shock and vulnerability on her father's death when she was only 11. All these experiences together lay bare the emotional roots that predisposed her to dedicate her life to the cause of the workers and the liberation of the Blacks in South Africa.

Her Jewish literacy, which is demonstrated in the multitude of cultural allusions in the diary, both religious and secular, demonstrate the distance that the 80-year-old Ray of the autobiography has travelled from her Jewish roots that permeate every aspect of her life in the diary. Thus, in contrast to the distant memories that are recorded in the autobiography, this small diary, written at the age of just 14, not only accompanied her physical migration from Latvia to Cape Town, but personifies her spiritual migration from her Jewish roots to internationalism.

Notes

1. Allison Drew, *Discordant Comrades: Identities and Loyalties on the South African Left* (Aldershot: Ashgate, 2000), 1, 6–10, 36–7, 46–8 and 52–4; H.J. and R.E. Simons, *Class and Colour in South Africa, 1850–1950* (Harmondsworth: Penguin Books, 1969), 184 and 257–261; Gideon Shimoni, *Community and Conscience: The Jews in Apartheid South Africa* (Hanover, NH and London: University Press of New England, 2003), 8–9.
2. Ezra Mendelsohn, *The Jews of East Central Europe between the World Wars* (Bloomington, IN: Indiana University Press, 1983), 241–2.
3. Ray Alexander Simons, *All My Life and All My Strength*, ed. Raymond Suttner (Parktown, Johannesburg: STE Pubishers, 2004), 42–6.
4. Simons, *All My Life and All My Strength*, 50, 55 and 62.
5. Under South Africa's Apartheid laws people, meetings, organizations and publications could be banned. A typical banning order would restrict a person to a particular magisterial district, require them to report regularly to the police, prevent them from associating with more than one person at a time and prevent them from visiting public places and institutions. Additionally nothing a banned person said or wrote could be published. There was no

avenue of appeal against a banning order, About.com, African History, http://africanhistory.about.com/od/glossaryb/g/def_banned.htm.
6. Milton Shain and Miriam Pimstone, "Ray Alexander (Simons), 1913–2004," http://jwa.org/encyclopedia/article/alexander-simons-ray; Tanya Barben (Simons), e-mail, August 26, 2012.
7. http://raymemorycentre.org.za/?p=164.
8. Simons, *All My Life and All My Strength*, 351.
9. See Patricia Van der Spuy, "'Our Book': A Personal Reflection on Ray Alexander Simons' *All My Life and All My Strength*," *Kronos* 72, no. 31 (Winter/Spring 2005): 223–7.
10. Interview with Tanya Barben, August 2011.
11. Yiddish poetry diary, Jack & Ray Simons collection, BC1080, 2.12. Special Collections Department, University of Cape Town Libraries, University of Cape Town. (Unpublished). English translation by Veronica Belling.
12. See D. Shneer, "Izi Kharik," in the *Yivo Encyclopedia of the Jews of Eastern Europe*, editor-in-chief Gershon Hundert (New Haven, CT and London: Yale University Press, 2008), 1: 885–6.
13. Virginia Woolf's phrase, cited in I. Papirno, "What Can Be Done With Diaries," *Russian Review* 63 (October 2004): 562.
14. Ibid., 562–4.
15. Philipe Lejeune, *On Autobiography* (Minneapolis: University of Minnesota Press, 1989), 4.
16. Max Weinreich, *Der Veg Tsu Undzer Yugnt: Yesoydes, Metodn, Problemen, fun Yidisher Yugnt-Forshung* [The way to our youth: foundations, methods, problems, of the research of Jewish youth] [in Yiddish] (Vilna: Yidisher Visnshaftlekher Insitut, Optsvayg Yugnt-Forshung, 1935), 349–50; Barbara Kirshenblatt-Gimblett, Marcus Moseley, and Michael Stanislawski, "Introduction," in *Awakening Lives: Autobiographies of Jewish Youth in Poland before the Holocaust*, ed. Jeffrey Shandler (New Haven, CT and London: published in cooperation with the Yivo Institute for Jewish Research, Yale University Press, c.2002), xxiii.
17. In the Soviet Yiddish orthography the Hebrew words that are traditionally written without vowels, are vocalized phonetically in the way of the words of Germanic and Slavic origin. See D. Katz, *Words on Fire: the Unfinished Story of Yiddish* (New York: Basic Books, 2004).
18. ORT, *The Yivo Encyclopedia of the Jews of Eastern Europe*, http://www.yivoencyclopedia.org/article.aspx/ORT.
19. Yiddish diary, 32, Jack & Ray Simons collection (see note 11).
20. Jochin Hellbeck, "Laboratories of the Soviet Self: Diaries from the Stalin Era" (PhD diss., Columbia University, 1998), cited in Papirno, "What Can Be Done With Diaries," 567.
21. Shandler, *Awakening Lives*.
22. Kirshenblatt-Gimblett, Moseley, and Stanislawski, "Introduction," xviii.
23. Ray Alexander Simons, interviewed by Steven Robins and Immanuel Suttner, July 20, 1993 and January 1996, Cape Town, in *Cutting Through the Mountain: Interviews with South African Jewish Activists*, ed. Immanuel Suttner (London: Viking, 1997), 30.
24. Yiddish diary, 12.
25. Simons, *All My Life and All My Strength*, 36; Yiddish diary, 7–9.
26. Yiddish diary, 7–8.
27. Photograph, Tanya Barben, private collection.
28. Yiddish diary, 10.
29. Ibid., 10–11, 17, 32, 35, 61 and 63.
30. Ibid., 18.
31. Simons, *All My Life and All My Strength*, 352.
32. D. Levin, "Latvia," in the *Yivo Encyclopedia of the Jews of Eastern Europe*, 1: 997.
33. Yiddish diary, 3.
34. Ibid., 7.
35. Ibid., 5. English translation by Veronica Belling.
36. Ibid., 4 5.
37. It was not possible to establish for certain the nature of the school, but as the Hebrew network of schools in Eastern Europe was called 'Tarbuth', one presumes that the Committee school that was conducted in Yiddish would have been affiliated to the Bund, especially as the principal is described as a Communist.

38. Simons, *All My Life and All My Strength*, 33.
39. Yiddish diary, 4–5.
40. Simons, *All My Life and All My Strength*, 31.
41. While in Latvia, Ray, like all Jews in Eastern Europe, observed their birthdays according to the Jewish calendar, a lunar calendar, so that their birthdays fell on a different date in the Christian calendar each year.
42. The *Shma* refers to the prayer, "Hear O Israel the Lord our God, the Lord is One" (Deuteronomy 6: 4–15).
43. Yiddish diary, 10.
44. Simons, *All My Life and All My Strength*, 30–31, 33 and 40; Yiddish diary, 6–7.
45. Simons, *All My Life and All My Strength*, 30.
46. Yiddish diary, 12.
47. Ibid., 12.
48. See H. Kazovsky, "Kultur-Lige" [Culture League], in *Yivo Encyclopedia of the Jews in Eastern Europe*, 1: 953–6.
49. Yiddish diary, 15.
50. Poetry diary.
51. Yiddish diary, 11–12 and 15–16.
52. Ibid., 16–17.
53. Ibid., 13.
54. Simons, *All My Life and All My Strength*, 88.
55. Ibid., 34 and 38.
56. Ibid., 38.
57. Yiddish diary, 13.
58. Her love of reading also features in the autobiography. However, in the diary she also discusses the contents of the articles and books that she is reading.
59. Kirshenblatt-Gimblett, Moseley, and Stanislawski, "Introduction," xxxi.
60. Simons, *All My Life and All My Strength*, 35.
61. She refers to the story, "Hershele der Doktor" (Hershele the Doctor), Yiddish diary, 5.
62. See K.B. Moss, "Not *The Dybbuk* but *Don Quixote*: Translation, Deparochialisation, and Nationalism in Jewish Culture, 1917–1919," in *Jewish Culture Front: Representing Jews in Eastern Europe*, ed. B. Nathans and G. Safran (Philadelphia: University of Pennsylvania Press, c.2008), 196–240.
63. Yiddish diary, 30; F. Dostoevsky, *The House of the Dead* (London: J.M. Dent, 1911, reprint 1939), 368.
64. Yiddish diary, 52.
65. See references to Anatole France in L. Begley, *Why the Dreyfus Affair Matters* (New Haven, CT: Yale University Press, c.2009).
66. Yiddish diary, 30 and 61.
67. Shomer was the pen name for N.M. Shaykevitsh; for Yiddish romantic fiction, see D. Miron, *A Traveler Disguised: A Study in the Rise of Modern Yiddish Fiction in the Nineteenth Century* (New York: Schocken, 1973), 28–9.
68. Yiddish diary, 13.
69. Simons, *All My Life and All My Strength*, 39, 41; Suttner, *Cutting Through the Mountain: Interviews with South African Activists*, 37–8.
70. Yiddish diary, 7.
71. M. Freilich, "TOZ," in *Yivo Encyclopedia of the Jews in Eastern Europe* (see note 12), 1891–2.
72. OZE sought to create an all-Russian Jewish welfare system with the goal of promoting the study and knowledge of medical and sanitary practices, detecting and curing diseases among Jews, preventing epidemics and creating living conditions conducive to the normal physical and mental development of Jewish children, YIVO/OZE, http://www.yivoencyclopedia.org/article.aspx/OZE.
73. Yiddish diary, 34–6 and 38.
74. Joachin Hellbeck, *Revolution on My Mind: Writing a Diary Under Stalin* (Cambridge, MA: Harvard University Press, 2006), 349.
75. See Alyssa Quint, "Personal Hygiene and Grooming," in *Yivo Encyclopedia of the Jews of Eastern Europe*, 2: 1345–7.

76. Hellbeck, *Revolution on My Mind*, 358.
77. Yiddish diary, 39–40.
78. Joel Berkowitz and Jeremy Dauber, ed., trans. and intro., *Landmark Yiddish Plays: A Critical Anthology* (Albany: State University of New York Press, c.2006), 257–90.
79. Yiddish diary, 43, 45 and 59.
80. Ibid., 43.
81. "Simon Petlyura" (1879–1926), *Encyclopedia Judaica* (Jerusalem: Keter, 1972), 13: 340–41.
82. See Kelly Scott Johnson, "Schwarzbard: Biography of a Jewish Assassin" (PhD diss., Harvard University, 2012).

Harvard man, American dough boy, Mississippi Jew: the papers of Samuel (Sam) Leyens Switzer in Virginia

Maura Hametz

Department of History, Old Dominion University, Norfolk, Virginia, USA

Archives function both as repositories of documents and materials and as sites of memory collection and classification. This article explores the provenance and process of collecting and archiving through the lens of the collection of personal papers of Samuel Switzer, a Northern educated Southerner, World War I soldier, and a Jew. It examines how the interplay of Switzer's various identities affected the donor's and archivists' perspectives on the collection's importance and relevance and demonstrates the impact of these viewpoints on the collection's presentation and use by scholars.

Dear Lady,

Please notice the date which is the eve of Pesach I think. The Jewish Welfare Service in Beaune had a service tonight but I did not go although I wanted to badly. To-morrow, I am going to try to get some matzohs, if possible.[1]

So wrote Sam Switzer, a soldier attending the American Expeditionary Force's Beaune University in France. How did Switzer's letter, written on 14 April 1919 to his mother in Vicksburg, Mississippi, land in Special Collections at Old Dominion University's Perry Library in Norfolk, Virginia? The answer seems relatively simple: Switzer's niece, Bettie Minette Cooper, who settled in Norfolk with her husband in the early 1960s, offered her uncle's papers to the university on permanent loan in 1980. The materials in the collection migrated to Norfolk from Vicksburg on the death of Sam Switzer. Cooper, a philanthropist and community activist, who has served in a variety of local organizations from the Virginia Symphony and Young Audiences of Virginia to the Chrysler Museum and YMCA of South Hampton Roads as well as in Jewish organizations from Temple Ohef Sholom in Norfolk, Virginia to the Southern Jewish Historical Society, was responsible for managing her uncle's estate. She first sought out the archivist at the university near her home to conserve Switzer's World War I era maps, which were too large for her to store and in need of preservation. While Old Dominion University (ODU) did not have a large archive, the heavy presence of the American military in Norfolk, the university's role in catering to military personnel and their families, and the interest of many of the university's students in military history made the collection attractive to the archivist. After the maps were donated, Cooper decided to offer Switzer's correspondence and memorabilia.

The provenance of Switzer's letters and ODU's accession of the Switzer collection are clearly documented and seem straightforward. However, as Richard Cox reminds us, there are 'no innocent deposits'.[2] Switzer's and his mother's preservation of the materials, Minette Cooper's decision to offer them to Perry Library, and the ODU archivist's decision to accept the collection, organize it, and conserve it, hint at the perceived value of the materials, a value assessed at three levels: (1) by the creators of the materials (and in this case the creators' descendant, the donor); (2) by the archivists evaluating the materials and conserving them, and; (3) by the researchers who consult and use the collection.[3] The collection's path to ODU's library testifies to the importance of family networks and patterns of internal migration in the preservation of personal histories. The contents offer a perspective on the lives of wealthy, acculturated Jews in the American South that contributes to the mosaic of perspectives emerging in Jewish American history which has traditionally focused on the immigrant experience of the turn of the twentieth century.[4]

The creators and individual memory

At the creator's and the donor's levels, the collection testifies to the persistence of individual memory and the memory of a family, and, in this particular case, to the 'memory aims' of Minette Cooper, Switzer's niece. Growing up in a prominent Southern family with a strong philanthropic, intellectual, and cultural bent, Cooper inherited a keen sense of the importance of personal and societal history, a commitment to carry on the works and traditions of her family, and a responsibility to promote cultural education and preservation. She became the 'preserver' of her generation, sorting through family papers, choosing what she felt had either intrinsic or sentimental value. She then dispersed materials to various archives and collections. The papers of William Haas, Sr., and William Haas, Jr., related by marriage, went to the American Jewish Archives (AJA).[5] Established in 1947 and housed at the Hebrew Union College – Jewish Institute of Religion in Cincinnati, the AJA 'identifies, collects and preserves records of enduring value that document American Jewish life' with the aim to demonstrate 'the diversity and distinctiveness of the North American Jewish community'.[6] Cooper felt that the papers of Haas senior, a businessman, and his son, a journalist for the *Mexico Ledger*, both prominent citizens and philanthropists in Mexico, Missouri, would find an appropriate home there. Her Uncle Sam Switzer's rare and valuable books on Judaic subjects, Cooper donated to her congregation Ohef Sholom.[7] While the temple in Norfolk, Virginia provided a home for the books, it was not an appropriate site for Switzer's correspondence and other materials documenting his education at elite north-eastern US institutions, his experiences in World War I, his travels around the world, and his life in Vicksburg.

In considering what to do with Uncle Sam's papers, Cooper had a variety of choices. The historical society in Vicksburg, Mississippi would probably have been interested as Switzer was a prominent citizen and native son. Perhaps archivists at Phillips Exeter Academy in Exeter, New Hampshire or Harvard University in Cambridge, Massachusetts would have found Sam's correspondence and papers worthy of accession; he was an alumnus of both institutions.[8] As the materials offer a glimpse of American Southern Jewish life in the early decades of the twentieth century, AJA (where Cooper donated the Haas papers) might have been interested. Certainly, the Southern Jewish Historical Society Archives (SJHS), housed in Special Collections at the Addlestone Library at the College of Charleston, South Carolina, which specializes in 'family and community histories related to the Jewish experience in the South, and collections and items of exceptional intrinsic or research value relating to Southern Jewry' would have been a natural choice.[9] Among Cooper's many philanthropic and volunteer endeavours was a stint on the SJHS board. She served as the Society's president and donated her papers relating to SJHS work to the archives there.

Donation of Sam Switzer's papers to the AJA or SJHS archives would have marked the collection and Sam Switzer's experience as part of the history of American and Southern Jewry. Both archives are what archivist Laura Millar categorizes as 'activist archives', founded with a specific mission and developing collections that advocate for the history of a particular group.[10] AJA and SJHS encourage broad public use of their archives, but at both of these sites the collections would have been catalogued with an eye to their contributions to American and/or Southern Jewish history. Sam Switzer's papers would have been most accessible to scholars researching questions related to the archives' Jewish mission.

Instead, Cooper placed the correspondence and ephemera in Special Collections at ODU. She offered two reasons. First, she was pleased with the university's treatment of records relating to the City of Norfolk's development that her husband's family had deposited there.[11] Second, she wanted the collection to be accessible to her three sons and their families, living in Norfolk and Washington DC. She wanted her children and grandchildren growing up amidst cousins and relatives of her husband, members of the Cooper and Miller families with deep roots in the Hampton Roads, Virginia area, to feel a part of her family and to understand the richness of their ties to Vicksburg and the lives of their Switzer and Leyens relatives.[12]

Emotional ties guided Cooper's decision to offer the papers to ODU, and the importance of these sentiments linked to the materials, mostly letters and Sam Switzer's personal documents, is evident in two ways. First, Cooper maintains ownership. The collection is at ODU under an agreement for permanent loan.[13] Second, other materials that might have been attached to the collection, but did not carry the same emotional weight or have the personal perspective, have been dispersed to other archives. For example, in 2004, long after the Switzer collection had been placed at ODU, Cooper donated a large photograph of Sam Switzer's father Simon Switzer standing in front of Switzer-Newitter (the predecessor to the family's Valley Dry Goods Company in Vicksburg) to the AJA archives in Cincinnati.[14] The donation to the AJA archives may reflect Cooper's emotional distance from her uncle's father and her willingness to donate the photograph outright. It may also reflect Cooper's judgement with respect to the collection's value and her assumption regarding the scholarly audience that might find it of interest.

The archivists and collective memory

The choice of ODU's Special Collections affected the ways in which Switzer's papers would be shared in a public space and the ways in which they would be read. ODU's Special Collections is a 'hybrid archive', an archive that functions as a repository for internal institutional materials and acquires collections of interest from outside donors. It is organized according to the university's priorities, catalogued by the university's archivists, and presented to make it appealing to a diverse community of scholars and researchers using it for myriad purposes to explore a wide variety of themes.[15]

As Richard Cox suggests, 'Whatever comes into archives and however it gets there might be beside the point because archives are a way station on the road to a collective memory'.[16] Once the materials were deposited at ODU, they ceased to be merely Uncle Sam's papers. They became MG (Manuscript Group) 37 'The Papers of Samuel Leyens Switzer', grouped with more than 50 other manuscript collections containing 'correspondence, diaries, legislative and mayoral files, campaign files, family papers, scrapbooks, photographs, business papers, and legal files' in Special Collections, a repository with strengths 'related to African-American history, the Civil War, local history, Norfolk school desegregation, politics, military history, and Women's [sic] history'.[17] Appropriated from the family, Switzer's papers began to reflect the priorities and aims of ODU's archivist. The naming of the collection marked its passage from a collection of materials relating to individual or family reminiscence to a tool for construction of public memory. Minette Cooper's remark, 'I never recall him being called Samuel', in reference to the listing of 'The Papers of Samuel Leyens Switzer', testifies to the transfer of the collection's stewardship.[18]

The archivist arranged the materials chronologically. The collection begins with a letter from Sam to his mother written in 1911 that describes life at Exeter Academy (Hanover, NH). The final pieces of correspondence, written in Vicksburg, date from July 1957. The bulk of the holdings reflect on Switzer's experience of World War I – his years at Harvard (1915–1917), in military training (1917–1918), on the French front (1918), and in France and Germany (until June 1919). Materials relating to Switzer's life in Vicksburg after the war are considerably sparser.[19] The relative paucity of documents from Switzer's later years reflects Cooper's choices. Unable to preserve everything her Uncle Sam had collected, Cooper sorted through his effects. Some scattered papers related to temple business and history went to the family's congregation, Anshe Chesed in Vicksburg. Cooper weeded out much of the later correspondence that appeared mundane and impersonal, and much was discarded. Switzer's early letters she kept and eventually placed at ODU.

Special Collections' appropriation of these materials is underlined both in the finding aid and in the biography of Switzer that appear on the library's website to guide the researching public's use of the collection. The touch of the archivist's hand, judgement, and intents in preserving the collection are evident. The finding aid and biography reveal what Eric Ketelaar has described as the importance of the 'multi-layered, multi-faceted meanings hidden in archivalization and archiving'.[20] The biographical sketch, prepared in 1980 on acquisition of the materials and subsequently posted on-line, begins with a mention of Switzer's birth in 1896 to a 'prominent Vicksburg, Mississippi family'. It traces his education, experience in World War I, and return to civilian life in Vicksburg, where he lived as a bachelor, successful businessman, and community philanthropist. It ends with the note, 'Samuel Leyens Switzer died on April 14, 1960, in Vicksburg, Mississippi. His family remembered him as being "fervently American as a nationality and Jewish as a religion"'.[21]

The introduction of the family's voice in the final line hints at a difference between the perspectives of the donor and the archivist. As Elisabeth Kaplan suggests, archives play a role in 'the construction of particular forms of identity and the sublimation of others'.[22] The donor's vision and assessment of the public value of Switzer' papers clashed with the archivist's assessment of the collection and desires to exercise responsible stewardship to encourage its use.[23] The clash between Cooper and the archivist also related to aspects of 'social memory' associated with the collection's preservation and use.[24] Cooper saw the papers through the lens of personal experience with her uncle, and her impulse was to reconstruct his past based on her impressions. His service in World War I linked him to World War I soldiers and their universal or common experiences. In Cooper's view, World War I had an indelible effect on Switzer's life. She attributes his lifelong bachelorhood to the wartime trauma and the lasting psychological effects of his war experience.[25] The archivist, without this personal connection, focused on categorizing Switzer and classifying his experience to provide research 'signposts' and 'map' the collection for researchers' use.

Tensions between the donor and the archivist were evident in a letter Cooper wrote shortly after the collection was loaned in 1980, in which she offered a correction to the draft biography. The biography emphasized Switzer's Jewishness, particularly near the end where it reflected on his philanthropic and social activities in Vicksburg. Cooper asked that Switzer's Americanness and the importance of the collection in conveying aspects of American society and American life be recognized equally and remembered.[26] Cooper had salvaged these papers that documented Sam Switzer's contribution as an American hero of World War I. The archivist prioritized his place in history as a Jewish American. The emphasis on his later life and Jewish activities in Vicksburg in the archivist's biography is particularly striking as few papers relate to his post-World War I experience. Cooper had purposely donated them elsewhere. The final line of the ODU biography reflects a compromise between the donor and the archivist. The phrase 'fervently American as a nationality and Jewish as a religion' was inserted in the last line, admitting the importance of Switzer's overlapping allegiances as a Harvard man, an American soldier, a Southerner, and a Jew, but it was placed in quotation marks and distinguished as part of the family's wishes, separating the family's voice from that of the archivist.

A Jewish archive?

Cooper's argument for the recognition of Switzer's Americanness gets to the heart of broader Jewish dilemmas, bringing to light questions relating to Jewish assimilation, acculturation, and self-identification in American society. It also reflects her perspective on American mainstream tendencies to see Jews as separate or distinct and to associate them first and foremost with their religious heritage. The collection's relevance to Jewish life can be established in the context of Switzer's family history and on the basis of the content of some of the correspondence. However, insistence on the 'Jewishness' of the collection sublimates other identities that were at the heart of the preservation of the collection and are equally or perhaps even more strongly preserved in the surviving materials.

References to Jewish ritual, practice, and culture are scattered throughout the documents, but Jewishness is not a predominant theme. Evidence of Jewishness and associations with Judaism appear most frequently in Switzer's letters written at Harvard. Several times, he mentions going to temple and joining relatives in the Boston area for lunch.[27] He writes to his mother about an invitation to join ZBT (Zeta Beta Tau), the Jewish fraternity. Established in 1898 at the Jewish Theological Seminary, by the 1910s ZBT had several north-eastern chapters and one at Tulane in New Orleans. It catered to Reform Jews, most of whom were members of the American Jewish elite of German origins.[28] The invitation recognized Switzer's social standing. The initiation fee was a steep $40, and the fraternity only accepted 10 people.[29] It also suggested his acceptance among the privileged Jewish elites who, as the decade wore on, used fraternal and other social organizations to 'exercise the entire gamut of internal communal prejudices', differentiating themselves from recent immigrants seeking advancement through education.[30]

No further mention of the organization appeared, and ultimately it does not seem that Switzer joined. Either he decided against it or was not one of those selected for membership. Nonetheless, his circle of friends and acquaintances appears to be primarily a Jewish one, a reflection of the social realities of Boston and Cambridge society. Switzer clearly embraced his privileged place but also recognized the underlying prejudices and social disadvantages that Jews faced in the United States. At Harvard, while he fitted in with the acculturated wealthy Jews, he was certainly not one of the old stock traditional Harvard students who proceeded with an attitude of 'cultivated indifference'. Rather, he was most likely one of the 'unseemly nouveaux', looked down on as an 'aggressive Jew', an 'energetic' middle class (by Harvard standards) student who viewed the college 'as a means of social advancement'.[31] Switzer was aware of the social hierarchy and of his place in it. In a letter describing the social world of Cambridge he explained why Jews, in particular his young married cousin, might be less than satisfied with the local social scene. 'Cambridge is inhabited by two social extremes' – the 'roughnecks' or 'lower class of labouring people' and the 'descendants of the Pilgrim forefathers, etc.' His cousin would not notice the former, he noted, and 'the latter would not notice' her, 'she not having blue blood'.[32]

The traditions of anti-Semitism in Cambridge were well-established. In 1904, for example, Dean of the Lawrence School of Science at Harvard University Nathaniel Shaler published a chapter entitled 'The Hebrew Problem' in *The Neighbor: The Natural History of Human Contacts*, a tome warning of the dangers of immigration. Shaler did not revile Jews or place them at the low level of Africans, but he saw them as occupying an ambiguous social position and did not advocate mixing with them.[33] By 1922, Harvard President A. Lawrence Lowell proposed a plan to limit the admission of 'boys who have come, or whose parents have come, to this country without our background', a veiled attempt to limit Jewish enrolment, which had increased from 6% in 1908 to 22% in 1922.[34]

Switzer's level of commitment to Jewish ritual is not clear. Like Joseph Proskauer from Mobile, Alabama, Switzer appears to have grown up in a Reform Jewish household 'not piously orthodox but observant', surrounded by friends and acquaintances of a variety of faiths, and believing, perhaps, that 'all religions were good' but his 'was somewhat the best'.[35] Certainly, Switzer eschewed Jewish practices related to *kashrut* (Jewish dietary law). He mentions attending a party in Boston praising the 'lobster salad – lots of pretty women'. He reports spending time with his cousin Miriam, but found the religious atmosphere stifling, telling his mother, 'I told her I had enough religion to last me a year'.[36]

Other comments suggest that Switzer was not devoted to rituals although he felt his Jewishness strongly. From France in April 1919, he wrote to his mother saying that he *thought* it was 'the eve of Pesach'. He suggested that he 'wanted badly' to go to services sponsored by the Jewish Welfare Board but did not go. Switzer said he would 'try' to obtain *matzohs* but had not prepared in advance for the holiday. In the Passover season, he wished to 'read some religious book', but admitted that he had left his bible in Paris and prayer book in Kruft (Germany).[37] He valued his copy of the *Abridged Prayer Book for Jews in the Army and Navy of the United States* provided by the Jewish Welfare Board (JWB) enough to keep it as a memento of his service abroad. It is among the materials in the collection at ODU.[38] But its significance to him was probably not related to daily use or specific religious content. A token of his World War I experience as an American Jewish soldier, the prayer book would not have met Switzer's devotional needs after the war. Its content was the product of a compromise between orthodox and liberal Jewish groups. Religious leaders across the spectrum were dissatisfied with it, and as a result of the controversy, the JWB had restricted the prayer book's distribution to those serving overseas.[39]

Switzer was part of a Jewish community in Vicksburg dating back to the 1820s.[40] The family's congregation, Anshe Chesed (People of Loving Kindness), was founded in 1841 and incorporated in 1862. In 1874, the congregation joined the American Hebrew Congregations, placing it securely within the Reform tradition.[41] The temple building in use throughout Switzer's lifetime dated from 1868. The Young Men's Hebrew Benevolent Association, formed in 1871, was affiliated with B'nai B'rith and later became known as the B'nai B'rith Literary Association or B.B. Club.[42] As in many other 'small places', or towns with small Jewish populations, B'nai B'rith formed the nexus for local Jewish social life – 'the congregation, the club, the centre of charitable activity, and the literary and debating society'.[43] At the turn of the century, the Vicksburg B.B. Club, housed in an ornate building erected in 1892 then rebuilt after a fire in 1915,[44] was noted for lavish entertaining, hospitality, and excellent (non-kosher) cuisine. In the 1920s, charter member of the synagogue's sisterhood Birdie Field also practised Christian Science, a testament to the community's tolerance for diverse personal religious practices.[45] Taking over the congregation in the 1930s, Rabbi Brav found a 'remarkable unity' in the Jewish community that he attributed to his predecessor Rabbi Sol Kory's ability to accommodate Jews of various religious lifestyles and beliefs.[46]

Scattered correspondence suggests that while not wedded to orthodoxy, Switzer remained deeply committed to his congregation, congregational life, and the relationship of Jews to the larger community in Vicksburg.[47] Switzer's experience with Jewish organizations, in particular with the B.B. Club, reflected the secular values of many acculturated American Jews. For men in particular, social clubs played a role as important as synagogues in offering an arena in which to articulate their religious affiliation.[48]

Established in New York by German-Jewish immigrants dedicated to humanitarian causes and, in particular, to ameliorating 'the deplorable condition of Jews in this, our newly adopted country', at its founding in 1843 B'nai B'rith was a benevolent society seeking to provide insurance and aid to widows and children. Its commitment to charitable works and humanitarianism led the organization to a neutral stance in the Civil War, and it served those suffering on both sides of the conflict.[49] Disputes over the eligibility for membership in the 1870s led to decentralization and the development of a federated organizational structure. Local lodges maintained considerable freedom of action, but the organization's core commitment to Jewish humanitarian causes in the United States remained strong, and B'nai B'rith expanded its efforts to serve Jews around the world.[50] While the organization provided considerable support and advocacy for Jews in Palestine, it did not emphasize Zionism or Israel in the manner of Hadassah, the national Jewish philanthropic organization founded in 1912, which took Zionism and support for Israel as its central focus.[51] B'nai B'rith's neutrality in the Civil War and its 'secular ethnicity' and 'pluralist integration' approach in the first half of the twentieth century were in tune with the sentiments of Vicksburg's Jews, whom Rabbi Brav described as a 'community of non-Zionists'.[52]

Race, ethnicity, and nation

Minette Cooper's insistence on equal attention in the collection to Switzer's Jewishness and Americanness reflects the dilemma that confronted wealthier acculturated Jews like Switzer in turn-of-the-century America (and continues to haunt American Jews today) – the conundrum of 'determining how Jewish they wanted to be'.[53] This question lay at the heart of debate in the 1890s when the American Jewish Historical Society was founded. The society, which pledged its commitment to 'not sectarian but American' values, distanced itself from the religiosity and 'foreignness' of immigrant Jews.[54]

In the American South, where nation, religion, and race intertwined, Jews' associations were complicated. In *The Provincials*, Eli Evans, native of Durham, North Carolina, recounts the conflicts and complications of being Jewish, American, and Southern. At the turn of the century, '[t]he Jews were first of all white, or at least men who could pass for white'. However, they were not Christians and evoked a sense of distrust and foreignness that made them 'alien' to most Southerners accustomed to the 'sameness all around'.[55] According to Eric Goldstein, some Jews welcomed the racial discourse emerging in the late nineteenth century. It allowed them to voice their distinctiveness from mainstream American society and exhibit a 'degree of communal assertiveness' while, at the same time, it provided 'emotional security' by placing them securely in the larger white world.[56]

Switzer was of the generation that after several decades of Jewish acculturation had been 'swallowed up in the terrain of the Southern mind and soul', who '[g]rowing up as Southerners' had 'absorbed the regional defiance and unrestrained pride, the memories of rising to sing "Dixie" in grammar school assembly and, in history class, the surging poignance of reading Lee's farewell to his troops'. While Jewish men of his generation were keenly aware of their 'alienness', they shared the Southern sense of nostalgia and romanticization of the American South. As Evans suggests, they were 'white boys to the Negro', who would 'know deference and come to expect it of the blacks'.[57] Although they were associated with trends toward urbanization, industrialization, and modernity linked at the turn of the century to cultural degeneracy, Jews nonetheless resided on the white side of the black/white colour line.[58]

As a young man, Switzer certainly imbibed the social prejudices and racial attitudes characteristic of the turn-of-the-century South. In a letter to his mother written in 1916, he complained that he had been forced 'to hang around the smoker for a good long time' on a crowded train to New York on account of a white woman 'with more nerve than sense'. The woman in question had sent her maid, a 'coal black Ethiopian', to sit with her child in the seat opposite Switzer's. His revulsion to 'the ebony damsel', who he claimed 'was perfuming the opposing receptacle for bodies in a sitting position', led him to abandon his seat to seek haven in the 'burnt-leaf cabin'.[59] Switzer's harping on the black woman's offence to his olfactory senses echoed common racist criticisms levelled against Jews as well as blacks, charges that the inferior races could be identified by their bodily secretions and distinctive odours. Switzer's self-induced exile to the smoking cabin reflected broader Southern social and legal trends favouring increased racial separation. Rail cars were one of the first sites of legal segregation in the postbellum South.[60]

In 1914, Switzer wrote two 'themes' for his classes at Harvard, one a 'Criticism on Kipling' and the other 'The Life of the Average Southern Negro'. Both essays reflected the turn-of-the-century fascination with racial identity and white hierarchy derived from emerging European theories of racial science.[61] The former on Kipling was in line with the standard curriculum and the study of British, Anglo-Saxon, and white supremacy abroad. The latter relied on Switzer's experience as a Southerner.[62]

The quickening pace of Jewish immigration and mass immigration from Eastern Europe that changed the American landscape in the first decades of the twentieth century nearly doubled the American Jewish population in the years from 1907 to 1918 and caused considerable disquiet in the ranks of established American Jews in large urban centres.[63] Throughout the United States, Jews were increasingly associated with foreignness and 'cast beyond the pale of whiteness'.[64] The mass migration had less effect in small towns in the South like Vicksburg, where the relatively small percentage of Jews forced them to participate more in non-Jewish society. Accustomed to acceptance as whites in the polarized racial climate of the South, Jews like Switzer were most likely taken aback by prejudice and racism directed at Jews in cities like Boston.[65]

Nonetheless, due to the shifting racial tides, Switzer would have seen changes in his Vicksburg congregation. Vicksburg Rabbi Sol Kory's efforts to welcome Eastern European immigrant families and assist orthodox newcomers met with resistance and criticism.[66] Throughout his tenure at Anshe Chesed from 1903 to 1936, the native-born Mississippian was deeply involved in secular and religious philanthropic causes. Eventually, he succeeded in integrating the new immigrants into the congregation. He took care to spread his philosophy and reminded young congregants like Switzer of their responsibilities to local religious life. 'The future lies in you boys and having faced the realities and gotten down to the fundamentals our religious life will be shaped by you', Kory wrote to Switzer in France.[67] Switzer returned after the war and took on his role as a leader in the Vicksburg Jewish community.

How Switzer's experience of the war, life abroad, and developments in Vicksburg and in the United States in the decades following World Wars I and II, including the rise of the Civil Rights Movement in the American South, affected his racial and political attitudes is difficult to gauge. Evidence suggests the emergence of liberal sympathies among the leaders of Vicksburg's Jewish community by the 1950s. Scholars debate Southern Jews' position in and contributions to the American civil rights movement. Some Southern rabbis are noted for their role in promoting civil rights, but most appear as quiet, reticent voices for social change.[68] Holders of Anshe Chesed's pulpit do not fit this mould. Switzer and members of other prominent Vicksburg Jewish families who sat on the temple's board hired and supported outspoken men with records of commitment to social justice.[69]

After Sol Kory, Anshe Chesed's rabbis during Switzer's lifetime included Stanley Brav (1937–1948), Samuel Schillman (1948–1953), Leonard Rothstein (1954–1956), and Adolf Philippsborn (1956–1961).[70] All, including Kory, attended Hebrew Union College in Cincinnati. Founded in 1875, HUC was the first American institution of Jewish higher education and provided training for the Reform rabbinate. From its inception, the institution emphasized communal work and 'progressive', 'modern' spiritual leadership.[71]

Among Vicksburg's rabbis, Stanley Brav was the best known for his political activism. A pacifist, passionately involved in issues of social justice and peace, he promoted women's rights and civil rights.[72] His opposition to white supremacist Mississippi governor and United States Senator Theodore Bilbo garnered nationwide attention. In 1945, the leftist New York newspaper *PM* published a statement by Bilbo claiming that Mississippi Jews supported his racial position and that they 'all' had voted for him. The Vicksburg rabbi responded with an indignant letter. Bilbo then denounced Brav and suggested that the rabbi 'move to New York', presumably to join in what the Senator intimated to be the Jewish communist conspiracy threatening the nation. In the Congressional Record in July 1945, Bilbo maintained, 'I have outstanding Jewish friends in Vicksburg who have always supported me'. He claimed to know the 'good Jews of Mississippi, who are fine citizens, many of whom ... are in thorough sympathy with the ideals and principles of the South and [are] not negro-lovers – Jews who believe in the white race and white supremacy'. The fiery exchange received state- and nation-wide attention. Anshe Chesed's president initially condemned the rabbi in a chastising letter, but the temple's board withdrew the letter and gave Brav a vote of confidence.[73] Brav kept his pulpit and continued his vociferous opposition to racism. In particular, he fought to thwart Bilbo's re-election in 1946.[74] He was one of only two whites to testify against Bilbo in Federal Court in December 1946. The congregation did not protest at his activism, and less than a year later in 1947, in honour of the tenth anniversary of his service, gave him the gift of 'a handsome Oldsmobile car'.[75]

In 1948, Brav left the congregation for a larger congregation and to return to family in Cincinnati. In his memoirs, he mentioned the 'serious controversies' that arose with regard to the 'all-pervasive racial problem' and noted having been 'frequently asked to curtail such pulpit references' in Vicksburg. But while his outspokenness certainly caused discomfort in some segments of the Mississippi community, he remarked that he had felt, 'accepted and respected in spite of, if not because of my unpopular views'.[76] In this respect, the Jews of Vicksburg seemed to share the dilemma of Jews throughout Mississippi and the South, many of whom appeared to sympathize to varying degrees with civil rights efforts, but who were reticent to openly oppose racial norms or breach accepted racial etiquette for fear that activism would carry too high a price.[77]

Rabbi Leonard Rothstein, who joined Anshe Chesed in 1954, had a long history of outspoken activism, dating back decades to social advocacy at his congregation in Alexandria, Louisiana from 1907 to 1918. After serving in World War I, he went to Pine Bluff, Arkansas, where his opposition to the local school board's decision to allow a member of the Ku Klux Klan to speak in the public schools divided his congregation Anshe Emeth. In 1923, he left Arkansas and moved north to St. Paul, Minnesota, where he criticized the 'narrowness and blindness of the [Arkansas] community at large'.[78] The Vicksburg community was surely aware of Rothstein's history and activism when considering him for Anshe Chesed's pulpit in 1954. The decisions to hire Rothstein and Brav suggest that rabbinical outspokenness must have been acceptable to the Vicksburg community.

It may be that elite social status, involvement in Jewish social activities, and lifelong bachelorhood shielded Switzer from the 'segregation at sundown' (or social segregation and exclusion outside of the integrated world of commercial endeavours and business transactions) that plagued Jewish families seeking social acceptance in the mainstream South.[79] But even Brav noted the high level of integration of Jews in Vicksburg. In addition to membership in Jewish organizations like B'nai B'rith and the YMHA, the rabbi found himself a member of the YMCA, the Rotary Club, the Advisory Board of the Salvation Army, and the National Park Golf Club.[80] Possibly Vicksburg, with its emphasis on commerce and very small and old-established Jewish population with very few immigrants was less fearful and more open in its social acceptance of Jews than other communities in Mississippi and the Deep South.

With respect to Switzer's personal attitudes, racism does not appear in the documents after World War I. Switzer was among the prominent members of his Vicksburg congregation, and he worked closely with the rabbis during their tenures, perhaps most notably serving as the president of the first Jewish Welfare Federation in Mississippi, established by Brav.[81] After Rothstein retired in 1956, Switzer continued their relationship and saw him as a friend. He purchased the books now at Ohef Sholom in Norfolk, Virginia from Rothstein when the rabbi moved out of his home and into a nursing facility.[82] Although Switzer's motivation could have been entirely humanitarian and personal, the transaction indicates a degree of social intimacy and mutual respect free from ideological discord. A hint of liberal bent later in life lies in Switzer's lifelong membership in B'nai B'rith. In 1954, the organization took a strong stand in support of the Supreme Court's decision striking down the 'separate but equal' principle. Thousands of members throughout the South chose to resign, but Switzer remained a member until his death in 1960.[83]

An American archive?

ODU's collection relates primarily to Switzer's World War I experiences. Issues related to social class, race, and life in the American South have equal or greater weight than Jewishness in the collection, which testifies to the interwoven threads of 'braided' identity – American, Southern, and Jewish – that constitute the fabric of Southern Jews' lives. The collection reveals the 'compatibility of Southern and Jewish traditions', a seamless existence that allowed Jews in the South to 'feast on matzoh brei as well as moon pie'.[84]

The care with which Cooper assembled Switzer's correspondence and mementos relating to his military service suggests that she took pride in his experiences as an American, a Southerner, a soldier, and a veteran. The preserved papers testify to Switzer's participation in the US Army Training Camp at Plattsburgh in 1916 and the Military Instruction Camp at Harvard in 1917. He then joined the American Expeditionary Forces in France in a trajectory typical for a Harvard recruit.[85] A preserved letter from the Training Camp Division for the south-east, headquartered in Charleston, South Carolina, suggests that even before he went abroad, officers in the American military sought Switzer out as a leader among his Southern peers. They called on him as a fellow Southerner to help attract recruits from Mississippi.[86]

In addition to the dozens of letters written from military training camp and from Europe, the Switzer collection includes post-war correspondence that focuses on memories of the war, correspondence with veterans' organizations, documents and news clippings, and other papers related to Switzer's military service. Scattered post-war folders include correspondence asking Switzer to recount the circumstances of his being awarded the Distinguished Service Cross for defending a bridge position in July 1918. They also include exchanges with fellow servicemen.[87] In this respect, American nationalism, patriotism, and military service form the thematic thread in the collection. The creators' and donor's emphasis on the experience of the Great War meshes with contemporary intellectual currents and scholar's interests. It invites study in line with the broader public fascination with the extraordinary circumstances of World War I and remembrance in its aftermath.[88]

Video footage of Switzer's 1937 trip around the world (converted to DVD format) that depicts daily life in capitals of East Asia, in Turkey, and at the Universal Exhibition in Paris bears no imprint of Jewishness. The record of this trip, for which Switzer had 'twelve feet (4 meters) of tickets', affords a glimpse of life on the eve of outbreak of war in Asia and the Pacific. It contains no hint of the virulent anti-Semitism already gripping Nazi Germany and Europe that would explode in the Holocaust.[89]

Challenging assumptions: Americanness, Jewishness, and migration

The collection was not consciously created as a Jewish archive, nor does the bulk of the material deal with Jewish themes. Yet the archivist's impulse was to underline Switzer's Jewishness, a reflection of his judgement of the materials' value to researchers. Scholars' utilization of the papers has demonstrated the value or impact of the archivist's 'mediation'.[90] Prior to the autumn of 2009 and autumn of 2010, when the Switzer collection formed the basis for a project assigned in an ODU graduate seminar on historical methods, the materials were consulted primarily by scholars studying American Jewish soldiers' experience of World War I. The graduate students who consulted it found that the collection offered much fodder for the exploration of various issues relating to the French front, American censorship, the relationship between the home front and soldiers abroad, and the American experience in Europe just after World War I. The collection's value lies in the combination of identities it depicts – of Sam Switzer as a Northern-educated, elite Southern Jew from Vicksburg, Mississippi and a war hero.

Early twentieth-century Jewish history in the US is viewed most often through the lens of immigration and through the eyes of poor, 'foreign' immigrants and their experiences of chain migration or of acculturation. Where it is examined in the context of American history in the decades following the Civil War, it is often conceived and explored in a regional context.[91] The Switzer papers underline the interrelation of the Northern and Southern Jewish communities and North and South. They suggest the need to examine assumed dichotomies between urban and small town Jews. They demonstrate that wealthy Jews migrated readily between communities in the north-eastern and southern United States, taking advantage of established commercial, social, and kinship networks. Historians like Deborah Dash Moore have identified Jews' attachment to and concentration in cities, or their 'urban regionalism', as a foil to sectionalism, a basis for shared identification across typical American regional divides.[92] But Sam Switzer's experiences and the experiences of his family, while characterized by commercial ties to north-eastern cities and elite education, cannot be considered urban. Vicksburg remained a small community, with a population that grew from 15,000 to 25,000 over the course of Switzer's lifetime. The Jewish population declined from a high of 688 in 1907 to 280 by 1950.[93]

Ties to Vicksburg defined Switzer's and his family's existence. The Switzer family's experiences echo those of the prominent Lehman family. With major interests in Alabama and New York related to the cotton trade, members of the Lehman family moved relatively freely between North and South pursuing commercial opportunities in interdependent trade networks. While the Lehmans eventually quit Alabama for larger metropolitan centres as they expanded their financial empire, their experience challenges commonly held assumptions of regional divides in the US.[94] Operating on a smaller scale than the Lehmans, the Switzers had a similar experience of traversing the North/South divide. They established the Valley Dry Goods Company in Vicksburg in the 1880s and worked with family members and agents in New York and Boston. Unlike the Lehmans, the family did not abandon the South. Sam Switzer's branch remained ensconced in Vicksburg. But, Switzer did travel north to Phillips Exeter Academy and then to Harvard. There, he was enmeshed in a circle of aunts, uncles, and cousins educated in elite Northern institutions including Cornell University and Yale University, many of whom lived in New York and Boston.[95] The trek northward to attend school or university near to Northern relatives was not an uncommon experience for Southern boys and young men. Proskauer's 'Southern boyhood' in Mobile ended with his matriculation at Columbia University in 1892.[96] Contacts between North and South and the constant flow of goods and capital forged interdependence. This was reflected in family networks and community development north and south of the Mason–Dixon line.[97] Social mobility and economic circumstances affected Jewish self-identification and the construction of Jewish communities.[98] Switzer's experience testifies to the importance of social class as well as kinship ties that enabled Jews to traverse traditionally conceived sectional or cultural divides in the United States.

In terms of migration, the deposit of the Switzer collection in Virginia may represent the family's movement 'full circle'. Minette Cooper came to the Tidewater region of Virginia because it was her husband's family's home, but the Switzers had roots in Virginia. Sam's father Simon Switzer had migrated from Staunton, Virginia to Vicksburg, when he married Flora Leyens, a Mississippi native.[99] The Valley Dry Goods Company was named for Virginia's Shenandoah Valley, a mark of Simon Switzer's nostalgia for his home.[100]

With respect to questions of the Switzer collection's Jewishness and indeed of the broader dilemma of defining what constitutes a 'Jewish archive', examination of the collection and its provenance offers no definitive answers. It depends on which materials or voices in the archive are privileged, by whom, and for what purpose. Just as archivists understand that the meaning of records 'can be deconstructed and reconstructed, then used by scholars, over and over again',[101] so too can the archive be reconsidered and re-evaluated as a site for the 'production of knowledge'[102] according to its location, context, and purpose.

Acknowledgements

The author wishes to thank B. Minette Cooper for making her uncle's papers available, for sharing the rich history of her family, and for reading a draft of this paper with a keen, critical eye. The author also acknowledges the gracious assistance of former Special Collections Librarian and University Archivist Sonia Yaco at Old Dominion University, now at the University of Illinois-Chicago, and the anonymous reviewers for their helpful suggestions and comments. The Kaplan Centre at the University of Cape Town and the Parkes Institute at the University of Southampton provided a climate conducive to sharing and refining this work.

Funding

The Institute for Jewish Studies and Interfaith Understanding at Old Dominion University provided travel monies and support for this research.

Notes

1. Special Collections and University Archives, Patricia W. and J. Douglas Perry Library, Old Dominion University Libraries, Norfolk, VA 23529 (hereafter SCUA-ODU), Papers of Samuel Leyens Switzer (MG 37), (hereafter Switzer Coll.), letter, Sam Switzer to Flora Switzer, April 14, 1919, Box 2, Folder 11.
2. Richard Cox, *No Innocent Deposits: Forming Archives by Rethinking Appraisal* (Lanham, MD: Scarecrow Press, 2004).
3. Ibid., 31.
4. Consistent, although by no means constant, references to Jewishness and Switzer's ties to Jewish social and cultural networks throughout his life justify the reference to acculturation rather than assimilation.
5. The Haases were the father and brother of Cooper's Aunt Bertha, the wife of her uncle Sam Kleisdorff. Author's interview with B. Minette Cooper at her home in Norfolk, Virginia, March 20, 2011 (hereafter Cooper interview); email communication from B. Minette Cooper to the author, May 17, 2012 (hereafter Cooper email).
6. The Jacob Rader Marcus Center of the American Jewish Archives, "About the AJA: General Information" and "About the AJA: AJA Collection Policy," http://americanjewisharchives.org/.
7. Cooper interview; Cooper email.
8. Switzer was awarded a special AB degree from Harvard University in 1919 that recognized those who had volunteered for war service after completing most but not all of their degree requirements. Switzer's experience at Harvard and information on the awarding of the degree *in absentia* appear in SCUA-ODU Switzer Coll., Box 1, Folders 4–14, passim. Frederick S. Mead, ed., *Harvard's Military Record in the World War* (Boston: Harvard Alumni Association, 1921), lists those who earned this degree. The entry for Switzer reads "(war degree)18(19)," 928.
9. "Southern Jewish Historical Society: Archives," http://www.jewishsouth.org/archives.
10. Laura A. Millar, *Archives: Principles and Practices* (London: Facet Publishing, 2010), 42–4.
11. SCUA-ODU, Papers of Dudley Cooper and Ocean View Amusement Park (MG 31). Minette Cooper also donated, in 2012, a collection of Virginia Squires programmes from 1970 to 1976, relating to the American Basketball Association team on which Julius Erving played from 1971 to 1973, and correspondence relating to Young Audiences of Virginia, SCUA-ODU, Papers of Minette Cooper (MG 110).
12. Cooper interview.
13. SCUA-ODU, Archivist's Control Folder (MG37).
14. The Jacob Rader Marcus Center of the American Jewish Archives, "Oversize Photograph," http://americanjewisharchives.org/catalog/Record/vtls000007467.
15. Millar, *Archives*, 37–9.
16. Cox, *No Innocent Deposits*, 234.
17. Old Dominion University, "Special Collections and University Archives," http://www.lib.odu.edu/specialcollections/manuscripts/index.htm.
18. Cooper interview.
19. "The Papers of Samuel Leyens Switzer (MG 37)," http://www.lib.odu.edu/special/manuscripts/switzer.htm.
20. Quoted in Randall C. Jimerson, *Archives Power: Memory, Accountability, and Social Justice* (Chicago: Society of American Archivists, 2009), 215.
21. "The Papers of Samuel Leyens Switzer (MG 37)," http://www.lib.odu.edu/special/manuscripts/switzer.htm.
22. Elisabeth Kaplan, "We Are What We Collect, We Collect What We Are: Archives and the Construction of Identity," *The American Archivist* 63 (2000): 127.
23. On archivists' professional responsibilities, see Millar, *Archives*, 46–7.
24. On social memory see Francis X. Blouin, Jr. and William G. Rosenberg, *Processing the Past: Contesting Authority in History and the Archives* (Oxford: Oxford University Press, 2011), 97–101.
25. Cooper interview.
26. SCUA-ODU, Archivist's Control Folder (MG37), letter, Minette Cooper to University Archivist James Sweeney, September 10, 1980.

27. SCUA-ODU Switzer Coll., Box 1, Folders 4–14, passim.
28. Marianne Sanua, "Jewish College Fraternities in the United States, 1895–1968: An Overview," *Journal of American Ethnic History* 19, no. 2 (2000): 10. The initials ZBT originally referred to the organization's Hebrew biblical motto Zion Be-mishpat Tipadeh (Isaiah 1:27).
29. SCUA-ODU Switzer Coll., letter, Sam Switzer to Flora Switzer, May 2, 1915, Box 1, Folder 12.
30. Sanua, "Jewish College Fraternities," 11.
31. Joan Hedrick, "Harvard Indifference," *The New England Quarterly* 49 no. 3 (1976): 352, 357, 379.
32. SCUA-ODU Switzer Coll., Sam Switzer to Flora Switzer, April 14, 1919, Box 2, Folder 11.
33. Leonard Rogoff, "Is the Jew White? The Racial Place of the Southern Jew," *American Jewish History* 85 no. 3 (1997): 212.
34. Oliver Pollak, "Antisemitism, the Harvard Plan, and the Roots of Reverse Discrimination," *Jewish Social Studies* 45 no. 2 (1983): 114. Pollak quotes Lowell.
35. Joseph M. Proskauer, "Southern Boyhood," in *Autobiographies of American Jews*, ed. Harold U. Ribalow (Philadelphia: The Jewish Publication Society of America, 1973), 133, 137. Proskauer was an appellate court judge then entered into private practice. He served in various political positions. From 1943 to 1949, he was president of the American Jewish Committee. "Appellate Division First Department, Joseph M. Proskauer," http://www.courts.state.ny.us/courts/ad1/centennial/Bios/jmproskauer2.shtml.
36. SCUA-ODU Switzer Coll., letter, Sam Switzer to Flora Switzer, undated, Box 1, Folder 2 and letter, Sam Switzer to Flora Switzer, September 22, 1914, Box 1, Folder 4.
37. SCUA-ODU Switzer Coll., letter, Sam Switzer to Flora Switzer, April 14, 1919, Box 2, Folder 11.
38. The book is preserved in SCUA-ODU Switzer Coll., Box 4, Folder 2.
39. Jessica Cooperman, "'A Little Army Discipline Would Improve the Whole House of Israel': The Jewish Welfare Board, State Power and the Shaping of Jewish Identity in World War I America" (PhD diss., New York University, 2010), 174–8.
40. Lee Shai Weissbach, *Jewish Life in Small-Town America: A History* (New Haven, CT: Yale University Press, 2005), 40.
41. "Vicksburg: Anshe Chesed Cemetery," National Park Service US Department of the Interior, Vicksburg National Military Park, http://www.nps.gov/vick/forteachers/upload/jewish%20cemetery-2.pdf.
42. "Encyclopedia of Southern Jewish Communities: Vicksburg, Mississippi," http://www.isjl.org/history/archive/ms/vicksburg.htm.
43. As described in the 1890s from a congregation in District 6 (the northern Midwestern states), quoted in Edward Grusd, *B'nai B'rith: The Story of a Covenant* (New York: Appleton-Century, 1966), 113.
44. "Vicksburg: Anshe Chesed Cemetery," "Encyclopedia of Southern Jewish Communities: Vicksburg, Mississippi," http://www.isjl.org/history/archive/ms/vicksburg.htm.
45. Weissbach, *Jewish Life in Small-Town America*, 229, 234.
46. Stanley Brav, *Dawn of Reckoning: Self-Portrait of a Liberal Rabbi* (Cincinnati: Sholom Press, 1971), 141–2.
47. "The Papers of Samuel Leyens Switzer (MG 37)," http://www.lib.odu.edu/special/manuscripts/switzer.htm.
48. Eric L. Goldstein, *The Price of Whiteness: Jews, Race, and American Identity* (Princeton, NJ: Princeton University Press, 2006), 12–13.
49. Deborah Dash Moore, *B'nai B'rith and the Challenge of Ethnic Leadership* (Albany: State University of New York Press, 1981), 24–6.
50. Dash Moore, *B'nai B'rith*, 29, 254, and "B'nai B'rith Roots," http://bnaibrith.org/about_us/bbi_roots.cfm.
51. "Our History," Hadassah – The Women's Zionist Organization of America, Inc., http://www.hadassah.org/site/c.keJNIWOvElH/b.5651301/k.AE75/Our_History.htm.
52. Dash Moore, *B'nai B'rith*, 251; and Brav, *Dawn of Reckoning*, 160.
53. Quoted in Kaplan, "We Are What We Collect," 133.
54. Quoted in ibid., 127, 142.

55. Eli Evans, *The Provincials: A Personal History of Jews in the South* (Chapel Hill: University of North Carolina Press, 2005), 38.
56. Goldstein, *Price of Whiteness*, 11–12.
57. Evans, *Provincials*, 41.
58. Goldstein, *Price of Whiteness*, 36.
59. SCUA-ODU Switzer Coll., letter, Sam Switzer to Flora Switzer, April 30, 1916, Box 1, Folder 14.
60. Rogoff, "Is the Jew White?," 209.
61. Ibid., 204–7.
62. SCUA-ODU Switzer Coll., letter, Sam Switzer to Flora Switzer, December 8, 1914, Box 1, Folder 7.
63. The American Jewish population grew from 1,777,185 to 3,390,301 according to Pollak, "Antisemitism," 114.
64. Goldstein, *Price of Whiteness*, 31.
65. Ibid., 59–63.
66. Weissbach, *Jewish Life in Small-Town America*, 162.
67. SCUA-ODU Switzer Coll., letter, Sol Kory to Sam Switzer, April 16, 1919, Box 2, Folder 11.
68. The contours of the debate are outlined in Mark K. Bauman, "Introduction," in *The Quiet Voices: Southern Rabbis and Black Civil Rights, 1880s to 1990s*, ed. Mark K. Bauman and Berkley Kalin (Tuscaloosa: University of Alabama Press, 2007), 4–12, 16–18.
69. Cooper interview.
70. "Encyclopedia of Southern Jewish Communities: History of Anshe Chesed Congregation, Vicksburg, Mississippi," http://www.isjl.org/history/archive/ms/HistoryofAnsheChesed.htm.
71. "Hebrew Union College – Jewish Institute of Religion: History," http://huc.edu/about/history.shtml.
72. A description of Stanley Brav appears in Theodore H. Wohl and Amiel Wohl, *He Really Had Something to Say: The Ideas of Rabbi Samuel Wohl: A Biographical Presentation and World Perspective of Scope and Compassion* (Jersey City, NJ: KTAV Publishing House, Inc., 2005), 97–8.
73. Brav, *Dawn of Reckoning*, 175.
74. Stanley Brav, "Mississippi Incident," *American Jewish Archives* (June 1952): 59–65, http://americanjewisharchives.org/journal/PDF/1952_04_02_00_brav.pdf. Bilbo was not re-seated in Congress. He died in August 1947.
75. Brav, *Dawn of Reckoning*, 178–80.
76. Ibid., 167–8, 181.
77. Marvin Braiterman, "Mississippi Marranos," in *Jews in the South*, ed. Leonard Dinnerstein and Mary Dale Palsson (Baton Rouge: Louisiana State University Press, 1973), 351–9. He describes a Mississippi Jewish community he visited while working for civil rights and desegregation. See also, Goldstein, *Price of Whiteness*, 52.
78. "Encyclopedia of Southern Jewish Communities: History of Pine Bluffs Congregations," http://www.isjl.org/history/archive/ar/HistoryofPineBluffCongregations.htm, and Carolyn Gray LeMaster, *A Corner of the Tapestry: A History of the Jewish Experience in Arkansas, 1820s–1990s* (Fayetteville: University of Arkansas Press, 1994), 57.
79. Rogoff, "Is the Jew White?," 213 n. 41 attributes this to Harry Goldin.
80. Brav, *Dawn of Reckoning*, 143.
81. Ibid., 144.
82. Cooper interview, and Dash Moore, *B'nai B'rith*, 228–9.
83. Cooper interview.
84. Stephen J. Whitfield, "The Braided Identity of Southern Jewry," in *Dixie Diaspora*, ed. Mark K. Bauman (Tuscaloosa: University of Alabama Press, 2006), 431, 446–7.
85. Mead, *Harvard's Military Record*, ix–xvi, outlines the typical path for Harvard students.
86. SCUA-ODU Switzer Coll., letter, H.G. Hooker, Training Camp Division to Sam Switzer, July 7, 1917, Box 1, Folder 23.
87. SCUA-ODU Switzer Coll., Box 2, Folders 15–39, passim.
88. On culture and the memory of World War I, see Jay Winter, *Sites of Memory, Sites of Mourning: The Great War in European Cultural History* (Cambridge: Cambridge University Press, 1995), 2–5.

89. SCUA-ODU Switzer Coll., DVD, Interfile. A copy of this DVD is also available at the AJA archives in Cincinnati in 2008, "Trip Around the World 1937," http://americanjewisharchives.org/catalog/Record/vtls000017281.
90. On archivists' mediation and activism in shaping archives, see Blouin and Rosenberg, *Processing the Past*, 143–8.
91. William R. Ferris et al., "Regionalism: The Significance of Place in American Jewish Life," *American Jewish History* 93 no. 2 (2007): 113–14.
92. Ibid., 115–16.
93. Weissbach, *Jewish Life in Small-Town America*, 342.
94. Elliott Ashkenazi, "Jewish Commercial Interests between North and South: The Case of the Lehmans and the Seligmans," in *Dixie Diaspora* (see note 84), 195, 203–5.
95. References to relatives in the north-east appear in Switzer's Phillips Exeter and Harvard letters in SCUA-ODU Switzer Coll. See also mentions of North/South family networks in Leo Turitz and Evelyn Turitz, *Jews in Early Mississippi* (Jackson: University Press of Mississippi, 1983), 54.
96. Proskauer, "Southern Boyhood," 138.
97. Ashkenazi, "Jewish Commercial Interests," 206.
98. Ferris et al., "Regionalism," 127.
99. Turitz and Turitz, *Jews in Early Mississippi*, 53.
100. Cooper interview. The Valley Dry Goods Company remained in the Switzer Leyens family until 1985. See David S. Sampliner and Mark I. Greenberg, *Discovering Jewish Heritage Across the South* (Jackson: Goldring Woldenberg Institute of Southern Jewish Life, 2001), 35.
101. Quoted in Jimerson, *Archives Power*, 215.
102. Nupur Chaudhuri, Sherry J. Katz, and Mary Elizabeth Perry, *Contesting Archives: Finding Women in the Sources* (Urbana: University of Illinois Press, 2010), xiii.

Index

Abuhazeira, Rabi (Baba Sali) 63
Adler, Alfred 95
Adorno, Theodor 43
AEIOU project, Austria 77
African National Congress (ANC) 111
Aleppo Jewish heritage centre (Israel) 56
Alexandrovich, Rochel Esther *see* Simons, Ray Alexander
American Hebrew Congregation 130
American Jewish Archives (AJA) 125–6
American Jewish Historical Society 131
American Jewish identity 128–36
Anderson, Benedict 63
Anshe Chesed (Jewish congregation) 130, 132–3
Anski, Shin 112
anti-Semitism: and smell 43–4, 47; in the US 129
Aristotle 50
Ashkenazi Jews 48, 49, 50–1
assimilation, of immigrants 13–17, 56
Association for Jewish Refugees journal 88
Auschwitz Museum 78, 88
Australian Migration Heritage Center, New South Wales 81
'Auswanderer-Ausstellung' exhibition, Hamburg 81

Baba Sali (Rabi Abuhazeira) 63
Babel, Isaak 47–9
Babylonian Jewry Heritage Centre (Israel) 56, 57, 58, 59, 60, 61, 62, 64, 65, 66
Ballinstadt, Hamburg ('Port of Dreams' museum) 80
Beilis blood libel affair 47
Beinart, Katy 6–25
Beinart, Rebecca 8
Beinart, Woolf 9–10, 13–15
Belling, Veronica 110–23
Benjamin, Walter 12, 44
Ben-Porat, Mordechai 66
Benz, Wolfgang 38
Bernstein, Michael Andre 29
Bhabha, Homi 77
Bilbo, Theodore 132–3

biography, and the archive 93–5
Bloch, Felix 105
B'nai B'rith 130, 133–4
Bohr, Niels 101
Born, Max 101
Bourdieu, Pierre 61, 68
Boyarin, Jonathan 13, 85
Brav, Rabbi Stanley 132–4
Brodsky, Ana 76
Buhler, Charlotte 113
Bund (Jewish Workers' Party) 110, 116

Cairns, Stephen 6
Cape Town, South Africa 10
Carter, Paul 6, 8
Centre of the Jews of Cochin (Nevatim, Israel) 59
Chambers, Iain 77
Cité nationale de l'histoire de l'immigration, Paris 77
Civil Rights Movement, USA 132
Clacherty, Glynis 83
Clifford, James 77, 84
Communism, and Judaism 116–17
Communist Party of South Africa 110–11
conferences, on migration 82–3
Congress of South African Trade Unions (SACTU) 111
Cooper, Bettie Minette 124–8, 131, 134, 136
correspondence, personal, as archive 27–41
Cox, Richard 125, 127
Csikszentmihalyi, Mihaly 87
Curie, Irene 105
Curie, Joliot 105

Darling Salt Pans and Produce Company (South Africa) 14
Darmstadt Technical University, Germany 67
Darwin, Charles 50
Deleuze, Gilles 85
Deutsche, Rosalynn 77
Deutsches Auswandererhaus, Bremerhaven 80
Deutschkron, Inge 37
diaries 112–13

INDEX

Diaspora: and migration 84; and Zionism 60, 65
Dietrich, Marlene 82, 87
Dik, Isaac Meyer 118
Dirac, Paul 101
Dona Gracia Museum, Tiberias 61
Don't Look Back (art installation) 15
Dostoevsky, Fyodor 118
Dreyfus, Alfred 118

Edelstadt, Dovid 112
E'ele betamar (Yemenite Jewish association) 58
Ehrenfest, Paul 101
Einhorn, David 112
Einstein, Albert 105
Elsasser, Walter 101
Eva Zeisel Papers 94, 99, 106 *see also* Zeisel, Eva
Evans, Eli 131
Exile 60, 66

Farewell Concert (art installation) 19
Federation of South African Women (FEDSAW) 111
Fermi, Laura 96
Field, Birdie 130
Filaratoff, Ann 9
Foer, Jonathan Safran 24
Fonrobert, Charlotte 85
Food and Canning Workers' Union (FCWU), South Africa 111
Foucault, Michel 85
France, Anatole 118
Freud, Sigmund 44, 52
Freudenheim, Fritz 84
Frug, Shimon 112

Gamow, George 103
Garfield, Rachel 13
German Heritage Museum *see* Museum of the German Speaking Jews
Germany, and Jewish emigration 36–8
Ghostwriting (art installation) 23, 24
Gibbons, Joan 25
Gilbert, Shirli 86
Goldshtein, Aleksandr 47, 50–1
Goldstein, Eric 131
Gorky, Maxim 118
Grossmann, Atina 28
Guattari, Felix 85

Haas, William (Sr and Jr) 125
Hadassah 130
Halper, Leib 112
Halton, Eugene 87
Hametz, Maura 124–36
Harvard University 94, 129
Hatefuzot, Beit 63

Hebrew Union College, Cincinnati 132
'Heimat im Koffer,' 2008 (exhibition) 77
Heine, Heinrich 45–6, 49
Hellbeck, Jochin 114
heritage centres, and identity 55–68
Herzl, Theodor 61
Hess, Sabine 82–3
Hinrichsen, Jan 77–8, 84
Hirschbein, Peter 119
Hitler, Adolf 37, 100
Holocaust: commemoration 56, 67; survivor memories 29, 49, 56
Hooper-Greenhill, Eileen 67
Horkheimer, Max 43
Houtermans, Fritz 97, 98, 101, 102, 103, 105, 106
Hull, England 17–19
Hungarian Jewry Centre *see* Memorial Museum of Hungarian Speaking Jewry
Hungarian National Library, Budapest 95
Huyssen, Andrea 58

Immigration Museum, Melbourne 79
Ingold, Tim 25
International Child and Youth Care Network 83
International Socialist League (ISL) 110
Israel: immigration to 56, 59; museums and heritage centres 55–68
Italian Jews, Museum of (Israel) *see* Museum of Italian Jews (Israel)
Italian National Institute for the Exchange of Foreign Currency 39

Jabotinsky, Vladimir 119
Jewish American history 128–36
Jewish Museum, Berlin 84
Jewish Museum, Camden, London 44–5
Jorvik Viking Centre, York 44, 51–2
Jüttens, Ingrid 87

Kapitza, Piotr 101, 103
Kaplan, Elisabeth 127
Katsis, Leonid 49
Ketelaar, Eric 127
Kharik, Izi 112
Kharkov, Ukraine 94, 98, 99, 100, 103
Klemperer, Victor 36, 38
Koestler, Arthur 95, 97, 98, 104, 105–6
Kory, Rabbi Sol 130, 132
Krakozkin, Raz 60
Kristallnacht 38
Kultur-Lige (Workers' Party, Latvia) 114, 118
Kushner, Tony 39

Landau, Lev 99, 100, 102–3, 104
Latvia, Jewish life in 110, 113–19
Laue, Max von 106
Lawson, Nigella 44
Lazar, Weiner 86

INDEX

Lazarsfeld, Paul 95
Lederer, Emil 95
Lefèbvre, Henri 77
Lehman family 135
Leib, Mani 112
Leipunsky, Aleksandr 99, 101, 102, 104
Lejeune, Philippe 113
Lévi-Leleu, Michel 88
Libyan Jewish Centre (Bat-Yam, Israel) 58, 59
Libyan Jewish Heritage Museum (Or-Yehuda, Israel) 61, 65
Litvin, Savelii 46
Lowell, A. Lawrence 129
Lukács, Georg 95, 97
Lyotard, Jean-François 62

Mandelshtam, Osip 47, 49–50
Mann, Barbara 85
Mantel, Hilary 15
Mashhadis 63
Memorial Museum of Hungarian Speaking Jewry (Israel) 56, 57, 58–9, 61, 62, 63, 64, 66, 67
Mendelssohn, Moses 49
Mendes, Dona Gracia 61
Meurer, Ulrich 86
Migration Studies 84
Millar, Laura 126
Mondry, Henrietta 43–52
Moore, Deborah Dash 135
Moroccan Museum, Jerusalem 59
Mothlante, Kgalema 111
Museum of Immigration, London 79
Museum of Italian Jewish Art (Israel) 59, 62, 64
Museum of Italian Jews (Israel) 56, 59
Museum of the City of New York 79–80
Museum of the German Speaking Jews (Israel) 56, 57, 59, 61, 63, 66–7
museums: of Jewish heritage 55–68; of migration 77–84
music, and migration 85–6

Nazi Germany 36–8, 93
Nermut, Hanan 88
Network Migration in Europe 82
New York, Museum of the City of 79–80
New York Museum of Arts and Design, Center of Olfactory Art 52
Nissimi, Hilda 55–68
Nora, Pierre 58, 63
Nuremberg laws 37

Obreimov, Ivan 101, 102, 104
Offere (short film) 15–16
Oikonomou, Maria 86
Old Dominion University (ODU), Norfolk, Virginia 124–7

Origination (art project) 8
Ostjude 45

Pearce, Susan 17
Pearlman, Edith 9, 16, 17–22
Pearlman, Israel 21, 22
Pearlman, Leopold 9, 17–18
Perri, Cataldo 82
Perrin, Jean 105
Petlyura, Simon 119
Philippsborn, Rabbi Adolf 132
Pincus, Lily 36
Placzek, Georg 97, 102, 104, 105
Poehls, Kerstin 82–3
Polanyi, Karl 96
Polanyi, Laura 95, 96–7, 99
Polanyi, Michael 96, 97, 104
Polanyi Collection, Hungarian National Library, Budapest 95–7
Polanyi family 94–9
Pollacsek, Mihály 96
Proskauer, Joseph 129, 136
Proust, Marcel 43, 45, 48, 51

Reisen, Avraham 112
Riefenstahl, Charlotte 103
Rogoff, Irit 77
Romanian Jewry Centre 63
Rosenfeld, Morris 112
Rothstein, Rabbi Leonard 132, 133–4
Rozanov, Vasily 46–7, 49–50, 51
Ruhemann, Martin 102, 103, 104
Russian Jewish literature 46–51

Saraga, Esther 27–41
Schillman, Rabbi Samuel 132
Schlör, Joachim 76–92
Schwarzbard, Sholem 119
Sebald, W. G. 11, 23
Seghers, Anna 95
Sforim, Mendele Moykher 118
Shaler, Nathaniel 129
Shammas, Anton 77
Shemtov, Vered 85
Shiloni, Yisrael 56
Shmulowitz, Solomon 86
Shomer 118
Shubnikov, Lev 99, 101, 103, 104
Simons, Jack 111–12, 115
Simons, Ray Alexander 110–20
Sinelnikov, Kiril 99, 101
Slobin, Mark 86
smell, and memory 43–5
Smith, Neil 77
Soja, Edward 77, 85
South Africa: Communist Party 110; immigration to 13–17, 110–20; trade union movement 111

INDEX

Southern Jewish Historical Society (SJHS) 126
Soviet Union, and the Ukrainian Physico-Technical Institute (UFTI) 99–101
Sperber, Manès 97
Spitalfields, London 79
Staas, Christian 76
Stalin, Josef 99, 100–1, 105
Stellenbosch, South Africa 15
Stricker, Michael 96, 97
Stricker, Sándor 96
Strindberg, Auguste 118
suitcase, as symbol of migration 76–89
Suleri, Sara 77
survivor guilt 30
Switzer, Samuel Leyens 124–36
Szapor, Judith 93–109
Szilárd, Leo 95
Szondi, Leopold 95

Tan, Shaun 77
Teller, Edward 102
Though I have missed you so very much (walking tour) 19–23
Tisza, Laszlo 102–3, 106
Transferre (archive representation) 17
Trapeznikova, Olga 101, 103
Tschofen, Bernhard 77
Tsenkhenshtein, Semen 46
Turkish Heritage Centre (Israel) 57, 63

Ukrainian Physico-Technical Institute (UFTI) 94–5, 98, 99–101
Ury, Else 87–8

Valley Dry Goods Company, Vicksburg 126, 135, 136
Van de Graaff, Robert J. 101
Vansant, Jacqueline 30
Varaklan, Latvia 110, 113, 115, 116
Vezér, Erzsébet 97
Vicksburg, Mississippi 124, 125, 127, 130, 132–3, 135

Weiner, Charles 99
Weinrich, Max 113
Weissberg, Alexander 94–5, 97–9, 101–2, 102, 104–6
Weisskopf, Victor 97, 103–4
Winchevsky, Morris 112, 117
Wohl, Cecile 95, 96

Yehoash 112
Yemenite Jewish association (E'ele betamar) 58, 59
Yemenite Museum, Rosh-Hay'ayin 62–3, 65, 66
Yiddish 113, 114, 116
YIVO (Yidisher Visnshaftlekhe Institut), Vilna 114
YIVO Encyclopedia of the Jews of Eastern Europe 115
Yoffe, Leib 116

Zeisel, Eva 94–5, 96–9, 104, 105
Zeisel, Hans 97–8, 104
Zionism 60–1, 65
Zuckmayer, Carl 94